Flowers and Herbs
of Early America

Flowers and Herbs of Early America

By Lawrence D. Griffith

Photography by
Barbara Temple Lombardi

Colonial Williamsburg
The Colonial Williamsburg Foundation
Williamsburg, Virginia

In Association with
Yale University Press, NEW HAVEN & LONDON

Published in 2008 by The Colonial Williamsburg Foundation in association with Yale University Press

Library of Congress Control Number: 2008926453

ISBN: 978-0-87935-238-7 (CWF: hardcover : alk. paper)
ISBN: 978-0-300-14536-6 (Yale: hardcover : alk. paper)

Designed by Helen M. Olds
Printed in Singapore

Colonial Williamsburg is a registered trade name of The Colonial Williamsburg Foundation, a not-for-profit educational institution.

The Colonial Williamsburg Foundation
PO Box 1776
Williamsburg, VA 23187-1776
www.colonialwilliamsburg.org

20 19 18 17 16 15 14 13 12 11 10 09 08   1 2 3 4 5 6 7 8 9

To Curtis Scott Moyer
and in memory of my
parents, W. P. Griffith
and Frances W. Griffith
—LDG
To Michael
—BTL

Contents

President's Message

The Colonial Williamsburg Foundation is fortunate to have the generous support of individuals and foundations that help advance our mission. Gifts from Janet and Fred Brubaker of Somerset, Pennsylvania, Teresa and Ken Wood of Chester Springs, Pennsylvania, and the Mars Foundation of McLean, Virginia, have made possible this exquisitely photographed and meticulously researched book of Colonial Williamsburg's Historic Area flowers and herbs. Colonial Williamsburg curator of plants Lawrence Griffith and photographer Barbara Lombardi have authored a significant contribution to the body of literature on plants in early America.

Janet and Fred Brubaker are long-time friends of Colonial Williamsburg and have been frequent visitors. Their devotion to history and citizenship education and the enjoyment they derive from leisurely strolls through the Historic Area gardens inspired them to support publication of this book through the Janet and Fred Brubaker Foundation.

Also long-time donors to Colonial Williamsburg, Teresa and Ken Wood are especially interested in Colonial Williamsburg's gardens and education outreach efforts, specifically teacher training. Ken serves on the board of the Pennsylvania Horticultural Society while Teresa is a regional representative for Longwood College. After viewing some of Barbara Lombardi's exquisite photographs for the book, the Woods decided to lend their support—a commitment for which we are most grateful.

The Mars Foundation, a stalwart benefactor of Colonial Williamsburg, provided a grant to our Landscape and Facilities Services Department for a three-year study of plants once familiar to colonial Virginia, but lesser known today. We are most grateful for this support, enabling us to continue our commitment to researching and presenting historically accurate plants in the Historic Area.

On behalf of my colleagues on the board and staff of the Colonial Williamsburg Foundation, I express deep appreciation to Mr. and Mrs. Brubaker, Mr. and Mrs. Wood, and the Mars Foundation for this beautifully conceived collaboration. Their commitment ensures a lovely, enduring record of these early American plants for generations to come, helping us to fulfill the mission of Colonial Williamsburg—that the future may learn from the past.

Colin G. Campbell
The Colonial Williamsburg Foundation

Foreword

In their endeavor to identify plants from the colonial era that are appropriate for use in Colonial Williamsburg's gardens and to photographically preserve the beauty of those plants, Lawrence Griffith and Barbara Lombardi have produced a distinctive work that will appeal to all who love gardens and the plants found in them. Whether you are a horticulturist or gardener, either serious or recreational, you will be intrigued by the details and history, both narrative and pictorial, of these treasures from gardens of a former time.

The Colonial Williamsburg Foundation is a remarkable cultural institution dedicated to teaching colonial American history in nontraditional ways, primarily by interpreting eighteenth-century Virginia, especially the city of Williamsburg, to twenty-first-century guests. The restoration of Williamsburg began in 1927. From the beginning, every attempt was made to provide an authentic setting to serve as both foreground and background to the interpretation of the many things that happened here. The Historic Area, the original core of eighteenth-century Williamsburg, today includes over four hundred restored or reconstructed buildings and more than one hundred gardens.

The flowers and herbs found in Colonial Williamsburg's gardens have always been a subject of interest and affection on the part of our guests. From its earliest days, Colonial Williamsburg has continually endeavored to document American colonists' familiarity with, and use of, native and imported flora by identifying written instances of those plants in historical records. As Colonial Williamsburg's Historic Area took shape, generations of horticulturists and landscape architects found evidence with which to green the landscape of the restored city. That work, by former Colonial Williamsburg researchers, remains valuable. However, scholarship on plants that were available to American colonists continues to proliferate, as has access to data via the Internet. To take advantage of these advances, Colonial Williamsburg undertook to revisit the question of which plants were available to colonial Virginians.

In the spring of 2001, the Mars Foundation of McLean, Virginia, generously awarded a grant to the Colonial Williamsburg Foundation so that the Landscape and Facilities Services Department could reacquaint itself with the resources that inform its choice of plant material in the Historic Area and to begin to consider changes to the plants used there. We were both reevaluating the old canon of plants and commentary and searching for new plants and fresh documentary sources to continue to underwrite our commitment to a historically authentic plant palette.

Lawrence Griffith, curator of plants, who is a skilled researcher and equally an accomplished gardener, undertook to explore the flowers and herbs known to have been in Williamsburg and coastal Virginia in the eighteenth century. Not only did Lawrence sift through the available literature, he also obtained seeds for each of the plants and grew them. His skills as both a practical gardener and a plant historian gave him unique insight into these plants, which is demonstrated in this work.

Thus, Lawrence conducted this two-pronged investigation. First, using the resources at Colonial Williamsburg's John D. Rockefeller, Jr. Library and the College of William and Mary's Earl Gregg Swem Library, he documented the evidence that places plants in early Virginia. Second, through real-time field trials conducted in the Lewis House garden on Colonial Street in Colonial Williamsburg's Historic Area, he ascertained the merits and durability of many of the plants that have traditionally been part of our plant list but that had fallen out of use. He was also able to suggest new plants suitable for planting in Historic Area gardens.

While Lawrence seeded, cultivated, and evaluated these plants, Barbara Lombardi, Colonial Williamsburg photographer, became a regular visitor to the garden capturing photographically the nuances of these captivating plants.

Thus, this book is a notable collaboration of Lawrence Griffith's research and gardening skills and Barbara Lombardi's photographic talent and eye for beauty. In his introduction, Lawrence suggests that these plants might be considered part of the colonial American herbal. Perhaps this book is the beginning of a discussion on that point.

Gordon Chappell
Director, Landscape and
Facilities Services Department
The Colonial Williamsburg Foundation

Introduction

What a pleasant thing it is for a Man (whom the Ignorant thinke to be alone) to have Plants speaking Greek and Latine to him, and putting him in minde of Stories, which otherwise he would never thinke of?

—William Coles, 1657

For the many millennia that humankind has been posing questions about plants and attempting to discern their purposes, their relationship to civilization has been of two kinds: ornamental and utilitarian.

It is only recently that we've come to view plants overwhelmingly for their ornamental appeal. Until the seventeenth century, plants were thought of only in terms of their usefulness. This was the case to such an extent that an influential belief emerged in the first millennia called the doctrine of signatures. It argued that, if the texture of a walnut looked like that of a human brain, then the walnut must be applicable for afflictions of the head; if the leaf of the *Cynoglossum*, hound's-tongue, looked just like that, a hound's tongue, it must be good for the relief of dog bites.

Alongside the birth of observational science in the sixteenth and seventeenth centuries, an aesthetic appreciation of plants gained hold. It was during this time that Europe saw the birth of botanical gardens and ornamental flower books. England in the seventeenth century had the horticultural precociousness inherited from the Roman occupation. By the early 1600s, England's garden aesthetic was well honed. Even in rural areas in Britain, with the emergence of the middle class during the Elizabethan age, yards became enclosed and abutted the house, and the concept of the cottage garden was born. By contrast, in 1607, British colonists stepped ashore into Virginia's virgin forest—a landscape utterly different from blossoming British horticulture. Whereas homeland Britons were beginning to enjoy the aesthetics of gardening, their colonizing brethren were concerned with survival.

From the beginning, there was an awareness of the natural abundance and beauty of Virginia. The noble Capt. George Percy, an early deputy governor of the colony, is often quoted:

Fair meadows and goodly tall trees, with such fresh waters running through woods as I was almost ravished at the first sight thereof. . . . the ground all flowing over with fair flowers of sundry colors and kinds as though it had been in any garden or orchard in England; there be many strawberries and other fruits unknown; we saw the woods full of cedar and cypress trees, . . . we kept on our way in this paradise.[1]

The colonists' first priority when it came to plants was food. From a survey of several first-account narratives, we know that the following food plants were available, either wild or farmed by the Amerindians: maize, beans, pumpkins, acorns, walnuts, mulberries, strawberries, chestnuts, chinquapins, cherries, plums, gooseberries, persimmons, tuckahoe, groundnuts, mushrooms, melons, "*maracock* [passionflower]—a wild fruit like a kind of pomegranate," "peaches they dry in the sun for winter-use. . . . earth-nuts, which they call *Tuccaho,*" and "Martagon-Roots [lily], and esteem them dainties."[2]

Though America bore the brunt of a continental climate, not the gentle maritime climate of England, there is evidence that the English also tried to cultivate crops they brought from home. Capt. Gabriel Archer documented the cultivation of British grains in Virginia less than a month after landing at Jamestown: "[June] 2, 3 [1607]. Tuesday, Wednesday. . . . setting of corn." The English used the word *corn* to mean any of their native grains (i.e., wheat, barley, rye). Archer's attestation is affirmed by George Percy's record, which reads, "The fifteenth day of June [1607]. . . . We

had also sown most of our corn on two mountains [mounds]; it sprang a man's height from the ground." Archer also observed, "All our garden seeds that were carefully sown prosper well." William Strachey, secretary of the colony, seconded Archer's comments: "And we have made trial of our own English seeds, kitchen herbs, and roots, and find them to prosper as speedily as in England."[3]

Strachey and Archer both refer to various "apothecary drugs" found among the native plant materials. Familiarity with native plant materials may well have extended to ornamentals, for, even in the very first years of the colony, the chapel at the fort at Jamestown was "to be kept passing sweet and trimmed up with divers flowers."[4]

As to the disposition of the earliest gardens and their arrangement, we can only infer from the historical documentation that the fort and the grounds immediately in the fort's vicinity provided what tillable ground the colonists had during the first several years. However, even in 1612, in a promotional pamphlet, Robert Johnson related, albeit secondhand, "that every man may have his lodging and dwelling place apart by himself, with a sufficient quantity of

Typical English country house with forecourt and garden.

ground allotted thereto for his orchard and garden to plant at his pleasure, and for his own use."[5]

By 1615, Ralph Hamor reported on a thriving colony with "handsome house[s] . . . and twelve English acres of ground adjoining thereunto very strongly impaled; which ground is only allotted unto him for roots, garden herbs, and corn." Orchards were important, and, according to Hamor, Sir Thomas Gates had in "his garden at James town many forward apple and pear trees come up of kernels set the year before."[6]

By the mid-seventeenth century, small- to medium-sized plantations became established, and their grounds were developed and arranged chiefly around three agricultural components: tobacco, livestock, and food crops. Though the quest for food was paramount, and drove the development of settlement patterns, herbs and flowers might have played a subsidiary role to vegetables and crops.[7]

It is the gardens of the large landowners, rather than those of the yeoman farmers, for which we have significant physical and documentary evidence. Two gardens emerge in the middle to late seventeenth century that, due to their size and archaeological durability, shed light on the arrangement of gardens on their respective properties. Bacon's Castle and Green Spring plantation are emblematic of prosperous mid-seventeenth-century plantations.

In 1650, the wealthy Arthur Allen, probably a merchant, obtained the first lands that came to constitute the holdings of Bacon's Castle in Surry, Virginia. Archaeologists believe that by 1690 a substantial garden, approximately 195 feet by 360 feet, was established adjacent to the house. The rectangular garden was in a symmetrical arrangement of six main planting beds and two smaller subsidiary beds. The garden shadow survives because the original footprint of the garden was so deep, so dramatic, and so symmetrical.[8]

Although the garden undoubtedly served a utilitarian purpose, evidence of garden pavilions and starting beds, set to the north to capture the summer's sun, suggests to some that the garden also had ornamental aspects. The border beds especially would have provided an opportunity to plant a live enclosure embellished with ornamentals. Thus, we have evidence of a clear articulation of garden space and an indication of ornamental features in a garden dating to the first century of colonization.[9]

Green Spring plantation was the seventeenth-century home of Sir William Berkeley, who was appointed governor of Virginia in 1641 and came to the colony in 1642. In 1643, he obtained via court order 984 acres named Green Spring, because of a fresh spring there. By 1649, Sir William was growing fifteen hundred fruit trees at Green Spring. During his second term as governor, from 1660 to 1667, he was fully involved in the management of a large and complex plantation, including the cultivation of grapes for wine, rice, flax, tobacco, and mulberry trees for silk production. The estate activities included timber production and the breeding of horses and cattle as well.[10]

Kent Brinkley, landscape architect, has suggested that separate pleasure and kitchen gardens were set to the northeast and east of the original manor house. The fact that a mount currently exists in the vicinity of the presumed pleasure garden, a European taste, lends weight to the idea of a dedicated pleasure garden. A court figure in London, Berkeley would have been sensitive to the latest landscape design fashion.[11]

As the century turned, the capital of Virginia moved from Jamestown to

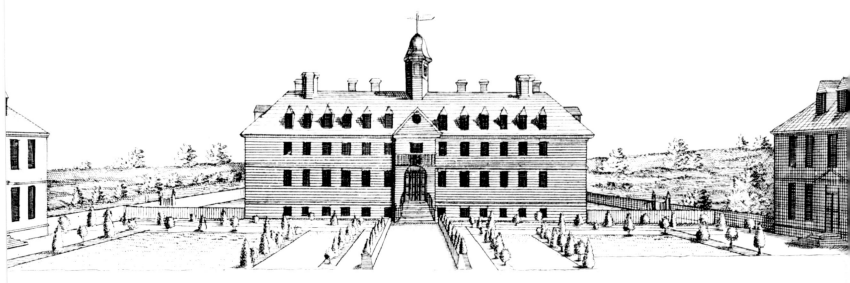

Detail from the Bodleian Plate.

Williamsburg, the colony became prosperous, and the Enlightenment dawned. Within this more settled, more affluent culture, a plethora of gardening sites emerged. In Williamsburg, two public buildings, the Wren Building and the Governor's Palace, dictated a prestige in gardening that other elite gardeners would mimic.

Designed to be imperial, the Governor's Palace garden in Williamsburg represented the acme of colonial garden design. In 1710, a proposal to the Burgesses was made:

That a Court-Yard, of dimentions proportionable to the said house, be laid out, levelled and encompassed with a brick wall four foot high, with ballustrades of wood

thereupon, on the said land, and that a Garden of the length of two hundred fifty-four foot and of the breadth of one hundred forty-four foot from out to out, adjoining to the said house.

Reference was also made "That a Flower Garden behind [north of] the House" be enclosed as well.[12]

Evidence gleaned from the Bodleian Plate, an engraved copper plate showing the layout and facades of the College of William and Mary, the Governor's Palace, and the Capitol, suggests that a late-seventeenth-century formality was originally envisioned for the area to the north of the Palace. The diamond-shaped parterres, which are clearly indicated on the plate, argue that a tightly organized,

hierarchical, Dutch-inspired garden was likely installed, neat and well manicured.

The same type of garden, reflecting the meticulous details of parterres and topiary, graced the eastern side of the Wren Building: textbook Dutch Palladian with its symmetry, its evergreen topiaries, and its well-ordered precision. A kitchen garden lay on the western side of the building behind the wings of the chapel and great hall.[13]

Three other significant properties of the early eighteenth century about which we have somewhat detailed information are William Byrd II's Westover, the early-eighteenth-century phase of Green Spring, and John Custis's Six Chimneys.

Located in Charles City County between Williamsburg and Richmond, Westover, the famous home of the Bryds,

must rule on the ground. With wooden stakes and string, I imposed a neat grid, set to planting seed, and watched for germination, barely recognizing each minute seed crop as it materialized. It wasn't long before I had a crop of plants that in many cases were head high.

Over the next several years, I grew 180 species of plants, primarily annual flowers and various herbs, from seed directly sown into soil. Directly sowing seed in a garden setting without benefit of modern greenhouses or even historically accurate cold frames or hot frames was a task that I had rarely done. The ease with which modern gardeners come by their plants belies the difficulty of starting large quantities of seed in situ.

While all propagation was, for the initial two years, exclusively by seed directly sown in the ground, by the third year a thirst for new crops and limited bed space meant that a few crops were sown under glass at the landscape nursery. Also, in such cases as Indian-shot (*Canna indica*), a tropical tuberous-rooted perennial, it is time efficient to purchase the tubers rather than invest in the many years of significant time and labor involved in raising these relatively rarified crops.

As I gardened, I kept a journal. I noted the day each species was planted, when it germinated, when it first flowered, the duration of flowering, and the day it was pulled from the garden. If at all possible, plants were allowed to develop their seed, which was either harvested by hand or allowed to self-scatter. I observed general growth habits and how easily each plant might be incorporated into various types of gardens. I got to be judge and jury.

One of the things I quickly learned was that two hundred dollars in seed gives a far greater garden in less time than the equivalent investment in gallon-sized perennials, a quarter of which would probably die in the first year. Eight-dollar perennials, or three-dollar annual herbs, represent an exponential increase of the price of each initial seed. That added value represents the grower's considerable investment in the germination of the seeds, their growth, and getting them to market. The home seed gardener assumes all that labor. The challenge would be considerable, I acknowledged, but it would certainly winnow out the weak and demonstrate which plants could feasibly be sown in the open.

In considering the hundreds of possible plant choices, my decisions were both instinctive and methodical. Instinctively, I grew plants such as the hound's-tongue (*Cynoglossum officinale*), ragged robin (*Lychnis flos-cuculi*), and costmary (*Chrysanthemum balsamita*) just for the sake of their names. I grew short plants like pennyroyal (*Mentha pulegium*), all-heal (*Prunella vulgaris*), and strawberry blite (*Chenopodium foliosum* 'Strawberry Sticks') and tall plants like crested cockscomb (*Celosia argentea* var. *cristata*) and the joe-pye weed (*Eupatorium purpureum*). I came to know, completely by chance, the cinnamon-colored American groundnut (*Apios americana*), whose convoluted shape is mystifying, and the swamp milkweed (*Asclepias incarnata*), whose predation by orange aphids is equally so. Plants about which medicinal claims are made came to my notice: St. Mary's thistle (*Silybum marianum*), blessed thistle (*Cnicus benedictus*), and motherwort (*Leonurus cardiaca*). "Fever" plants and palliative herbal teas are legion, including anise hyssop (*Agastache foeniculum*), horsemint (*Monarda punctata*), and boneset (*Eupatorium perfoliatum*).

With respect to method, I studied the Foundation's plant list as well as

plant lists of other institutions. I consulted ancient and Renaissance herbals and gardening encyclopedias as well as other period works. I quickly came to the realization that the canon of plants during the medieval and Renaissance periods was circumscribed and that the body of plants known or used in the colonies was even further restricted by the sheer distance from the mother country.

The many plants that I studied

might be considered part of the colonial American herbal, if we may coin such a term. An herbal, in its most specific sense, is a book about plants and their uses. Although there is no specific, written colonial American herbal, per se, there is a compendium of plants that represents those native American plants and imported species that were of use and interest in the colonial period.

As I began to experiment with

plants, and as I watched them mature to the point of bearing and dispersing seed, I realized that there would be dispersal patterns from the seed-bearing plants. I conceived of these groups of seedlings as "colonists" and judged whether they would be transient, stable, or aggressive.

As I had guessed, the garden held to its strict geometry through the first year, though, even by the fall of the first season, certain crops predominated, the

larkspur (*Consolida orientalis*) primarily, and colonies formed, impregnable to other seeds if not the good garden fork. The second summer of flowering was equally successful, but the grid that I had established the previous year was morphing as self-sown seedlings emerged where they had been blown by wind and rain. What I learned is that the plants have a say in all this and that they find the places that they like and

predominate. My sixty-nine plots began to vary in size as plants spilled onto the now-obsolete garden paths.

Although it was not my original intention, a form of gardening was emerging. I was developing a very modified cottage garden, that patch of ground intensively cultivated and planted with a chaotic combination of annuals, perennials, herbs, and vegetables that self-perpetuate by seed and the wise will of the gardener. I qualify "cottage garden" in the sense that, as mentioned earlier, a cottage garden in the mid-Atlantic region, given our hot, humid climate, is a misnomer. But, as my work led me to a garden given over to vast quantities of annuals, a few perennials, a goodly number of herbs, small trees, and four roses, I began to fantasize that the phenomenon in some way mimicked the lore of that English garden. Nevertheless, with persistent weeding and watering, I found that you can create a cottage garden–like feel in a small space with a handful of seed.

My garden, however, was not to demonstrate a manner of gardening. It was not its mission to solve the question of how the colonists gardened. It was to demonstrate the types of plants they

might have grown and the feasibility of their growth.

While this book serves to document my work and research, it is written for the twenty-first-century gardener interested in colonial plants: to inform, to entertain, and mostly to provide a choice of period plants to grow in your own garden. Archaically, the majority of plants were thought to have practical purposes while only a small minority were plants of ornament. So, I have divided the plants in this book into the two categories, but I have made each assignment based on how the plant is largely appreciated today. Thus, the ornamental plants now represent a majority.

However, the appreciation of the ornamental nature of older species of plants presents a number of pitfalls for the over-expectant gardener. Typically, flower size is not what the modern gardener may expect, and length of bloom seldom satisfies the intentions of those who want season-long color from a single crop. Intensive hybridization over the past two and half centuries has accustomed modern eyes to expectations of floral grandeur and extravagant duration of bloom. But, once we become accustomed to the reintroduction of original

plant species and their humbler blooms, gardens of delicate flowers quickly become a new, acquired taste.

Realizing and photographing those fine details was the astute and practiced eye of photographer Barbara Lombardi, who brought to the project her various lenses, capturing the stunning beauty of the minutest of flower parts and divulging the complexity of their construction. While it might seem counterintuitive to use macroscopic photographs in a book devoted to period plants, the age of microscopy started in the seventeenth century, and, by the eighteenth century, plant taxonomists were using the microscope to visually dissect the sexual parts of flowers and thereby classify them.

Juxtaposed with the vivid photography are period illustrations. These lovely watercolors, gouaches, and colored engravings, largely from the sixteenth through early nineteenth centuries, provide not only artistic representations from the era in question but also comparisons of early renditions of species with modern ones. We can determine how much, or how little, change the floral or herbal subjects have undergone. The disparity is sometimes quite dramatic.

This book does not attempt an encyclopedic treatment of all the herbaceous species that might have been encountered by colonial Americans. Rather, it is a selective, discursive recounting of my experience with, and research about, a selection of annuals, biennials, and perennials that I grew in the field, firsthand, and about which I researched extensively. Criteria for inclusion included their success in the field, their worthiness in a garden setting, and

whether they were amenable to photography, which is a strong element of this book. This collection represents a small sample of perhaps the thousands of plants and their endless varieties that were entertained by, speculated upon, and used by persons of learning and common folk alike in the American colonial period on both sides of the Atlantic.

For the purposes of this work, plant names, taxonomy, are consistent with that of the United States Department of Agriculture (USDA) Plants Database, which "provides standardized information about the vascular plants, mosses, liverworts, hornworts, and lichens of the U.S. and its territories." The author recognizes the database as an arbitrary but reputable choice among others, and the database is considered the standard by other authorities in the field. Taxonomic information was also gleaned from *Hortus Third* (2000) and the Royal Horticultural Society's *Dictionary of Gardening* (1956), which conveniently provides dates of introduction to English horticulture of plants listed in the work. Many times Taylor's

Gardening Guides were also consulted with respect to zone hardiness and other plant behaviors.[21]

A productive, beautiful garden can be created from seed sown in the ground during a single season in Virginia if one uses a palette of annuals, herbs, and perennials that flower during their first year. The use of these plants, in a merry conflation, was for me horticulturally satisfying, intellectually stimulating, and of significant practical use. I hope these simple plants and their growth will be rewarding for you as well.

A Note on the Sources

By the end of the eighteenth century, plants were making their way around the world. Many plants native to the Middle East, South America, and Asia had made their way to England and often on to North America. Dutiful plant encyclopedists, such as Philip Miller, diligently recorded the routes whereby plants moved around the globe.

The histories of plants can be traced largely through old herbals and florilegia, though other sources are also helpful. An herbal is simply a compendium of plants and their purported purposes. A florilegium, a word derived from Latin that means flower book, is a work devoted exclusively to pictures of flowers. The Western herbal dates to the third century BC while the earliest florilegium was published only around 1590. While to assemble a florilegium is a work of monumental artistic merit, to compile an herbal was not just to know the names of hundreds of plants but to understand what they did, what properties they held, where they were found, when they flowered, when they set seed, and how their roots, leaves, stems, and flowers were used.[1]

Our earliest source, Theophrastus, in his third-century BC herbal *Enquiry into Plants,* saw plants primarily as medicine,

fiber, and food. But, in his discursive way, he established a method of observation and a discipline of cataloging that bears the birth pains of modern science.[2]

Aristotle and Theophrastus, both pupils of Plato, were sequentially head of the famous Lyceum, the philosophical school in Athens. Upon Aristotle's death, Theophrastus inherited the leadership of the Lyceum, Aristotle's library, and the garden at the Lyceum, giving us the literal, geographical alpha point for Western botany. Theophrastus's botanical lectures were compiled by his students and published after his death. This posthumous compilation is the first Western herbal, Theophrastus is Western botany's genesis, and Western botany unwinds from him.[3]

The next obvious source is Dioscorides, the eminent first-century Greek physician and surgeon who served in the Roman army. The true nature of Dioscorides's herbal is evident in its title, *De materia medica,* which translates as "of medical matters." Although functioning like an herbal because it is plant based, this text is more a compendium of first-century medical remedies whose constituents are the plants, and in some cases minerals and animal parts. Dioscorides compiled over one thousand remedies using approxi-

mately six hundred plants and plant products. For almost fifteen hundred years, Dioscorides was regarded as the ultimate authority on plants and medicine.[4]

During the Dark Ages and late medieval times, herbals survived solely as manuscripts, copied by hand. A number of these medieval manuscripts are known to exist, though they are barely more illuminating from a botanical standpoint than the classical authors upon whom they rely. They are laden with warmed-over superstition, such as the aforementioned doctrine of signatures and the myth of the four humors (hot, dry, wet, and cold), which were thought to rule the human body.[5]

With the advent of printing and as culture and capital began to swell during the Renaissance, European courts vied for botanical superiority. The Medici family of Florence began their horticultural legacy in the sixteenth century with the founding of the botanical garden at Pisa. By the sixteenth century, the Renaissance permeated cold, central Europe, and the great German herbal by Leonhart Fuchs was published in 1542. It, as with all other herbals before and after it, references the commentary of the ancients: Theophrastus, Dioscorides, Galen, and Pliny.[6]

Fuchs, who was a medical doctor by training, incorporated direct observation and hands-on knowledge of plants into his herbal, an innovation at the time. Fuchs's herbal is helpful in demonstrating that there existed, as of 1542 when it was published, a canon of plants that was reported about for roughly two thousand years. This work is primarily a medical manual; its ornamental appeal is limited.

Until this time, printed herbals, if they were illustrated, were pictured with woodcuts, some more crude than others, often "borrowed" from other artists and works. While these can be enormously helpful in making graphic matches with contemporary plants, colored illustrations enhance their familiarity. Fuchs's illustrated and colored but unpublished Vienna Codex (ca. 1566) is a single work of art, some of whose colored illustrations have been published recently.[7]

Equally as valuable as a reference, but in a different way, was the slightly later *Hortus Eystettensis* (The garden of the bishop of Eichstätt) (1613), republished in 1989 as the *Besler Florilegium*. A florilegium (flower book) rather than an herbal, it was devoted exclusively to the flowers grown in the thirteen gardens set within the walls of the castle of Eichstätt in Germany. This set of colored engravings, often called the most beautiful, was a revolution in the sense that it contained no herbal data, had no medicinal pretensions. While not providing contemporary scholars practical notes on the plants' origins, habits, or uses, it provides crucial graphic evidence of the bonanza of ornamental varieties developed from humbler roots, such as the snapdragon (*Antirrhinum majus*) and the foxglove (*Digitalis purpurea*). It is apparent in the double larkspur varieties (*Consolida orientalis*) that the post-Elizabethan Stuarts and their European brethren were imbibing in the flashiest delights that plant selection and breeding could afford.[8]

Graphically important also is *The Florilegium of Alexander Marshal*, produced around 1653 but not published until 2000, one of the rarest and certainly one of the loveliest examples of botanical art in the world. Marshal's watercolors of individual stems express a subtlety and beauty unmatched in his time. Consisting of several hundred vellum pages, 284 species from 73 genera are represented. Included are sixty varieties of tulips (*Tulipa gesnerana*), thirty roses (*Rosa* spp.), sixty carnations (*Dianthus caryophyllus*), thirty-eight auriculas (*Primula auricula*), and forty-five anemones (*Anemone coronaria*). This narrow collection of species reflects a wide taste for these florists' flowers at this point in horticultural history. Florists' flowers were those breeds of flowers, which also included the hyacinth (*Hyacinthus orientalis*) and ranunculus (*Ranunculus asiaticus*), that specialized growers called *florists* bred with especial vigor. At that time, florists primarily bred and grew potted flowers, as opposed to the cut flower trade adopted by modern florists.[9]

Incontrovertibly central to our discussion is John Gerard's *Herbal, or General History of Plants*. The second edition from 1633 describes about 2,850 plants and includes over 2,500 woodcuts. This publication provides both graphic depictions of plants, in the form of woodcuts, and lengthy herbal lore, including prescriptive uses and name and place derivation. Although Gerard was alleged to be a plagiarist and his woodcuts assuredly a generation away from first run, his 1597 edition and the second edition of 1633, enlarged and amended by Thomas Johnson, offer recognizable woodcuts for the majority of plants and commentary in readable English. Its availability to the British public, its availability to modern gardening enthusiasts, its comprehensible English, and its recognizable woodcuts make it a central work when deducing the movement of plants across Europe. Like many before me, I've chosen to cite the 1633, rather than the original 1597, edition because the 1633 is more comprehensive and more readily available today.[10]

Sources begin to proliferate as the seventeenth century progresses. Curiosity in Europe incited the investigation of the New World by such plantsmen as John Tradescant Jr. In 1638, he made a voyage to Virginia and returned with several hundred plants then unknown in Britain. A second trip ensued in 1642. The Tradescant plant catalogs of father and son, which date from the middle of the seventeenth century, are seminal to understanding the dates of plant introductions into England and from where, in many cases, those plants came.[11]

Another Englishmen who left a legacy of plant data is an Oxford divine, John Banister. Banister was recruited to venture to America by Henry Compton, who was to become bishop of London and Banister's horticultural patron. Banister arrived in Virginia in 1678. By 1680, he had completed his catalog

of Virginia plants, which he named "Catalogus Stirpium Rariorum." In the late 1680s, Banister was still collecting specimens and sending them to Bishop Compton in London. In May 1692, Banister was accidentally shot while botanizing on the Roanoke River.[12]

As for Banister's "Catalogus Stirpium Rariorum," it didn't see the light of day until it was subsumed into naturalist John Ray's major work, *Historia Plantarum* (vol. 2, 1688). Although Banister's catalog is in Latin and is simply an index of plant names, it is helpful in placing native and introduced plants in Virginia in the fourth quarter of the seventeenth century.[13]

Another record left was that of John Josselyn, an English traveler who spent two spells in New England in the second and third quarters of the seventeenth century. In 1672, he published *New-Englands Rarities Discovered*, a slim volume that has been called provincial in its scope and its few woodcuts near valueless. But, it does give a glimpse into that time in American culture and substantiates plant identities from other contemporary sources.[14]

Like John Banister, John Lawson, another explorer, met a tragic end in the New World. And, like Banister, he left us a valuable resource. In his very description

tive *A New Voyage to Carolina* (1709), he recounted his trek through Carolina territory, his role in the establishment of the towns of Bath and New Bern, and his acquaintance with the aboriginals. His natural history of the country sounds like the stock descriptions that preceded him for nearly one hundred years.[15]

He was, however, prolific when enumerating the "*Corn* [grains] *of* Carolina:" rye, barley, oats, and so forth. Of the "*Herbs of* Carolina," he was equally lengthy, giving a nearly complete list of the diet of the Carolinians at the dawn of the eighteenth century. Especially helpful is his enumeration of "Pot-herbs" of European origin. Several common herbs, such as thyme (*Thymus* spp.), hyssop (*Hyssopus officinalis*), rosemary (*Rosmarinus officinalis*), and lavender (*Lavandula* spp.), are listed, as well as more arcane medicinal herbs, blessed thistle (*Cnicus benedictus*), elecampane (*Inula helenium*), and vervain (*Verbena officinalis*), for instance.[16]

Already discussed, but seminal, is the correspondence between John Custis of Williamsburg, a plutocrat, and Peter Collinson of London, a cotton merchant and Quaker, published in 1957 as *Brothers of the Spade*. Representing twelve years from 1734 to 1746, it is the dedicated conversation between two men immersed in their personal fascination with gardening.[17]

Resources come in many kinds. John Clayton, the botanist, left two. He is the known author of *Flora Virginica*, an encyclopedia of Virginia plants written in Latin and published on his behalf in Amsterdam in two parts in 1739 and 1743. Even for the lay reader, his use of Latin genus names provides a starting point in the quest to identify the plants in his catalog. He also left 710 dried herbarium specimens, the majority of which are preserved in the Natural History Museum in London. Those herbarium specimens can now be searched and seen online at the museum's John Clayton Herbarium Web site. These two resources, *Flora Virginica* and the herbarium collection, provide a nearly microscopic assessment of plant life, primarily native and wild, in mid-eighteenth-century Virginia. Of Clayton, Thomas Jefferson said, "[He] is supposed to have enlarged the botanical catalogue as much as almost any man who has lived."[18]

Philip Miller, prolific author and curator of the Chelsea Physic Garden from 1722–1771, is a central figure to the study of mid-eighteenth-century English, and consequently American, horticul-ture. His *Gardeners Dictionary* (1731) provided the English-speaking public an exhaustive gardening manual and an encyclopedic array of plants collected at the center of European horticulture, the botanical gardens of the day: Leiden, Padua, Pisa, Paris, Montpellier, to name a few. The 1754 edition is widely published and available and is a perfect representation of the state of taxonomy mid-eighteenth century. The 1768 edition is crucial in that it was owned by both Thomas Jefferson and Lady Jean Skipwith, two avid and well-read colonial American gardeners.[19]

A later Philip Miller, illustrated encyclopedia is the beautiful, leather-bound, two-volume *Figures of the Most Beautiful, Useful, and Uncommon Plants Described in the Gardeners Dictionary, Exhibited on Three Hundred Copper Plates, Accurately Engraven after Drawings Taken from Nature* (1760). Philip Miller's great opus offers not only high-quality hand-colored copperplates but also snippets of historical commentary in English, as opposed to Latin.[20]

In *Figures of the Most Beautiful, Useful, and Uncommon Plants*, Miller presented a palette of plants that represented the fusing of Old World plants and exotic, newly discovered, tropical New World plants. In the same work are asparagus (*Asparagus officinalis*) and amaryllis (*Hippeastrum* spp.), alkanet (*Anchusa officinalis*) and amaranth (*Amaranthus* spp.). *Figures* is the loveliest and best hybrid of herbal and flower book. It includes plants of the dusty wayside, viper's bugloss (*Echium vulgare*) for instance, because of their medicinal value and their herbal pedigree through two thousand years. Yet, the glorious red canna (*Canna indica*) and crinum lilies (*Crinum* spp.) were also figured with little thought of their practical use. All the plants in *Figures* are crisply drawn, set at their best aspect, each in its own dignity, each of botanical significance in Miller's mind and in those of his botanically inclined patrons.

Another European of monumental proportions is the Swedish Carolus Linnaeus. In his pivotal *Species Plantarum*, he demonstrated his newly devised system of plant classification: binomial nomenclature, the naming of plants by two Latin names corresponding to their genus and species. Published in 1753, *Species Plantarum* is credited with having identified and classified all known plants at the time.[21]

American sources are substantially rarer than European ones. Two seed lists from about 1759 and 1761, assembled by Moravian farmers at their Bethabara settlement in North Carolina, provide a list of ninety-nine plants and plant products from that time, an invaluable resource. Although these seed lists represent a German influence, there is little difference between them and others save for their completeness.[22]

By 1766, Thomas Jefferson began to log his garden activities in the most replete and valuable garden diary of the late eighteenth and early nineteenth centuries. Citizen and philosopher extraordinaire, Thomas Jefferson was, among other things, a passionate gardener. In his Garden Book, which documents his horticultural activities at Monticello from 1766 until 1824, he took meticulous, almost daily notes of the progress of his yearly planting schemes.[23]

A lively and keen historical figure, Lady Jean Skipwith left a sketchy but useful list of plants in her notes of 1793 concerning her garden at Prestwould, the plantation in Mecklenburg County, Virginia, that belonged to her and her husband, Sir Peyton Skipwith.[24]

After the turn of the century, a proliferation of data ensued. In 1802 or 1803, Bernard McMahon published a commercial advertisement, commonly referred to as a *broadside*, wherein he announced 720 varieties of seed for sale at his Philadelphia nursery. Included are hundreds of "Seeds of Physical Herbs," "Seeds of Annual Flowers," "Seeds of Biennial Flowers," and "Seeds of Perennial Flowers."[25]

McMahon's second important contribution to the documentation of the availability of plants in early America is his 1806 *American Gardener's Calendar,* in which his "General Catalogue" recommends 3,700 garden plants. Described as Jefferson's gardening mentor, McMahon can hardly be underestimated. *The American Gardener's Calendar* is recognized as the "most comprehensive gardening book published in the United States in the first half of the nineteenth century."[26]

In addition to historical sources, enormously helpful to my work was also the highly comprehensive compilation of southern plant lists produced by the Southern Garden History Society and Colonial Williamsburg in 2000. Ranging from 1734 to the twentieth century, "Southern Plant Lists" brings together a variety of primary source documents, providing plant lists alphabetically by species, for the most part, making a search for plants that much easier.[27]

Thus, we can follow a general path of plants inherited from the ancients and distilled through the Anglo-European herbals into America. We can follow a plant's history from its first notation by Theophrastus until the time we find it in Jefferson's diary. In many ways, this is a specific botanical tradition, a green stream of plants that traveled with us as we made our intellectual and horticultural way from Athens and Rome north and west through Germany to Britain and over the seas to Virginia. In some cases, it is more a vague linguistic stream, the repetition of the same name to mean various plants, or names like *mallow* that have a Greek homonym and pertain to many plants of a similar kind.

Is the colonial American herbal, if we can or decide to propose one, only a permutation of the Greco-Roman herbal via England and Europe? No, it is more because of the native flora yet to be discovered and the fact that the navigation of the seas by European powers flooded European courts with new plants. The result was that, during the Age of Exploration, the Greco-Roman herbal had grafted onto it exotic plants from all over the world, with implications even in Williamsburg.

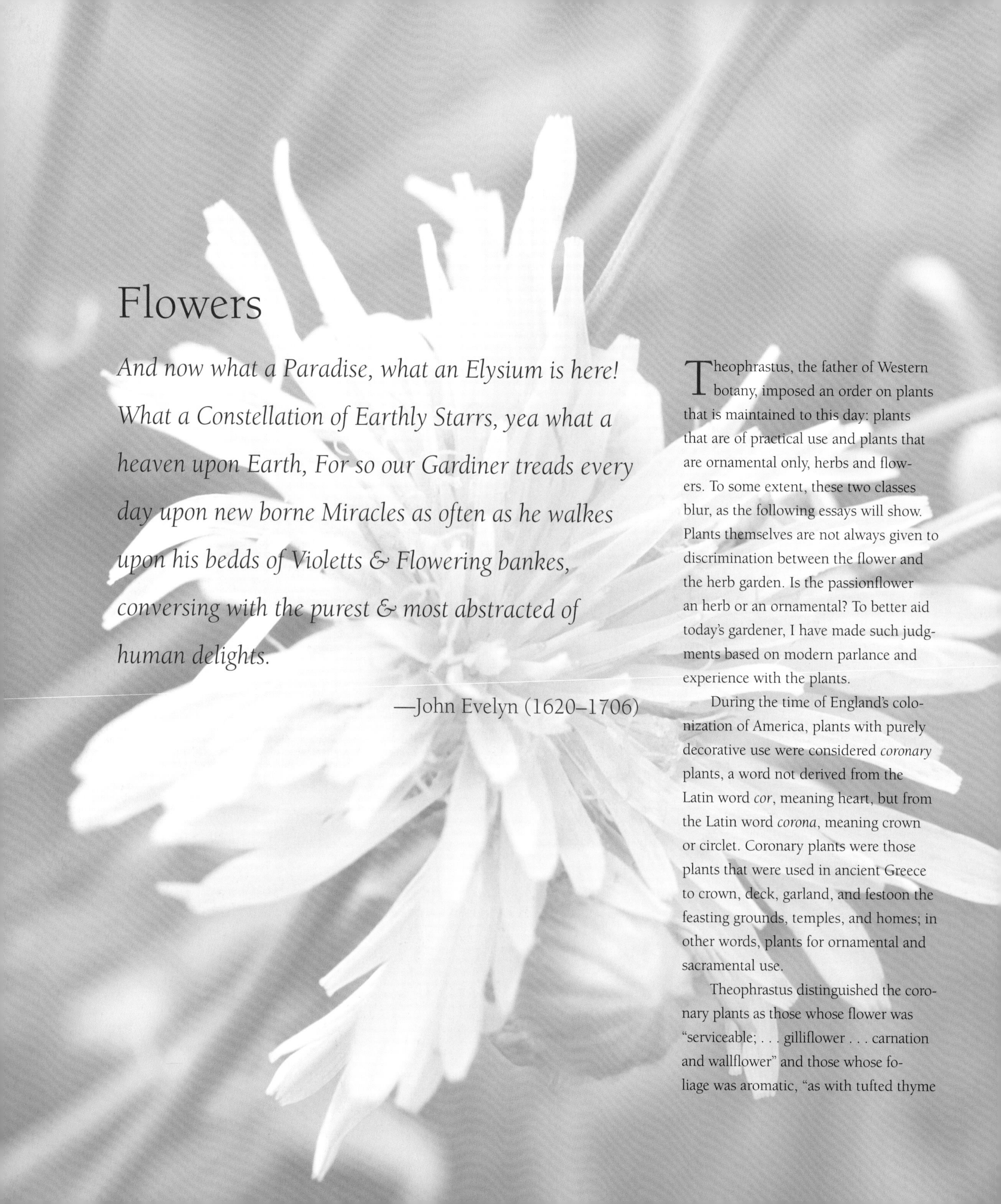

Flowers

And now what a Paradise, what an Elysium is here!

What a Constellation of Earthly Starrs, yea what a

heaven upon Earth, For so our Gardiner treads every

day upon new borne Miracles as often as he walkes

upon his bedds of Violetts & Flowering bankes,

conversing with the purest & most abstracted of

human delights.

—John Evelyn (1620–1706)

Theophrastus, the father of Western botany, imposed an order on plants that is maintained to this day: plants that are of practical use and plants that are ornamental only, herbs and flowers. To some extent, these two classes blur, as the following essays will show. Plants themselves are not always given to discrimination between the flower and the herb garden. Is the passionflower an herb or an ornamental? To better aid today's gardener, I have made such judgments based on modern parlance and experience with the plants.

During the time of England's colonization of America, plants with purely decorative use were considered *coronary* plants, a word not derived from the Latin word *cor*, meaning heart, but from the Latin word *corona*, meaning crown or circlet. Coronary plants were those plants that were used in ancient Greece to crown, deck, garland, and festoon the feasting grounds, temples, and homes; in other words, plants for ornamental and sacramental use.

Theophrastus distinguished the coronary plants as those whose flower was "serviceable; . . . gilliflower . . . carnation and wallflower" and those whose foliage was aromatic, "as with tufted thyme calamint bergamot . . . and the rest." The idea of flower collecting and garland making among the Greeks might sound apocryphal were it not for Theophrastus's account *"Of the seasons at which coronary plants flower."* His recitation of the coronary plants is a list of flora that is recognizable to the Western ear:

Of the flowers the first to appear is the gilliflower. . . . Along with the gilliflower, or a little later, appears the flower called the wild wallflower. These, of all the flowers that the garland-makers use, far outruns the others. After these come pheasant's eye and polyanthus narcissus (. . . the 'mountain anemone') and the 'head' of purse-tassels; for this too some interweave in their garlands. After these come dropwort violet, and of wild plants, gold-flower, the meadow kind of anemone corn-flag *hyakinthos*. . . . The rose comes last of these. . . .

The following belong rather to summer: rose-campion carnation *krinon* (lily) spike-lavender and the Phrygian sweet marjoram; also the plant called 'regret'. . . . The iris also blooms in summer, and the plant called soap-wort. . . . The fruit of the cotoneaster and the flower of the smilax, both of them wild plants, are also used in garlands.[1]

Botanically, the word *flower* has a very precise meaning, and what one often takes for a plant's flower is often only an exaggerated part of it or something else entirely: the flirty petals of the daisy, for instance, are only part of the flower structure; in the case of plants such as the poinsettia (*Euphorbia pulcherrima*), what we call the "flower" is actually modified leaves. This phenomenon impels us to appreciate plants for their full range of attributes: leaf shape and color, form, habit and seedpods, and so forth.

Though my heavily watered plot of weeds, half weeds, and fine coronary plants resembled a cottage garden, the style of your garden is up to you and the prevailing conditions. As you experiment, you will find crops that will flourish and become nearly homegrown. Horticulture evolves and moves on, adopting one style after another, pausing at times to take a look at the past. Gardeners imitating specific periods perhaps take the longest, and hardest, look back, but gardens can have many permutations to satisfy the modern gardener.

A few lines from the second-century BC poet Meleager provide an apt introduction to many of these fine flowers known from antiquity:

Anyte's lilies . . . narcissi pregnant with the clear songs of Melanippides, and . . . Simonides' vine-blossom; . . . the spice-scented flowering iris of Nossis. . . . and Erinna's delicious crocus. . . .
. . . Leonidas' fresh ivy-berries, and . . . the twisted tendrils of Pamphilos' vine . . . Kallimachos' sweet myrtle . . . Euphorion's rose-campion. . . .
. . . the first pomegranate-flowers of Menekrates. . . .
. . . Alexander's young olive-shoots. . . . marjoram, the flower of Polystratos' songs . . . Syrian spikenard . . . and the anemones of Sikelidas. Yes, and the golden branch of the ever-divine Plato. . . . mixed with the wallflower of Phaidimos, and Antagoras' finely turning ox-eyes, Theodoridas' sprouting, wine-loving thyme, and Phanias' corn-flowers . . . together with these early snowdrops of [my] own.[2]

Adonis

(Adonis aestivalis)
FLOWERING ANNUAL

Although Adonis is a post-colonial addition to American horticulture, its many merits make it an essential part of any garden reflecting the colonial era that also includes the early Federal period. Adonis's first American commercial mention occurs as "*Adonis* autumnalis" on an advertising broadsheet distributed by Bernard McMahon, a Philadelphia nurseryman, in 1802 or 1803. In his *American Gardener's Calendar,* published three to four years later, McMahon listed "*Adonis aestivalis*" as a hardy annual flower, meaning that it is capable of being sown in the fall for bloom the following spring.[1]

Though small flowered and ephemeral, Adonis became very popular in American gardens in the nineteenth century. The combination of abundant, glimmering cherry red flowers and luxuriant, ferny foliage guarantees its notice by any garden enthusiast strolling near a flowering clump. Its simple beauty and easy germination suggest its use as a fast-growing annual filler amongst drifts of more permanent plantings in a mixed, cottage-style garden, where annuals, perennials, and herbs find common ground in small, usually fenced areas or yards that abut the house.

Trial plantings of Adonis demonstrated that seed can be planted either in early fall (mid-September to mid-October) or in early spring (mid-March). Like other hardy annuals, such as calendula *(Calendula officinalis),* pansies *(Viola* sp.), and English daisies *(Bellis perennis),* Adonis tolerates mild southern winters and blooms prolifically the following spring. Fall-sown Adonis can bloom as early as mid-March, while spring-sown Adonis generally flowers by mid-June. Since Adonis is a self-seeding plant, gardeners can guarantee a nearly perpetual crop by sowing seed at two-week intervals and by allowing flowering plants to fully mature and set seed. While this means waiting for the plants to yellow and for the seed heads to form and scatter, your patience is rewarded the following spring when the new crop emerges.

This habit of reliably sprouting from self-sown seed earned Adonis a mythic quality among the ancient Syrians for whom it was a native plant. Sometime in antiquity, the flower became associated with the Middle Eastern fertility god Adonis, the mortal youth loved by Aphrodite. Upon his untimely death, Aphrodite transformed the spilled drops of her

lover's blood into the crimson flowers of this spring wildflower, achieving for him a suggestion of immortality. In fact, when Sicily was a Greek colony, a closely related species, *A. flammea*, was sown in his honor and used as an offering at his altars.[2]

Of the three best-known species, *A. aestivalis, A. autumnalis,* and *A. vernalis,* the first two are annuals, and the third a perennial. The first, *A. aestivalis,* is a native of southern Europe and Syria and was introduced into England in 1629. The closely related *A. autumnalis* is presumed to be native to central Europe as well as Britain, where it was known as pheasant's-eye or red Morocco. John Gerard testified in his 1633 *Herbal* that "the red floure of Adonis groweth wilde in the West parts of England among their corne." By the third quarter of the eighteenth century, it was collected from the cornfields near the River Midway in Kent and sold as a cut flower in London.[3]

Adonis's best use is in the mixed flower garden where its small but glorious flowers pinprick the garden with astonishing color. Whether sown in the fall or spring, Adonis germinates easily from seed directly sown in the ground at a depth of one-eighth inch. Some gardeners find a fall planting easier to accomplish. A fall planting in the trial garden resulted in vibrant, healthy flowering Adonis by the middle of March, persisting through April until the onset of seed production in May and June. Sown in either the fall or spring, Adonis is a boon to the spring garden, and gardeners' spirits, when the flowers pepper garden borders with cherry red vivacity.

Firsthand experience with Adonis recommends its use as a scattered, haphazardly seeded, recurring annual. Notable authors Ippolito Pizzetti and Henry Cocker suggest planting it as part of a mix among such things as yellow ranunculus (*Ranunculus ficaria*) and trollius (*Trollius europaeus*). In the cottage-style garden, it could mingle with the wallflowers (*Erysimum cheiri*) and larkspurs (*Consolida orientalis*), the annual corn poppies (*Papaver rhoeas*) and foxgloves (*Digitalis purpurea*), snapdragons (*Antirrhinum majus*) and calendulas (*Calendula officinalis*), and even find a niche amongst the winter greens (*Brassica* spp., *Barbarea* spp., etc.) and small spring onions (*Allium cepa*). Adonis performs well in the Tidewater Virginia climate by providing novice and experienced gardeners alike with another winter-hardy annual that harkens from the past and is reassuringly easy to grow.[4]

ADONIS, PHEASANT'S-EYE, FLOS ADONIS, BIRD'S-EYE
(*Adonis aestivalis*)

TYPE hardy annual
HEIGHT 18 inches
SPREAD 12 inches

HABIT
- bears ½-inch, glossy crimson flowers, sometimes in yellow varieties, and prominent seedpods
- sports ornamental, bright, green feathery foliage
- reliably self-sows
- resists most pests

NATURAL RANGE
Middle East, southern Europe

TIPS
- use in the annual, cottage-style, or mixed garden
- provide full sun
- sow seeds directly in the garden ⅛ inch deep March–April or very late August–very early October
- thin seedlings to 6 inches

Balsam Pear

(Momordica charantia)
FLOWERING ANNUAL VINE

Balsam Apple

(Momordica balsamina)
FLOWERING ANNUAL VINE

Curious all around, the vining balsam pear and balsam apple were among the most ornamental plants grown in the trial garden. Grown on teepees made from weedy tree-of-heaven (*Ailanthus altissima*) saplings, both bore elegant, deeply lobed leaves and crinkled, five-petaled yellow flowers after quickly sprouting during the warm days in late May. As the summer progressed, masses of luxuriant growth festooned all other flowers around them, causing much pruning and primping to keep the vines stable on their teepees. The balsam pear especially bore copious, elegant foliage before bearing its famous fruit, the "warty cucumber," which passed from green to yellow before dropping its crimson seeds.

Though closely related and similar in growth and appearance, the two vines have some significant differences. Something of a miniature version of the balsam pear, the balsam apple has daintier, deeply dissected leaves and smaller fruit and is a bit smaller overall in height and spread. The fruit of the balsam pear is the size and shape of a cucumber, somewhat grotesquely textured, with yellow pulp and bright scarlet seeds. The balsam apple yields a fruit more spheroid in nature, resembling a tomatillo in size.

The balsam pear has food and medicinal properties ascribed to it, but the balsam apple appears to be strictly ornamental.

Balsam apple's entry into Europe from the tropics was early enough to be included in Leonhart Fuchs's 1542 herbal, in which he said, "A recent introduction in Germany, now planted in many gardens," but ascribed no medicinal properties. As an ornamental, it appears in a later famous work, Basilius Besler's *Hortus Eystettensis* (1613), where it is paired with garden impatiens (*Impatiens balsamina*), with which it was purported to be related.[1]

The balsam pear was, prior to its introduction into Europe in 1710, well-known in its native regions of Africa, Asia, and eventually the Caribbean for its extensive medicinal uses. Its fruit and juices are thought conducive to proper bowel function and are used to treat ulcers, colic, colitis, and gas and to induce menstruation. Balsam pear is considered very effective in the treatment of worms, urinary stones, and fever. It is also an important food crop in the tropics, with unripe green fruits being added to curries or eaten raw, boiled, or fried and the young leaves and shoots cooked as vegetables. Tea made from balsam pear

is available at Asian food stores, where it is sold for use as an infusion as a tonic, diuretic, or gentle laxative.[2]

It was the ornamental quality of the balsam apple that probably induced Lady Jean Skipwith to grow it in her well-documented garden at Prestwould (ca. 1793), her home on the River Dan in Virginia. The vine's lobed leaves are particularly well modeled, and the elegant manner in which they comport themselves on the trellis, teepee, or other support makes this vine a valuable addition to the kitchen or flower garden proper.[3]

The cultivation of the balsam pear and balsam apple entails some effort. To start with, rich garden soil should be well mixed in place and "hilled" in the manner in which Native Americans would mound soil for their plantings of maize, beans, and melons. For each hill, make a teepee of three eight-to-nine-foot poles tied in place at the top. Using a posthole digger, chunk out three narrow holes eighteen inches deep on the periphery of the hill. Insert the poles of the teepee into the holes, and be sure the teepee is firmly established. The balsam fruits are

prolific growers in the heat, and their plant mass will easily topple an unsecured teepee. Sow seeds directly into the hills. These vigorous plants will quickly grow up to the tops of the teepees with help from the gardener.

Seed germinates quickly when soil temperatures approach eighty degrees and air temperatures are consistently warm to hot. With regular water and warm temperatures, you can expect abundant leaf growth, attractive five-petaled yellow flowers, and fruits of a curious nature. Despite the effort needed to maintain an aesthetic and bountiful crop of balsam apple and balsam pear, the graceful swags of foliage and fruit, festooning fences or teepees, make the whole effort very much worth it.

BALSAM PEAR, BITTER GOURD, BITTER MELON (*Momordica charantia*)

TYPE nonhardy tropical annual vine
HEIGHT up to 10 feet
SPREAD up to 10 feet

HABIT
• bears 1-inch yellow flowers
• sports ornamental, deeply lobed leaves
• bears interesting oblong fruit resembling "warty" cucumbers
• resists most pests
• retains medicinal uses in its native regions

NATURAL RANGE
Asian and African tropics; naturalized in American tropics

TIPS
• use in the annual, cottage-style, or mixed garden
• provide full sun
• sow seeds directly in the garden ½ inch deep May–June
• water regularly
• provide firm support

BALSAM APPLE (*Momordica balsamina*)

TYPE nonhardy tropical annual vine
HEIGHT up to 8 feet
SPREAD up to 8 feet

HABIT
• bears 1-inch yellow flowers
• sports small ornamental, deeply dissected, delicate leaves
• bears orange spheroid, handsome fruit
• resists most pests

NATURAL RANGE
Asian and African tropics; naturalized in American tropics

TIPS
• use in the annual, cottage-style, or mixed garden
• provide full sun
• sow seeds directly in the garden ½ inch deep May–June
• water regularly
• provide firm support

Globe Candytuft

(Iberis umbellata)

FLOWERING ANNUAL

Native to southern Europe, the annual globe candytuft was introduced into Britain by 1596. According to conventional gardening wisdom, it was Lord Edward, eleventh Baron Zouche, who grew the plant at Hackney on his return from the Continent and who gave seed to his friend John Gerard, the Elizabethan herbalist. Not long after, Gerard celebrated it in this way: "Candie mustard excelleth all the rest . . . for the decking up of gardens and houses."[1]

Many garden writers, in fact, have remarked that, though a small and rather simple flower, candytuft insinuates itself into the hearts of gardeners by a profusion of flowers and a range of natural colors. It is the proverbial sweet flower by the doorstep. Its common name, candytuft, is not a reference to its succulence or to any candied use of the plant, but rather it refers to its presumed country of origin, Crete, known as Candia by Elizabethans. John Parkinson, botanist to Charles I of England, explained the second half of the name: "We give it in English, the name of Tufts, because it doth fit the forme of the flowers best."[2]

Candytuft's introduction into colonial America was early, according to noted garden historian Rudy Favretti, who dates its probable use in the English colonies in North America to 1600–1699. An early American reference made to "candy tuff" appeared in an advertisement for seeds by John Townley in the *Boston Evening-Post* in 1760.[3]

Growing to a consistent eight inches in the trial garden, the globe candytuft lived up to its reputation as a redoubtable performer and a charming, sweet-natured plant. Like its sister species rocket candytuft (*Iberis amara* 'Coronaria'), it has a long blooming season. The flowering "tufts" or globes, which give this candytuft its name, commenced on June 21 and finished on August 8. Colonial Williamsburg's Historic Area gardeners were particularly attracted to this plant as it was the closest of any of the direct-sown annuals to behave like the classic bedding plant: short, uniform, and massing itself into a single cloud of color.

Self-scattered seed dispersed in the summer resulted in seedlings in the fall of that year, with blooming plants occurring the following spring. Self-sown wallflowers (*Erysimum cheiri*), also from the previous year, wiggled themselves amidst the candytuft, and the result was a very attractive mixture with adventitious winter cress (*Barbarea verna*) thrown in as

well. The three bloomed without apparent competition throughout April.

A modern cultivar of candytuft, 'Appleblossom', was grown in the trial garden to compare its color range with that of the simple species candytuft in order to observe that inevitable genetic drift. The resulting plants were more uniformly pink but no "pinker" than the "unimproved" varieties. Nor were they noticeably pinker than the candytuft painted sometime before 1587 by Jacopo Ligozzi, court painter to Francesco de Medici, Grand Duke of Tuscany. Ligozzi's paintings were said to "lack nothing but the breath of life itself," and the grand duke was presumably sufficiently satisfied with Ligozzi's skill to commission him, at considerable expense, to record candytuft, and many other fine flowers, in a set of botanical paintings, now owned by the Uffizi Gallery in Florence, Italy. Candytuft's naive, sweet nature led Alexander Marshal to include it, though only once, in his florilegium, another sumptuous work.[4]

GLOBE CANDYTUFT
(*Iberis umbellata*)

TYPE hardy annual
HEIGHT 8–16 inches
SPREAD 8–12 inches

HABIT
- bears 1–2-inch flowers in shades of pink and white
- fairly long bloom period
- reliably self-sows
- resists most pests

NATURAL RANGE
Mediterranean region

TIPS
- use in the annual, cottage-style, or mixed garden
- provide full sun; partial shade in hot climates
- sow seeds directly in the garden ⅛ inch deep March–April or in early fall for bloom the next spring
- thin seedlings to 6 inches

Castor Bean

(Ricinus communis)
FLOWERING ANNUAL

Though its history is steeped in medical and utilitarian lore, castor bean's appeal today is largely ornamental. Nevertheless, in the twenty-first-century historically sensitive garden, it can play both, useful and ornamental, roles.

The history of castor bean can be traced through our oldest botanical records dating to about the third century BC. The tremendous annual is found in *Enquiry into Plants*, the earliest known written herbal, compiled by students of the Greek scholar Theophrastus, who inherited the famous Lyceum in Athens and its library and garden from its cofounder Aristotle. Theophrastus mentioned only the fact that castor bean's leaves change in form as the plant ages.[1]

Throughout most of its history, castor bean has been seen solely as the source of castor bean oil, which is pressed from the seeds of the plant. Herodotus, the Greek historian writing at roughly the same time as Theophrastus, recounted that the Egyptians used it extensively, apparently for lamp oil among other uses. In the first century AD, Dioscorides included castor bean in his *De materia medica* and provided a recipe for the production of castor bean oil, which he says is "good for ulcers that penetrate the head, parasitical skin diseases, inflammation of the perineum, and obstructions and damage to the uterus. . . . Taken as a drink it draws out watery matter through the bowels, and it also draws out worms."[2]

With so many classical references to it, it is not surprising to find castor bean in the 1542 Renaissance herbal of Leonhart Fuchs. Fuchs, a physician who brought to the study of plants scientific observation and hands-on experience as well as a thorough reading of the classic botanical texts, said that "it grows nowhere in Germany unless planted. It occurs now in gardens everywhere."[3]

Introduced into Britain in 1590, John Gerard recorded it in his herbal (1633) saying, "Palma Christi [another common name for castor bean] groweth in my garden, and in many other gardens likewise." Gerard ascribed to it medicinal qualities, some of which are still expressed today in the vile evacuative actions of castor oil on the digestive systems of its victims.[4]

Landon Carter, the proprietor of Sabine Hall in Virginia in the eighteenth century, attended personally to the medical conditions of his family and servants. On one occasion when his daughter Judy

was ill, with what he called "a great relaxation and emptying" of the stomach, "in order to give some degree of warmth to the Nervous coat of her stomach," he dosed her with "4 drops tincture Castor."[5]

Despite its former medicinal uses, the castor bean, which is the seed of the plant, contains an extremely toxic substance, ricin. A derivation of ricin, rendered into an oil, was infamously implicated in at least one political assassination in London. Greek physicians considered the oil that is pressed from the seeds so toxic that they prescribed it only for external application.

But, by the late nineteenth century, after the perfection of an extraction process that removes most of the toxins, castor oil appeared in many pharmacopoeias as a purgative and emetic, and generations of children were cured of their constipation and tummy aches with a face-cringing teaspoon of the hateful oil.[6]

The idea of regarding plants as strictly ornamental objects was just beginning to dawn towards the end of the sixteenth century. Basilius Besler's *Hortus Eystettensis,* a book devoted exclusively to the decorative appeal of flowers, was published in 1613. Castor bean occupies a place in that world-famous flower book. Its dramatic leaves and phenomenal size would have appealed to an audience fascinated with the exotics streaming out of places then still barely known.[7]

It was probably castor bean's exoticism, rather than its herbal qualities, that first attracted Thomas Jefferson to it. He mentioned it in his *Notes on the State of Virginia,* written in 1781. Later, in 1811, he mentioned in his garden diary that he planted a row of palma christi around his plant nursery, perhaps intending to ward away moles, an attribute of castor bean long held among wizened country gardeners. It was planted in the trial garden for similar reasons and was mingled with sunflowers *(Helianthus annuus),* which, when spent, were cut out so that castor bean was able to attain its maximum height in a temperate climate—twenty-two feet in the case of one exceptional and amply-watered specimen.[8]

It is in this dramatic aspect that castor bean excels. In the trial garden, three plants were positioned and then encouraged to grow quickly with ample water, fertilizer, pruning, and primping so that by autumn they attained the stature of small exotic trees, eliciting extreme curiosity from guests. The plant's leaves, up to two feet across and shaped like five-fingered palms, provide a bold-textured bower under which more-fragile plants find shade. Its flowers, while unusually large, aren't colorful in the species, but modern cultivars have had bred into their leaves and flowers bright reds and dark purples, which are particularly effective in modern, tropical design.

Although castor bean is capable of providing quick height and bold seasonal interest, gardeners should be aware of the extreme toxicity of the seeds. Modern varieties of castor bean produce seedpods of prickly starbursts in dark reds that fall late in summer; the pods dry well and are useful in floral arrangements when the seeds are completely shaken out. Even the older, wild species provides a seed head of interest. But, the extreme toxicity of the seeds should be well respected, as should the propensity of previously sealed seedpods to burst open as they dry. A single seed can be fatal. Nevertheless, seed oil production is vital today in the manufacture of soaps, paints, lubricants, varnishes, and dyes.

CASTOR BEAN, CASTOR-OIL PLANT, PALMA CHRISTI (*Ricinius communis*)

TYPE nonhardy tropical annual
HEIGHT up to 20 feet
SPREAD up to 10 feet

HABIT
- bears very large, palmate leaves
- flowers are followed by prickly seed capsules bearing poisonous seeds
- can become treelike if lower leaves are removed
- resists most pests

NATURAL RANGE
Africa; naturalized in American and Asian tropics

TIPS
- use in the annual, cottage-style, or mixed garden
- provide full sun
- sow seeds directly in the garden ½–1 inch deep May–June
- remove seed heads to prevent toxic seed production

China Aster

(Callistephus chinensis)
FLOWERING ANNUAL

ASTER *gallicusleeantisimus.*

Florid isn't always a polite word. Strictly speaking, it means flushed with rosy color, but it is often taken to mean something very ornate or flowery. It can also imply something overblown, over the top. In the world of archaic flowers, China aster is as florid as they come. China aster's three-inch flowers are so much larger than other flowers known at the beginning of the 1700s that their appeal was immediate. When the flower arrived in London in the 1730s, Peter Collinson, a pivotal London plant collector, wrote to American plant collector John Bartram in Philadelphia calling the China aster "the Noblest finest Plant thee ever saw of that Tribe."[1]

China aster arrived in Paris from China in 1728 when a Jesuit priest sent seeds of it there, although Pierre d'Incarville is often credited with the introduction. Once in Europe, the plant's appeal only waxed, and one garden historian described China aster as adorning courtyards and parlors from Scotland to the Rhine by 1750. By 1752, the even-more flamboyant double forms reached Europe, and, in 1770, Sir Horace Walpole described the Luxembourg Gardens in Paris wherein "every walk is buttoned on each side by lines of flower-pots, which succeed in their seasons"—in all, nine thousand pots of China asters were used.[2]

Amazingly, within five years of the plant's seed collection in eastern Asia, the cultivation of China aster had half-circumnavigated the globe. It was likely growing in the elaborate garden that John Custis kept in Williamsburg at the four intensively developed acres surrounding the house called Six Chimneys. From their well-documented, horticultural correspondence, we know that Custis, a gentleman gardener, received seed of China aster around 1736 from Peter Collinson in London. By 1792, China aster was commercially available in American nurseries, appearing on a plant list attributed to William Faris, an Annapolis nurseryman.[3]

Although the investment in time from the sowing of the seed to the flowering of China aster is considerable (three months in the trials), the rewards are magnificent. The clump in the trial garden had as many as a hundred flowers simultaneously blooming in shades of pink, blue, purple, and white. Keep in mind, too, that, after the first planting, the cycle repeats ad infinitum through self-sowing. Seedlings of China aster, however, resemble the foliage of the common plantain (*Plantago* sp.), so care must be taken not to mistakenly weed them out. Sufficient water is necessary to keep the plants looking their best, and attention should be paid to spider mites and the fungal diseases fusarium wilt and aster yellows, which are endemic to this species. Crop rotation can alleviate fungal problems, and mites can be controlled by daily misting with water the undersides of the leaves.

These drawbacks should not daunt the intrepid gardener. China aster's contribution to floriculture is the pure, "florid," ornamental appeal of its large daisy and double-daisy flowers, much in the blue range, and a growth habit prodigiously easy. If well tended, it is nearly incessant in its late summer flowering, beginning in early August and persisting into mid-September, often a time when the bulk of a garden's color is past and the eye begs for it. In this respect, China aster is a genius of timing.

In the trial garden, China aster became part of a serendipitous companion planting involving the native American perennial common milkweed (*Asclepias syriaca*) along with self-sown seedlings of the early-blooming annual larkspur (*Consolida orientalis*), a lovely combination. The witty merit in this arrangement was that the foliage of China aster and the larkspur obscured the awkward milkweed, and the trio presented a succession of bloom throughout the growing season: the larkspur in the spring, the milkweed in the summer, and China aster in the fall, an effortless sequence.

CHINA ASTER, GARDEN ASTER
(*Callistephus chinensis*)

TYPE nonhardy annual
HEIGHT up to 4 feet
SPREAD 12–36 inches

HABIT
- bears flowers up to 3 inches in diameter in blue, pink, purple, and white
- sports oval, deeply lobed leaves
- provides a good supply of cut flowers
- susceptible to aster yellows, spider mites, and fusarium wilt

NATURAL RANGE
China

TIPS
- use in the annual, cottage-style, or mixed garden
- provide full sun
- sow seeds directly in the garden ½ inch deep after danger of frost
- water regularly
- provide support via staking
- mist the undersides of the leaves daily to prevent spider mites
- rotate planting location from year to year to alleviate fungal problems

Crested Cockscomb

(Celosia argentea var. *cristata)*
FLOWERING ANNUAL

The forms and colors of cockscomb are renowned for their diversity. The *plumosa* varieties are known for their plumelike flower forms while the *cristata* are known for their crested forms, often resembling the folded mass of the human brain. Celosias can range in color from the softest pink to the most garish red, and modern cultivars have also captured the yellow and gold color range.

Some horticulturists maintain that *C. cristata* is a separate and distinct species from *C. argentea*. For those who maintain this distinction, *C. cristata* is described in the literature as debuting in the English gardening realm in 1570, imported from tropical Asia. *C. argentea* followed later in 1740. In any event, celosias were established in England and infiltrated the American colonies by the middle of the eighteenth century.[1]

In John Gerard's herbal (1633), one of a series of illustrations shows a crested celosia with all of the hallmarks of its type, including the tight twisting of the floral head. Gerard wrote, "This in stalks and leaves is much like the purple floure Gentle *[Amaranthus caudatus],* but the heads are larger, bended round, and laced, or as it were woven one with another looking very beautifully like to Crimson velvet: this is seldome to be found with us; but for the beauties sake is kept in the Gardens of Italy."[2]

On December 26, 1738, Peter Collinson of London wrote to John Custis of Williamsburg that "What Seed I planted or sow'd," included "tall coxcombs." This attribution jibes with noted garden historian Rudy Favretti's affirmation that celosia is appropriate for colonial-era gardens of the 1700–1776 range. Throughout its perambulations in the gardens of Europe, cockscomb also accumulated a number of alternative names, including *prince's feather*. It is that name by which Jefferson called it in 1767 when he mentioned sowing "a flower like the Prince's feather."[3]

As soon as celosias entered the British gardening imagination, great pains were taken to improve on Mother Nature. The results were vivid colors and distorted, exaggerated shapes, not to everyone's liking: "We cannot pretend to grieve over celosias' gradual decline in popularity. . . . It is not . . . a genus to be cultivated by persons of discernment or refined taste," wrote twentieth-century authors Ippolito Pizzetti and Henry Cocker.[4]

The conventional red crested celosia probably earned the disdain of Pizzetti

and Cocker and many others, but it is the perfect cottage garden plant because of its propensity to self-sow during the same growing year and the wild varieties' abilities to reach nearly five feet in height and remain in bloom until frost. Though garish, in the mixed garden the bright color can be coordinated with other forward colors, and a wonderful mélange of warm hues can be achieved. Periodic cutting for dried flower material elongates the flowering season and doesn't stunt the plant's growth; in fact, it provides a season's supply of crimson holiday decoration.

Not to be outdone for its value in the garden, and probably more acceptable to the likes of Pizzetti and Cocker, the silvery pink celosia known by many as *Celosia argentea* 'Pink Candle' has an understated soft color that makes it more amenable to subtler color schemes. Though probably not a centuries-old variety, this lovely celosia may represent a close aesthetic match to older varieties. At five feet tall and in bloom for four months, this cockscomb was a strong annual performer and an easy germinator with pleasant, nearly constant flower color in the trial garden; it would be a formidable element in a cottage-like garden.

A strict nostalgic gardener, working within the tight historical parameters of the colonial era, would include the classic red celosia but might avoid the pink celosia. However, gardeners working primarily with annuals of early origin but not overly concerned with complete adherence to a specific century, and who are looking for another rewarding annual, would do well to grow 'Pink Candle'; its appearance, at least, surely doesn't smack of brand-new, but rather it gently insinuates itself into a colonial-style mix.

'Pink Candle' was perhaps the best annual performer in the field trials. Rising to five feet, it sports silvery rose spikes about four inches long and displays them for four months. So understated and elegant is the plant as a whole that, in a mixed annual border, it would be terrific in massed clumps in the midsection and background. Its rapid growth, heat resistance, and easy germination make it a good, quick filler in period perennial or mixed plantings. At its columnar height, its use as a bedding plant is problematic. But, with its subtle coloring and obedient, vertical habit, it can easily become the centerpiece around which a muted planting could be arranged. In a jumbled mixed garden, its gentle pink would mix well with *Ageratum houstonianum*, the old-fashioned pink perennial yarrow (*Achillea millefolium* 'Roseum'), the blue spikes of the perennial speedwell (*Veronica spicata*), and boneset's (*Eupatorium perfoliatum*) important white.

CRESTED COCKSCOMB, PRINCE'S FEATHER
(*Celosia argentea* var. *cristata*)

TYPE nonhardy annual
HEIGHT 4–5 feet
SPREAD 12 inches

HABIT
- bears spikes of red, yellow, pink, and white amaranth-like flowers
- provides a very vertical element in mixed plantings
- will rebloom if deadheaded
- self-sows readily if spent flowers are not removed
- resists most pests

NATURAL RANGE
Asian tropics

TIPS
- use in the annual, cottage-style, or mixed garden
- provide full sun
- sow seeds directly in the garden ¼ inch deep late May–June

Cypress Vine

(Ipomoea quamoclit)
FLOWERING ANNUAL VINE

Cypress vine is one of the plants that present a quandary for historic landscape managers, falling within the 1780 to 1800 gray area. The vine was documented in America in 1791 when Thomas Jefferson sent seed of this plant from Philadelphia to his two daughters, Mary and Martha, then at Monticello, Jefferson's plantation. In Williamsburg today, the St. George Tucker House, interpreted as a late eighteenth-century house and garden of a member of the higher Virginia gentry, might be an appropriate venue in which to grow this curious, heat-happy, and rare-for-the-time annual vine. Gardeners who can take full advantage of the last two decades of the eighteenth-century's contributions and are not bound by strict adherence to the colonial period are encouraged to add cypress vine to their spring seed lists.[1]

Cypress vine was brand-new to England when it was included in the appendix of the 1633 reprint of John Gerard's *Herbal*. As it was not suited to England's cool summers, it was given a cursory description for a plant so exotic, though its most important cultural habit was correctly identified: abhorrence of cold. "It is so tender a plant that it will not come to any perfection with us,

unlesse in extraordinary hot yeres, and by other artificiall helps." But, in the heat of Virginia, a hill of four or five seeds can yield twenty feet of vine dappled with fine, ferny foliage and small scarlet flowers. "It much delights the eie of the beholder," said Gerard, "and is therefore kept in pots in gardens of pleasure." The scarlet red of the flowers is particularly vivid, and even a sharply focused camera lens cannot reproduce the velvet quality and the three-dimensionality of the cushiony flowers.[2]

Cypress vine dates in Europe to at least as early as 1587 when the remarkable Jacopo Ligozzi's gouache on paper illustrated cypress vine's early presence in the dynamic horticultural atmosphere of Renaissance Italy. Cypress vine was also illustrated later in Philip Miller's *Figures of the Most Beautiful, Useful, and Uncommon Plants*, bringing it to the vivid attention of English garden lovers when he published his two-volume illustrated book in 1760. Miller said, "The Plant grows naturally in both *Indies,* from whence the Seeds were first brought to *Europe,* where it has been long cultivated," acknowledging cypress vine's early arrival in Europe. He added, "The Inhabitants of the *British* Islands in *America* call this

Plant *Sweet William*," perhaps a comment on the vividness of the red flower, which resembles the saturated hues of the traditional sweet William, the biennial *Dianthus* species long known and grown in England.[3]

In the trial garden, the first crop of cypress vine, planted in late spring, grew prolifically during a hot, dry summer. The crop was allowed to colonize an old picket fence until hard frost in November put an end to a summer of abundant flowering. Self-sown seed germinated abruptly early the next year, but a succession of forty-degree nights in mid-May halted the vine in its tracks, effectively killing the small, tender seedlings.

With renewed warm weather, however, new seedlings emerged, and pink- and white-flowered varieties appeared spontaneously during that summer.

Since it is a prolific self-seeder, its use comes with a word of caution. But, without a doubt, cypress vine solicited more questions than any other plant in the trial garden. The ferny foliage, of a light, robust green, elegantly drapes fence lines, creating swags of green interrupted by the vivid pinpricks of vibrant red. In all respects, cypress vine is enormously attractive, flourishing in the high heat of Williamsburg, thinking itself at home in the tropics until inevitable frost halts its headlong run.

CYPRESS VINE, CARDINAL VINE, STAR-GLORY, SWEET WILLIAM, QUAMOCLIT
(*Ipomoea quamoclit*)

TYPE nonhardy annual vine
HEIGHT up to 10 feet, with support
SPREAD 20 feet

HABIT
- quickly becomes rampant where happy
- bears ½-inch flowers in a deep red
- requires something on which to climb: fence, trellis, etc.
- self-sows very reliably
- provides quick results

NATURAL RANGE
American tropics

TIPS
- use in the annual, cottage-style, or mixed garden
- provide full sun
- sow seeds directly in the garden ⅛ inch deep after danger of frost
- thin seedlings to 12–18 inches

Devil's Claw

(Proboscidea louisianica)
FLOWERING ANNUAL

Devil's claw is an oddity with several curious characteristics. Its seedpods resemble two-fingered claws, recurved with thorny peril. In sharp contrast, its pink flowers, splotched with yellow, exude a sweet soapy scent and are distinctly ornamental. Its pedigree is confusing. It has been attributed to two families of plants, Pedaliaceae and Martyniaceae, and to two genera, *Proboscidea* and *Martynia*. Gardeners looking for seed should search for both genera because both are still in common usage. Authorities also disagree about its native region. Some say it is native to Mexico, while others say to the eastern seaboard south of Delaware, along the Texas coastline, to New Mexico. Perhaps its species name, *louisianica*, gives a broad idea as to the native region of this heat-loving, fast-growing, self-seeding annual.[1]

In Philip Miller's great opus, *Figures of the Most Beautiful, Useful, and Uncommon Plants* (1760), he wrote, "The Seeds of this Plant were brought from *Missisippi* to the Gardens at *Paris,* where it was first propagated; and the Plants ripened their Seeds there, some of which were sent me by Mr. *Richard,* the King's Gardener at *Versailles.* These were sown in the *Chelsea* garden [near London]; but they remained a year in the Ground a Year before they began to vegetate." Miller's use of "Missisippi" is interesting since he used the name well before the incorporation of the state. One assumes that this reference is to the region of the great river, placing us back again in the environs of Louisiana.[2]

When grown in the hot summer sunlight and humid air of Williamsburg, the plant exhibited none of the reticence to sprout that Mr. Miller recounted in his attempt in the cooler ground of the Chelsea Physic Garden. Seeds, soaked for twenty-four hours before planting, were sown well into the warm season when the soil had warmed to eighty degrees. The seedlings grew quickly and flowered a mere thirty-three days after the seeds were sown. Its cultivation is like that of okra (*Abelmoschus esculentus*): full sun, hot weather, and plenteous water.

Its presence in the garden is akin to a tropical borage (*Borago officinalis*), floppy and big leaved, with tremendous texture. But, its flowers couldn't be more different from borage's sumptuous blue. The soft pink flowers of devil's claw are large and massed on vertical stalks, and the yellow striped throat is easy to observe. In its native regions, the distinctive fruit,

DEVIL'S CLAW, UNICORN PLANT, RAM'S-HORN
(*Proboscidea louisianica*)

TYPE nonhardy annual
HEIGHT 30 inches
SPREAD up to 4 feet

HABIT
• bears 2-inch-long pendant flowers
• sports coarse, hairy foliage
• reliably self-sows
• resists most pests

NATURAL RANGE
Mexico, southern United States

TIPS
• use in the annual, cottage-style, or mixed garden
• provide full sun
• sow seeds directly in the garden ¼ inch deep May–June
• thin seedlings to 6 inches

which Miller's illustration so well details, is picked when tender and used for pickles. If the fruit is allowed to develop into hardened seedpods, they eventually dry and crack and disperse their seed in the vicinity. Self-sown seed reliably sprouts in spring, and a patch of devil's claw can easily be maintained throughout multiple years.[3]

Whether this plant's roundabout history from the New World to the French king's garden included a return to the New World and the eighteenth-century gardens of the Chesapeake region is doubtful. It did appear in a lovely illustrated botanical volume published in London in 1760 and in America in Philadelphian Bernard McMahon's *American Gardener's Calendar* of 1806. Its quick growth, its self-seeding reliability, and its facility for developing fascinating seedpods make it an essential element in the combination of annuals, biennials, and perennials that constitutes the modern mixed garden.[4]

Flax

(Linum usitatissimum)
FLOWERING ANNUAL

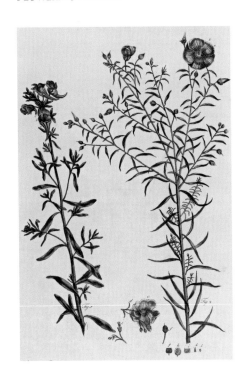

Flax, blue and beautiful, is not a garden plant; it is a field crop, its beaten stems yielding linen, an indispensable textile fiber used by Europeans and colonial Americans alike. For modern gardeners, centuries away from making their own clothes, flax is a lovely wispy annual ornamental with periwinkle blue flowers. Although short blooming, the willowy foliage turns to a bright gold as flax passes into maturity. Its best use in the modern garden is in a marginal setting where its ephemerality and informality don't intrude on more formal parts of the garden. In order to have the seductive blue flowers at all, inventive gardeners might leverage it in with other semiwild plants such as viper's bugloss *(Echium vulgare),* corn poppies *(Papaver rhoeas),* moth mullein *(Verbascum blattaria),* scabious *(Scabiosa atropurpurea),* and toadflax *(Linaria vulgaris).*

Flax was probably first used as a textile fiber by the Egyptians, although it was eventually adopted by the Greeks, Romans, and Chinese, among other peoples. Ultimately, Belgium developed a well-deserved reputation as the finest linen producer in modern times, but the golden fields of ripening Flanders flax are a disappearing sight as the world turns to cotton and new blends.[1]

In the first century, Dioscorides chose to concentrate on the therapeutic properties of flaxseed and flaxseed oil rather than on flax's historical use as a textile fiber, perhaps so patently known that he spared his readers. He said the seed, taken with honey and oil, had the same power as fenugreek *(Trigonella foenum-graecum),* "mollifying all inflammation inwardly & outwardly." Internally, he said, "it brings out also thinges from ye Thorax, being taken with Hony . . . & it doth asswage the coughs."[2]

John Gerard, the Elizabethan herbalist, typically, repeated Dioscorides's notes regarding flaxseed oil: "The seed of Line and Fenugreek made into powder, boiled with Mallowes, violet leaves, Smallage, and Chickweed, untill the herbs be soft; then stamped in a stone morter with a little hogs grease to the forme of a cataplasme or pultesse, appeaseth all maner of paine, softeneth all cold tumors or swellings, mollifieth and bringeth to suppuration all apostumes." Addressing other uses for the oil, he said that, when "pressed out of the seed, [it] is profitable for many purposes in physicke and surgery, and is used of painters, picture makers, and other artificers."[3]

Even modern herbal writers testify to the efficacy of flaxseed and flaxseed oil. The oil is high in alpha-linolenic acid, one of the omega-3 fatty acids, which are essential to human health and distinctly beneficial in the battle against cardiovascular disease, according to the American Heart Association. Additionally, flaxseeds, taken whole, act as a bulk laxative and draw toxins out of the digestive tract.[4]

In John Lawson's account of early Carolina history, *A New Voyage to Carolina* (1709), he made illustrating references to the growth and use of linen in the southern colony:

> The Women are the most industrious Sex in that Place, and, by their good Houswifry, make a great deal of Cloath of their own Cotton, Wool and Flax; some of them keeping their Families (though large) very decently apparel'd, both with Linnens and Woollens.

> The *French* are good Neighbours amongst us, and give Examples of Industry, which is much wanted in this Country. They make good Flax, Hemp, Linnen-Cloth and Thread; which they exchange amongst the Neighbourhood for other Commodities, for which they have occasion.[5]

Though it detests heat, germination of flaxseed in the trial garden proved effortless; seed sprouted in about a week or so. The prodigious number of seedlings grew quickly and very vertically, bearing slender stems with blue-gray foliage. The growth habit is wispy, and the effect is one of delicacy, belying the flax fiber's inherent strength. Flowering was strong for nearly three weeks and continued very sporadically while the seed cases ripened, turning golden brown on still-attractive stems, giving flax another common name, *golden flax*.

Although its place is not in the garden, a patch of it or a very small meadow planted with it is an indescribable sight, its delicate, light-blue flowers dancing all at a certain consistent height. In some situations, small meadows, fields, and orchards can become part of the garden. Since flax plants tend to be tall and leggy, a thick sowing of seed will provide wide drifts of attractive filler and background massing in the annual or mixed garden.

Although more crop than flower, a smattering here and there of annual flax, easily accomplished with seed and water, can be wedged and inched into pockets in the garden as quick, temporary filler. Annual blue flax, when in flower, is a happy event, and the modern retrospective gardener should find a way to weave it into a new, modern environment. Pest free and inherently attractive, flax is a flower crop suited to the experienced annual gardener as well as an easy plant for beginners and children to grow.

FLAX, COMMON FLAX, GOLDEN FLAX
(Linum usitatissimum)

TYPE annual
HEIGHT up to 4 feet
SPREAD 12 inches

HABIT
- bears ½-inch delicate blue flowers
- produces tall, narrow stems with delicate foliage
- foliage and seedpods turn golden as they mature
- resists most pests

NATURAL RANGE
Asia; now a cultigen

TIPS
- use in the annual, cottage-style, or meadow garden
- provide full sun; partial shade in hot climates
- sow seeds directly in the garden at or near the surface of the soil in April
- thin seedlings to 6 inches

Flossflower

(Ageratum houstonianum)
FLOWERING ANNUAL

Most modern gardeners are fond of the soft tufts of pale blue flowers that mark flossflower, but most are only familiar with the frustratingly squat, modern cultivars that predominate in garden centers. These modern types, sometimes as short as six inches, are derived from a far more delightful and taller species of ageratum found in Central America by William Houston (1695–1733), a ship's surgeon and plant collector.[1]

When exactly the ageratum species named for Houston reached the hands of English collectors is open to some debate. The Royal Horticultural Society cites 1822 as the year in which this ageratum was introduced into Great Britain. However, Philip Miller referenced *Ageratum houstonianum* in a 1768 edition of his *Gardeners Dictionary*. In that work, published in London, Miller wrote that this species "was found growing naturally at La Vera Cruz [Mexico], by the late Dr. William Houstoun, who sent seeds to Europe, which have so well succeeded in many gardens, as to become a weed in the hotbeds." Given Miller's 1768 reference, we can speculate that this plant was likely grown in at least some gentry English gardens prior the purported 1822 date.[2]

Although one prominent garden historian affirms that this ageratum's first American citation is comparatively late, 1836, it was at least percolating around Europe for roughly the previous hundred years in light of the fact that William Houston, who discovered it and for whom it was named, died in 1733. The difference in the degree of horticultural sophistication between precocious European horticulture and early America's young and plant-hungry new gardening tradition can be frustrating for gardeners looking for an American, eighteenth-century origin for their favorite nineteenth-century flowers.[3]

Trial plantings bore out Philip Miller's observation of this ageratum's potentially weedy nature. In fact, so persistent is this species of flossflower that the United States Department of Agriculture (USDA) now considers this species to be permanently distributed in Connecticut, Massachusetts, Florida, Alabama, Georgia, North and South Carolina, and Hawaii.[4]

That it so easily seeds itself from year to year can be a bane to some gardeners and a boon to others who are looking for regenerating herbaceous plants that allow a self-perpetuating palette of flowers that spans an entire

growing season. The robust fitness of this ageratum, which grows to two and a half feet and generates a free-flowing mass of flowers, makes it hard to overlook in the selection of carefree, antique annuals. The slight but noticeable variation in color of the flower, bluish but also pink and white at times, and the strong, maroon stems amplify the appeal of the plant. In bloom for nearly three months, the clump assumes a naturally graceful mound that seats itself casually into the landscape of the garden. In the trial garden, it mixed particularly well with the white bishop's weed (*Ammi majus*), the red small-flowered zinnia (*Zinnia pauciflora*), mixed four-o'clocks (*Mirabilis jalapa*), and the antique striped French marigold (*Tagetes patula* 'Striped'), in what became a complicated and content bundle of interwoven flowering stems all of which persisted, to some degree, till frost.

While Colonial Williamsburg would shy away from the use of this ageratum because of its probable late entry into American horticulture, gardeners comfortable with its 1768 English provenance and early nineteenth-century American introduction would be well-advised to include flossflower in their mixed annual planting schemes. In the residential garden, and in the gardens of plant connoisseurs and laissez-faire gardeners looking for carefree historically dated flowers, *A. houstonianum* is a reliable, long-blooming annual, subtle in its color and robust in its growth.

FLOSSFLOWER, AGERATUM, BLUEMINK
(*Ageratum houstonianum*)

TYPE nonhardy annual
HEIGHT 24–30 inches
SPREAD 24–36 inches

HABIT
- soft and mounding
- long blooming (May–November)
- reliably self-sows; can be weedy
- pest resistant

NATURAL RANGE
Central America

TIPS
- use in the annual, cottage-style, or mixed garden
- provide full sun; partial shade in hot climates
- sow seeds directly in the garden at or near the surface of the soil after danger of frost
- thin seedlings to 12 inches

Four-o'Clock

(Mirabilis jalapa)
FLOWERING ANNUAL

Nothing epitomizes a flower's fall from grace so much as the four-o'clock, or marvel-of-Peru. It reached prominence in Europe in the early seventeenth century, when parti-colored and bicolored flowered varieties became highly sought after. Its subsequent nose-dive in popularity throughout the twentieth century may have been related to the relative loss of the vintage variegated types; such specimens offer something beyond the invariable rose pink and yellow types typically found today.

In John Gerard's *Herbal* of 1633, he said that "the seed of this strange plant was brought first into Spaine, from Peru, whereof it tooke his name *Mirabilia Peruana,* or *Peruviana:* and since dispersed into all the parts of Europe." The marvel of the plant is the fact that, from the same seed, or from the same fleshy black tuber that the plant eventually forms, marvelous flowers in a variety of colors are produced. This trait led plant-hungry Elizabethans into a spiral of speculation concerning this flower of many colors. Gerard described every iteration of this phenomenon:

> [The] flowers . . . doe resemble
> the flowers of Tobaco . . . glittering

oftentimes with a fine purple or Crimson colour; many times of an horse-flesh; sometime yellow; sometime pale, and sometime resembling an old red or yellow colour; sometime whitish, and most commonly two colours occupying halfe the flower, or intercoursing the whole flower with streakes and orderly streames, now yellow, now purple, divided through the whole; having sometime great, sometime little spots of a purple colour, sprinkled and scattered in a most variable order, and brave mixture.[1]

Basilius Besler's remarkable florilegium (1613) includes the red and yellow–striped varieties. Similarly, Alexander Marshal's florilegium (ca. 1653) contains a watercolor of a variety of four-o'clocks with red and white–striped flowers.[2]

Its common name, *four-o'clock,* alludes to the fact that the flowers open only towards dusk, at four-o'clock at some latitudes. Thomas Jefferson, writing on July 18, 1767, remarked in his Garden Book, "Mirabilis just opened. very clever," evidence of his fascination with the sun-sensitive four-o'clocks. At the opening of the flowers at evening time,

 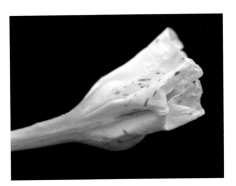 

FOUR-O'CLOCK, MARVEL-OF-PERU, BEAUTY-OF-THE-NIGHT
(*Mirabilis jalapa*)

TYPE nonhardy tuberous perennial
grown as a recurring self-seeding
annual
HEIGHT up to 4 feet
SPREAD up to 36 inches

HABIT
- bears 1-inch flowers in shades and
combinations of rose and yellow,
sometimes striped
- can be floppy without staking
- reliably self-sows
- resists most pests

NATURAL RANGE
American tropics

TIPS
- use in the annual, cottage-style, or
mixed garden
- provide full sun
- sow seeds directly in the garden ¼
inch deep May–June
- thin seedlings to 12 inches

the four-o'clock releases its sweet scent, making it a perfect plant for the fragrant after-dark garden. A combination of the sweet-smelling four-o'clocks, mignonette (*Reseda odorata*), and heliotrope (*Heliotropium arborescens*) would ensure an after-hours aromatic bonanza.[3]

Rudy Favretti, a veteran garden historian, considers four-o'clocks appropriate for historical gardens dating in the 1600–1699 range. However, the intervening years have not been kind to the four-o'clock's reputation. Considered rather common, they are seldom seen in selective modern gardens. But, if the determined gardener were to grow a modern cultivar such as 'Broken Colors', one that approximates the descriptions and graphic evidence of older varieties, the unrelenting yellows and reds might wane and he might find himself with the reliable, ever-present, and ingeniously

colored four-o'clocks such as were grown in the trial garden.[4]

Their culture is fantastically easy when seed is sown with the advent of hot weather and soil temperatures reach the eighty-degree range. Germination usually takes less than two weeks with growth occurring rapidly in warm weather. During the first year, the plants form tubers that are marginally hardy, but, in colder areas, they should be lifted in the fall and stored for use the next year. Though four-o'clocks multiply readily from seed, prized strains should be propagated via their tubers rather than via seeding since seeding allows genetic drift to take its random course. Be wary of unscrupulous bulb merchants, however, who offer four-o'clock tubers with fancy names at high prices: the savvy gardener can grow the same plants from a handful of seed.

Job's Tears

(Coix lacryma-jobi)
FLOWERING ANNUAL

Job's tears refers to the tears shed by the biblical Job who was unfairly accused by his neighbors and tested by God. The tears are represented on the plant by the seeds, which bear two white filaments symbolizing Job's lament. Though the white filaments are a great novelty, the plant's importance, ornamentally, in the garden is marginal. The four-foot foliage of this annual, tropical grass is only but so interesting. It is the historical use of Job's tears that should be of interest to gardeners.

Job's tears is known primarily for its production of one-quarter-inch, pea-like seeds that are completely round and that become very hard when dried. In southern Asia, from whence the plant originally comes, the seeds are used as a cereal grain. Once harvested and winnowed, the seeds are mixed into stews, soups, and broths; eaten raw as one would eat any small edible nut or seed; and fermented into an alcoholic beverage. The Chinese also pound the seeds into flour for use in cakes and breads. An astonishingly long list of folk remedies is appended to this extremely useful grain.[1]

Leonhart Fuchs, the German herbalist, mentioned Job's tears and included a colored illustration in the Vienna Codex, his greatest work, dating from the time of his death in 1566. The plant does not appear, however, in his earlier herbal of 1542. John Gerard's 1633 English herbal includes a woodcut illustration and short commentary about Job's tears. Gerard considered the plant's arrival in England to have been by way of Italy, where he said it grew very well. In his own climate, it had a reputation for not coming to seed, although he coaxed one season's worth, the "Sommer being very hot." Though Gerard didn't mention its important use as a grain or its historical reputation as a medical herb, he had heard, by way of France, that, with the seeds, "they do make beads, bracelets, and chaines thereof." Their use in rosaries is centuries old, and they are still a feature today in traditional Asian jewelry.[2]

The echo of Englishmen lamenting their cold climate is heard in Philip Miller's 1754 London account of his trials with Job's tears and in his description of its necessary germination in hotbeds and its eventual transplantation to the warm border. The fact that Job's tears is a sort of grain wasn't lost on Miller, who said the "poorer Sort of People" in "hot Countries" make a coarse sort of bread with the flour of "Coix." He also noted

the Portuguese habit of stringing the seeds as beads.[3]

Surprisingly, Job's tears appears today among the 710 dried specimens in the John Clayton Herbarium in the British Natural History Museum. These specimens were collected in Virginia by John Clayton, the American gentleman botanist, in the middle of the eighteenth century. The plant's presence in Clayton's collection definitively testifies to its incidence in eighteenth-century Virginia, but we know nothing more about its cultivation in the colonies. We don't know if Clayton collected it in the wild or from a garden, and no specific evidence suggests that Virginians made meals from its grain.[4]

Job's tears, Indian-shot (*Canna indica*), castor bean (*Ricinus communis*), cypress vine (*Ipomoea quamoclit*), and all the amaranths (*Amaranthus* spp. and *Celosia* spp.) represent but a few of the many tropical oddities that found their way into Virginian gardens prior to the middle of the eighteenth century. But, their mere mention in historical testimonials still begs the question of how to use them in the garden, how to leverage their exoticism within the context of more demure, temperate North American and Eurasian species.

Job's tears, which looks to some people like short corn, and Indian-shot, which looks like bigger corn, don't have the subtlety of leaf to quietly and elegantly inure themselves into a well-composed garden setting. One school would segregate them to different parts of the garden so that the combination of their simple long leaves wouldn't constitute too much of a voting block.

Others would say to grow the Job's tears around the base of the taller Indian-shot, the grassy disorganization of Job's tears under the larger disorganization of the Indian-shot. In a novelty garden, where the gardener is growing many species for the simple reason of experiencing them, the couplings and groupings of plants are less an issue, with workable and attractive combinations slowly winnowing themselves out in mixed garden–like fashion.

In the trial garden, the two plants were grown together, but the Indian-shot proved not hardy, while the seedlings of Job's tears proliferated the following summer. The cluster of Job's tears then expanded every subsequent year, a possible liability. But, using Job's tears as a real culinary-garden small grain is a distinctly possible concept because a small patch provides ample and easily collected seeds wherever it is grown. When fresh, with the character of small chickpeas, they can be sliced, salted, and added to salads or incorporated into cooked dishes.

JOB'S TEARS
(*Coix lacryma-jobi*)

TYPE nonhardy annual grass
HEIGHT 3–6 feet
SPREAD 3–4 feet

HABIT
- bears pendulous seedpods
- bears seeds with white filaments
- reliably self-sows
- tolerates heat if kept moist

NATURAL RANGE
southeastern Asia

TIPS
- use in the annual, cottage-style, or mixed garden
- provide full sun; partial shade in hot climates
- sow seeds directly in the garden ½ inch deep when the soil warms to 80°F
- thin seedlings to 6 inches

Larkspur

(Consolida orientalis)
FLOWERING ANNUAL

Larkspur is the heart and soul of the colonial-style garden. This lovely, colorful plant has been esteemed as an ornamental flower since the time of the ancient Greeks. According to Theophrastus in his ancient herbal, larkspur was one of the longer-blooming coronary plants and one used by the garland makers. Larkspur's habit of prodigious seed production and its propensity to colonize great swaths of the garden guarantee that next year's garden may be half larkspur if the gardener so decides.[1]

Larkspur remains immensely popular, and it is rampant in the historical record. Of the myriad annual larkspur species, three are well-known: *Consolida ambigua, C. orientalis,* and *C. regalis. C. regalis* has a natural distribution somewhat north of the other two, which are essentially Pan-Mediterranean. It is not surprising then that *C. regalis* should turn up in Leonhart Fuchs's German herbal of 1542, since its native range is squarely within Fuchs's purview. The rendering in Fuchs's herbal illustrates a plant that is still loosely flowered, prior to the elaborate cultivation that would render it, and the other annual *Consolida* species, fully doubled and massively dense, as seen in Basilius Besler's florilegium and other German flower books, just seventy years later.[2]

Few European annuals were cultivated with quite the passion as larkspur. In England, by 1633 when John Gerard's herbal was republished, varieties proliferated. Gerard pictured five in his herbal, including the "Great double Larks spur," being fully doubled, even ruffled. Out of the five larkspurs he mentioned, four "are set and sowne in gardens" while "the last ['the wilde Larks spur'] groweth wilde in corne fields," though not in England, but "frequently found in such places in many parts of Germanie." This is likely the larkspur illustrated by Fuchs.[3]

Larkspur remained a sensation in Europe throughout the seventeenth century. Alexander Marshal included six individual watercolors of larkspur in pink and blue, single and double forms, in his magnificent florilegium, thought to have been substantially finished in 1653. Contemporaneously, John Evelyn, a courtier and gardener, recommended *"Larkes heele"* for use "next the Walles," presumably where it benefited from stored heat: "Thus if the dubble-stock . . . & Lilies . . . grow next the Walles, let the *Tulip* succeede; with the *Iris, Calcedone,*

Narcissus, Carnations, Larkes heele in their *Series* for so likewise they . . . flower one after another."[4]

By the middle of the eighteenth century, larkspurs permeated emerging horticulture in the English colonies. An advertisement for flower seeds to be sold by John Townley in a 1760 *Boston Evening-Post* included "double larkin spur." And Thomas Jefferson clearly noted larkspur in bloom at Shadwell, his birthplace in Virginia, in 1767.[5]

When grown in the trial garden, *C. orientalis* performed beautifully and proved to be one of the showiest flowers in the garden. If kept watered and deadheaded, and if the spring stays cool, larkspur can be a rewarding, long-blooming annual. It is so prolific in its seeding that, by the second year, in some places, it can assume half of the available growing space and can colonize gardens with outrageously lovely pink, blue, and purple wands of four-to-five-foot larkspur.

To the twenty-first-century eye, many older varieties of flowers may look small and unimproved, not having been the subject of centuries of selective breeding. Consequently, many guests at the trial garden remarked on the variety of leaf textures, which is more apparent with small flowers. But, larkspur was the exception to this tendency to notice leaf before flower. One couldn't ignore ten- and fifteen-foot drifts of self-sown larkspur, which, in one wet, cool spring, lasted until the end of June.

Love-in-a-Mist

(Nigella damascena)
FLOWERING ANNUAL

Love-in-a-mist is a fleetingly lovely annual whose flowering is so sweet and stunning, and whose cultivation so easy, that its habit to swiftly flower is overlooked for the sake of having the brief flowers at all. The complicated architecture of the flower has led some to call it love-in-a-puzzle, love-entangle, and jack-in-prison. Others have called it odd, strange, and innocent looking, but the beauty of love-in-a-mist quickly beguiles the gardener and admirer alike.

Love-in-a-mist became part of the Elizabethan garden palette soon after it arrived in England in 1570 from southern Europe. Gerard (1633), never eloquent, called it "faire and pleasant, called Damaske Nigella," an imprecise attribution of origin to Damascus, Syria. It, in fact, has a far wider native dispersal, nearly Pan-Mediterranean. Philip Miller, however, also placed it in Syria when he referred to the various species of nigella in his glorious 1760 herbal: "This Plant grows naturally in the Corn Fields about *Aleppo,* from whence the Seeds were first brought to *Europe*." Aleppo is a city in Syria.[1]

Love-in-a-mist's association with the Middle East is ancient. Some cultures pressed the seed of this species for its essential oil to use as a base for cosmetics and perfumes. In fact, in his great German herbal, Leonhart Fuchs cited the usual trio of ancient plantsmen, Dioscorides, Pliny, and Galen, who regarded it as a cure for many ailments. Modern authorities know it as a seed with oil-bearing properties and as a cousin to *N. sativa*, black cumin, a species with dozens of culinary and folk medicinal uses.[2]

Its popularity and quick adoption by English gardeners resulted in love-in-a-mist becoming inextricably linked with the cottager's plot. Christopher Lloyd, the essential English gardener, explained why the plant was grown on English soil for four hundred years: "So long as you keep your garden cultivated, love-in-a-mist will return annually from its own seed, the largest seedlings developing from those that germinated in autumn and grew through the winter months," the best, most succinct explanation of the growth cycle of the "hardy annual" (perhaps an oxymoron to the uninitiated).[3]

Love-in-a-mist is one of the best-documented annual plants for our historic gardens. Its specific mention in an advertisement in Boston in 1760 invites

its use by gardeners desiring plants from the later eighteenth century.[4]

Its authenticity is matched by its ease of cultivation. Love-in-a-mist is one of those "bolters," flowers and greens that mature, flower, and seed quickly, especially in response to any real heat. But, its precocity in this respect is compensated for by the glory and complexity of the flower, the abundant bloom, and its signature seed heads, a staple of the dried floral artist. Complementing its flowering habit, its foliage is among the most pleasant in the plant kingdom, with delicate, wispy threadlike leaves in sumptuous green. An opportunity would be lost should the domestic gardener forego this traditional member of the real cottage garden, a hardy annual that keeps

age-old company with the larkspur (*Consolida orientalis*), corn poppy (*Papaver rhoeas*), yellow horned poppy (*Glaucium flavum*), and bachelor's button (*Centaurea cyanus*) in that storied gardenscape.

One season's experience is all you need to learn its easy tricks. Though best sown in autumn, love-in-a-mist proved winningly easy even when sown the third week of April. After flowering by the end of June and persisting for under a month, seed heads seemed to materialize immediately. New seedlings appeared in the autumn, were vigorous through cold November and December, and bloomed the following April. Love-in-a-mist, a plant of utter antiquity, can be enjoyed by modern gardeners in a variety of new cultivars and colors.

LOVE-IN-A-MIST, FENNEL FLOWER, LOVE-IN-A-PUZZLE, LOVE-ENTANGLE, JACK-IN-PRISON
(*Nigella damascena*)

TYPE hardy annual
HEIGHT 18 inches
SPREAD 12 inches

HABIT
- bears 1-inch delicate flowers
- prefers cool weather
- sports ornamental, feathery foliage
- reliably self-sows
- resists most pests

NATURAL RANGE
southern Europe, northern Africa

TIPS
- use in the annual, cottage-style, or mixed garden
- provide full sun; partial shade in hot climates
- sow seeds directly in the garden 1/8 inch deep March–April or August–September
- thin seedlings to 6 inches

Love-Lies-Bleeding

(Amaranthus caudatus)
FLOWERING ANNUAL

Love-lies-bleeding is probably so familiar that its provenance and history may have little meaning to gardeners too aware of its current reputation as coarse, gaudy, and common. But, the fuzzy tassels that are the hallmark of love-lies-bleeding are known to lengthen to two feet, provide months of amusement, and are a steadfastly Elizabethan statement in the very best American antiquarian gardens.

Imported into England in 1596, less than a century after the Spanish found love-lies-bleeding and other amaranths in Central and South America, this plant became the rage of the late-Elizabethan highbrow and, thereafter, a favorite in the flower borders of the Stuarts and in the cottage gardens of the yeomen. Its robust, tasseled flower heads were in a realm above the prim and sedate flowers of Renaissance England and Europe. John Gerard (1633) knew love-lies-bleeding as "Branched Floure-Gentle" and said that he "can compare the shape thereof to nothing so fitly as to the velvet head of a Stag, compact of such soft matter as is the same." Gerard was referring to the Scottish red deer, which annually sheds crimson felt from newly emerged horn. The common name shift from

"floure-gentle" to "love-lies-bleeding" occurred in 1665 when John Rea said, "This is an old flower and common, called by some Country women, *Love lies a bleeding*," although "floure-gentle" was still current.[1]

John Evelyn, a Stuart-era court figure and gardener, referenced love-lies-bleeding by its Latin name, *"Amaranthus* The *Flower-Gentle* {The noblest of all Annuals},"* and lauded it as the immortal amaranth, *"immortalisque Amaranthe,"* because of its use as a dried coronary flower. Early in the seventeenth century, love-lies-bleeding underwent yet another change in common name. In John Mortimer's *Whole Art of Husbandry,* he introduced his readers to "Princes Feathers": *"Amaranth* Flowers gentle, or Princes Feathers, are of great Variety." Philip Miller, writing in the mid-eighteenth century, recommended love-lies-bleeding for use in open borders or in pots. He emphasized that in England they need the benefit of germination in a hotbed early in the season, and then "It is in Beauty from the Middle of *June* till the Frost."[2]

Though purely an ornamental curiosity in England, love-lies-bleeding was a primary foodstuff in its native regions.

Miller commented that most species of amaranths were used locally as culinary plants, though as food, he thought, they didn't hold a candle to cabbage and spinach. He specifically stated that Central American natives used love-lies-bleeding as a boiled salad. Given its popularity in Europe in the seventeenth and eighteenth centuries, one wonders whether the Elizabethan English, though used to eating their own greens of orach (*Atriplex hortensis*), lamb's-quarters (*Chenopodium album*), and purslane (*Portulaca* sp.), saw any irony in their foppish delight with a plant that was a basic staple among indigenous peoples. Love-lies-bleeding continues to be cultivated in Mexico where young amaranth greens are used as a vegetable and the mature plants are harvested for their grain. In Peru and Bolivia, Purdue University horticulturists are trying to maximize the use of love-lies-bleeding as a commercial crop.[3]

It is as "Princes Feather" or "princess feathers" that love-lies-bleeding, or its myriad kindred of intermediate amaranths, became known to colonial Americans. References to "Princes Feather" or "princess feathers" in American gardening literature appear early, as with John Lawson's account in his 1709 *New Voyage to Carolina* of "Princes Feather, and *Tres Colores*." The first commercial mention of love-lies-bleeding occurred in a 1760 edition of the *Boston Evening-Post* in which John Townley advertised for sale the seed of "love lies bleeding" and "princess feathers." On April 4, 1767, Thomas Jefferson wrote in his garden diary that he planted seed for "Prince's feather" in his garden at Shadwell, his birthplace in Virginia.[4]

LOVE-LIES-BLEEDING, TASSEL FLOWER, PRINCE'S FEATHER
(*Amaranthus caudatus*)

TYPE nonhardy annual
HEIGHT 4–5 feet
SPREAD 36 inches

HABIT
- bears dramatic tassels of velvetlike flowers
- provides bold, coarse color and texture in the mixed garden
- susceptible to cucumber beetle predation

NATURAL RANGE
American, African, and Asian tropics

TIPS
- use in the annual, cottage-style, or mixed garden
- provide full sun
- sow seeds directly in the garden $1/8$ inch deep after danger of frost
- thin seedlings to 12 inches

Without a doubt, love-lies-bleeding was a part of our colonial past. But, what are we to do with a plant considered by so many today to be so vulgar, so common? Once celebrated by kings and botany's most lofty commentators, love-lies-bleeding now is relegated to the discount rack in hardware stores. Nevertheless, it still has the bold and colorful assets it had the day it was discovered and shouldn't be ignored by the independent-minded gardener in search of curiosities old and new. It is an essential annual for the mixed garden and a must for American colonial gardens where a dearth of a great selection of annuals can cramp the historic gardener who is also looking for abundant color. Given its dramatic verticality and the self-drying nature of the almost preposterous flowers, love-lies-bleeding deserves a place in the mixed garden in combination with the larger crimson and 'Pink Candle'

celosias (*Celosia cristata* 'Pink Candle'), striped French marigolds (*Tagetes patula* 'Striped'), and red small-flowered zinnia (*Zinnia pauciflora*).

It was determined in the trial garden that a late crop sown in July circumvented the cucumber beetle problem that can decimate this crop if it is planted earlier in the season. The germination and growth of love-lies-bleeding commenced after the end of the natural life cycle of the beetle. As if on cue, by early October, the late-sown plants sported their trademark tassels, which persisted into early December and the first significant fall frosts. As a late crop, sown in this manner, it took its place with similarly sown chicory (*Cichorium intybus*), bachelor's buttons (*Centaurea cyanus*), malva (*Malva sylvestris*), and the self-sown larkspur (*Consolida orientalis*), all of which returned the following year with little help from anyone.

Yellow Lupine

(Lupinus luteus)
FLOWERING ANNUAL

Lady Jean Skipwith was a masterful gardener who devoted much thought to the development of her elaborate garden at Prestwould, her plantation home in Southside Virginia. Our European yellow lupine, an ancient workhorse and a charming ornamental, was clearly one of the annuals that graced her garden. Her garden list, which dates to 1793, mentions yellow lupines, and a hand-written receipt shows that her husband purchased yellow lupine seed from Minton Collins of Richmond in 1793.[1]

North America is home to the majority of lupines, but Old World lupines have been cultivated in Europe and the Middle East for millennia, some say since as long ago as 4000 BC. Lupine seeds were found in Egyptian tombs dating to 2000 BC. Consumption of the white lupine (*Lupinus albus*) began at least with the Romans, who ate the dried seeds as nibbling food. White lupine seed, which is about the size of black-eyed peas, is still a commodity today and available in European food markets.[2]

Theophrastus (ca. 300 BC) addressed the white lupine by saying it belonged to that class of plants that will "not submit to cultivation at all," but, "if the seed is dropped where the ground is thickly overgrown, it pushes its root through to the earth and germinates because of its vigour." Theophrastus hinted at what is now well-known about lupines, that they dwell where the soil is poor and amend the soil by replenishing the nitrogen.

Virgil, a Roman poet writing over three hundred years later, addressed the ability of lupines to fix nitrogen. In book one of his agricultural poem *The Georgics*, he commiserated with farmers and described the poor soils that vexed them and what practices to adopt to affect a fair return from farming. "If the soil be barren, only scar / The surface," he warned, an admonishment against deep plowing, "Lest wicked weeds the corn should overrun." Then, speaking of thin soils in general, he said the wise farmer should let his soil lie fallow in alternate years:

> That the spent earth may gather
>   heart again,
> And, bettered by cessation, bear
>   the grain.[3]

Though the mechanism by which certain plants help to regenerate and restore nitrogen in soils was not

understood, their beneficence was recognized. Addressing the plants that nourish the soil in the intervening years, Virgil wrote:

> At least where vetches, pulse, and
>   tares, have stood,
> And stalks of lupines grew (a stubborn wood),
> The ensuing season, in return, may
>   bear
> The bearded product of the golden
>   year.[4]

In addition to this beneficial capacity to enrich soils, lupines were the subject of discussion among the more clinical and medically minded herbalists, including Dioscorides (first century) and Leonhart Fuchs (ca. 1545). They saw, in the white lupine especially, medicinal qualities too numerous to mention.[5]

Another species and the subject of our discussion, the yellow lupine was traditionally grown as a green manure crop and was tilled into the soil before it flowered to enrich the soil. New strains of the yellow lupine are now grown as field crops in central Europe and Russia, where flour, derived from the crushed seed, is often mixed with oat, pea, and bean flours in a wide array of breads and cakes.[6]

It is only in the English herbal that the yellow lupine was given its due. In Chapter 509, "Of the flat Beane called Lupine," John Gerard, the Elizabethan herbalist, addressed the yellow lupine: "It hath beautifull floures of an exceeding faire gold yellow colour, sweet of smell, made up into an eare, of the colour of the yellow violet, and somewhat of the smell." He was rarely so given to descriptive

praise; thus, we can confidently surmise that, by the mid-seventeenth century, the yellow lupine was a garden plant, an ornamental annual cultivated for scent and beauty. Squarely in eighteenth-century England, the Reverend William Hanbury, a gardener, echoed Gerard in his praise saying that the yellow lupine was equal "if not superior to any thing of the flowering tribe: It is so pure a sweet, so inoffensive, and exhilarating, that were I obliged to cultivate an Annual, and one only, it should be the Yellow Lupine."[7]

In the early twentieth century, new hybrid lupines, ripe with genome from New World species, sensationalized European floriculture, and the Russell lupines (L. 'Russell Hybrids') established themselves, late, in the centuries-old English cottage garden.

Lupines are surprisingly stubborn about the soils they will tolerate. Acidic soils are nearly essential for their survival, but heavy, peaty soils won't do. They insist on a light, sandy, silica-rich soil but one affording adequate if not copious moisture: a near contradiction. We must consider Theophrastus's warning that they resent cultivation and tend to prefer light, poor soils.

Nevertheless, yellow lupines proved moderately easy to germinate and start in the trial garden, though they resented the onset of hot weather, like almost all lupines. Sown in mid-March, the plants flowered at the end of May, bearing fourteen-inch stalks with concentric rings of deep yellow flowers. Although the soil in these initial beds was not as light and friable as it would become later, the plants' culture proved tolerably easy, especially given sufficient water. In subsequent

years, prodigious amounts of humus were added to the soil, lightening it. In what we thought was happier soil for the lupine, new seed was sown in the fall mixed with seed of the perennial pimpernel (*Anagallis monelli*) in the hope that the yellow lupines would bloom above a blue-flowered carpet of pimpernel. While the blue pimpernel performed admirably, the lupine failed to germinate. Variable seed quality and freshness, or change in acidity with the new soil additions? We never knew. It remains one of those mysteries of the garden for which gardeners usually unfairly blame themselves.

YELLOW LUPINE
(*Lupinus luteus*)

TYPE half-hardy annual
HEIGHT 24 inches
SPREAD 12 inches

HABIT
- bears spikes of yellow pealike flowers
- sports crisp green foliage

NATURAL RANGE
Mediterranean region, southern Europe

TIPS
- use in the annual, cottage-style, or mixed garden
- provide full sun
- sow seeds directly in the garden ¼ inch deep in March
- sow in well-spaded, acidic, light soil
- water regularly

Striped French Marigold

(Tagetes patula 'Striped')
FLOWERING ANNUAL

Following the Spanish invasions into the central and southern Americas in the early sixteenth century, varieties of newly discovered plants were swept back to Europe by returning fleets. Two inaptly named plants are said to have been part of that phenomenon: the African marigold (*Tagetes erecta*) and the French marigold (*Tagetes patula*). Common botanical wisdom explains these misnomers: Both marigolds became naturalized on the coast of northern Africa by fleets returning from Mexico, giving reason to the modifier "African." When the Holy Roman Emperor Charles V took Tunis on the African coast in 1535, the marigolds are said to have made their way to Europe, via France, in his wake; hence the modifier "French."[1]

The earliest visual image historians have of marigolds is seven early varieties in Leonhart Fuchs's unpublished Vienna Codex (1566). Among those images is a marigold with attenuated stems begging to become vines, very much like the older varieties of marigolds now available. Other illustrations in the same work show the early marigold to have already been available in single and fully double forms, demonstrating its natural variability in habit and bloom, a trait well-known to modern breeders and one that accounts for the plant's ready breeding.[2]

In growth and habit, the French and African marigolds are similar, although the African tends to grow taller and is usually associated with a double flower while the French is usually somewhat shorter with a single or semidouble flower. Both were popular in England in the seventeenth and eighteenth centuries, with John Parkinson saying about the African, "This goodly double flower, which is the grace and glory of a Garden in the time of his beauty."[3]

The variability and variety of the "striped" form fascinated the English and colonists alike. John Hill, a professional gardener working in London in 1757, described it as "the Colour . . . of an extreme dark, purplish Brown, and a gold Yellow; but in the Hand of Culture the Variety is endless." Plant historians hold that marigolds were present in colonial American gardens as early as the late 1600s, and Thomas Jefferson grew both the French marigold and the African marigold. Lady Jean Skipwith grew striped French marigolds at Prestwould, her estate in Southside Virginia. An invoice circa 1793 from Minton Collins of Richmond to Sir Peyton Skipwith, Lady

Jean's husband, shows the sale of "Strip'd French marygold."[4]

The striped French marigold offers sensational flowers on slightly impractical plants (perhaps the sole aim of the inventive gardener). They are appealingly ungainly in habit with a spiral of viney growth that sports vivid flowers the size of quarters. They are redoubtable bloomers that persist throughout long autumns when they assume an aura of ruddy foliage and faded, somewhat melancholy flowers.

The culture of the striped French marigold is eminently easy; nothing could be easier. It is a very vigorous plant, sporting muscular stems and aggressive roots. Its lanky habit is an asset when paired or tripled with other vining plants such as small-flowered zinnia (*Zinnia pauciflora*), ageratum (*Ageratum houstonianum*), annual scabious (*Scabiosa atropurpurea*), and whatever else might be there at the time. Striped French marigolds are not the annuals for precise and rectilinear planting beds. These are the floppy, sloppy things of the informal garden. In fact, the plants took well to aggressive pruning to shape their herbage; they proved very malleable in this respect. Since the plant is quite big, only a few are needed to add color to a mixed flower border in which they would mix well with plumed and crested celosias (*Celosia* spp.), the unctuous but dramatic love-lies-bleeding (*Amaranthus caudatus*), and China asters (*Callistephus chinensis*) when they come on in August.

STRIPED FRENCH MARIGOLD
(*Tagetes patula* 'Striped')

TYPE nonhardy annual
HEIGHT up to 36 inches
SPREAD 12–36 inches

HABIT
• lanky stems that profit from
  support
• floriferous
• self-sows
• resists most pests

NATURAL RANGE
Mexico

TIPS
• use in the annual, cottage-style, or
  mixed garden
• provide full sun
• sow seeds directly in the garden
  no more than ¼ inch deep after
  danger of frost
• thin seedlings to 6 inches

Nasturtium

(Tropaeolum majus)
FLOWERING ANNUAL

Upon its discovery by the Spanish conquistadors in Peru, the nasturtium was dubbed "Indian cress," the word *cress* indicating that it was regarded as a green salad leaf and eaten raw. Indeed, modern gourmands say the chopped leaves impart a pungent, peppery, and watercress-like flavor to mixed-greens salads.[1]

Of the two species most like modern nasturtiums, *Tropaeolum minus*, the small nasturtium, was the first to arrive on European shores in the sixteenth century. John Gerard described it in his *Herbal* (1633) as "Nasturtium Indicum": "Cresses of India. . . . The seedes of this rare and faire plant came first from the [West] Indies into Spaine, and thence into France and Flanders, from whence I received seede that bore with me both flowers and seede." Gerard described it as having "many weake and feeble branches . . . [which] occupie a great circuit of ground. . . . The leaves are round like wall peniwort. . . . The flowers are dispersed throughout the whole plant, of colour yellow, with a crossed starre . . . of a deepe orange colour."[2]

The nasturtium that we know best, *T. majus*, the large nasturtium, is thought to have arrived in England in 1686. An early English mention of the large nasturtium comes from Robert Furber's *The Flower-Garden Display'd* (1732), which includes prints of elaborate floral arrangements representing the flowers borne in each of the twelve months of the calendar. The caption reads, "*DOUBLE Nasturtium*, or the *Nasturtium Indicum with a double Flower*. This Plant we lately receiv'd from *Holland*; but it was first raised in *Italy*, and many Contrivances were used before it could be brought to *Holland*; it first bore a great Price, and was esteem'd as a great Rarity."[3]

The nasturtium's presence in colonial America is well documented. It appears definitively on Moravian farm plant lists compiled at the Bethabara settlement in North Carolina in 1759 and 1761. Closer to home, John Randolph of Williamsburg wrote in his *Treatise on Gardening* (1793) that nasturtium "should be sown in April or March, being extremely tender. If stuck they will climb a great height and will last till the frost come, and then totally perish. It is thought the flower is superior to a radish in flavour, and is eat in sallads or without." The pickled fruit of nasturtium makes for a good substitute for capers. Pickled nasturtium seeds are mentioned

in the colonial Moravian farm inventories from North Carolina where they are called "Capper—seeds of nasturtium, 'Kaper.'"[4]

Thomas Jefferson, in his Garden Book in 1774, attested to his use of the plant, mentioning that, at his grand vegetable garden at Monticello, he set his "Nasturcium in 35. little hills," which would have taken up considerable area. Perhaps this is a clue as to the esteem in which nasturtium leaves, flowers, and pickled seeds and buds were held at the dining table of a soon-to-be president.[5]

By the nineteenth century, in England and America, the nasturtium had become linked to the cottage garden, that evolving style of gardening that was more romance than necessity. In a hodgepodge garden, verdant mats of nasturtiums can carpet multiple square yards of ground with their charming near-round leaves and curious flowers in yellow, red, and orange. When grown with purpose, which means a cool corner and abundant moisture (but enough sun to ensure flowering), their luminous trailing vines green up the bare ground underneath taller plants, acting like a bed sham to hide the machinery of the garden.

In the trial garden, 382 nasturtiums were planted at four-inch intervals around three fifteen-foot-square beds. Kept well watered, they performed luxuriantly; trimmed and primped, they looked their best ambling onto garden paths. Even a late crop, sown well into August, can produce newly emergent foliage so attractive in its own right that the possibility of flowering is an afterthought. The mindful gardener should be aware, however, that nasturtiums are temperamental with regard to adequate moisture. Native to the mid-elevations of the Andes, they don't like searing sun and drought. But, in gardens where their needs are met, and where they can be planted prolifically, they can become a leitmotif, an element that strings the garden together.

Perhaps the most famous use of nasturtiums is achieved in Monet's garden at Giverny. There, nasturtiums stream across paths, and roses cantilever over garden arches, carrying color from the ground into the air with overachiever adroitness. This almost mythical use of nasturtiums is abetted by the cool, temperate French summers. Monet's deft trick with them only goads Virginian gardeners envious of green carpets, cool summers, and summertime salads dappled with vibrant flowers of Indian cress.

NASTURTIUM, INDIAN CRESS
(*Tropaeolum majus*)

TYPE nonhardy annual
HEIGHT 2–12 inches, more with
  support
SPREAD up to 10 feet

HABIT
• sprawling, ground hugging
• will climb if given twiggy support
• can self-sow

NATURAL RANGE
Andean South America

TIPS
• use in the annual, cottage-style, or
  mixed garden
• provide full sun
• provide trellising if desired
• provide consistent moisture and
  cool environment
• sow seeds directly in the garden ½
  inch deep after danger of frost
• thin seedlings to 6 inches

Scarlet Pentapetes

(Pentapetes phoenicia)

FLOWERING ANNUAL

Scarlet pentapetes is a plant about which many people get excited. After all, the sight of hundreds of crimson flowers on five-foot-tall stalks is not easily ignored. A tender annual in our climate, it is a native of China and India. It came to the attention of the great Swedish botanist Carolus Linnaeus by 1753 when he included it in *Species Plantarum,* a work that demonstrated his new theory of binomial nomenclature, the classification of plants by the analysis of their sexual parts and the naming technique using only two Latin names to describe a plant's genus and species. Scarlet pentapetes was included and exquisitely illustrated in Philip Miller's beautiful two-volume work *Figures of the Most Beautiful, Useful, and Uncommon Plants* (1760), in which he said that he received seed for it several times from India.[1]

Scarlet pentapetes was probably more familiar to eighteenth- and nineteenth-century plantsmen than it is to gardeners today. Neither the Royal Horticultural Society's *Dictionary of Gardening* nor *Hortus Third,* the American plant encyclopedia, contains a reference to the plant. It can, however, be found on a number of academic and botanical garden Web sites, including those of the University of Maryland and the Missouri Botanical Garden.[2]

Thomas Jefferson, part of a small, cohesive band of botanical enthusiasts, recorded specifically that he planted "Pentapetes Phoenicia" in his flower border at Monticello in 1811. An earlier reference to the plant can be found in Bernard McMahon's *American Gardener's Calendar* in 1806. But, as yet, no eighteenth-century reference has been found in the American horticultural canon. So, although scarlet pentapetes was apparently prominent in European horticultural circles in the eighteenth century, the record of the plant in American horticulture is blank prior to 1806. For that reason, Colonial Williamsburg horticulturists are reluctant to introduce it into the Historic Area gardens.[3]

Nevertheless, a plant as exciting as this represents opportunities for the historically minded home gardener. Firsthand experience with pentapetes proved it to be a glorious bloomer and a fantastic sight, with bloom occurring over more than three feet of the four- to five-foot height of the plant. The plant was a perfectly vigorous, shiny, boldly textured clump. The clumps sparkled in the sun because of the radiance of the

SCARLET PENTAPETES, SCARLET MALLOW
(*Pentapetes phoenicia*)

TYPE nonhardy annual
HEIGHT up to 5 feet
SPREAD 30 inches

HABIT
• bears 1-inch bright scarlet flowers
• provides stiff, vertical accent in the garden
• reliably self-sows
• resists most pests

NATURAL RANGE
China, India

TIPS
• use in the annual, cottage-style, or mixed garden
• provide full sun
• sow seeds directly in the garden ¼–½ inch deep May–June
• thin seedlings to 12 inches
• water regularly

scarlet flowers and the high gloss of the beautifully toothed leaves. This mirrors Philip Miller's 1760 observations: "The Figure of this Plant, which is engraven in the First Volume of the *Amsterdam Garden*, is far beyond Nature: The Leaves of the Plant are near twice the Size of those of the most vigorous Plant I have yet seen."[4]

This is high praise, and, as a garden plant, scarlet pentapetes couldn't have been more rewarding or required less work. The tropical mallows, almost as a rule, require only two things: abundant heat and abundant water. Within those parameters, tropical mallows such as cotton (*Gossypium* sp.), okra (*Abelmoschus esculentus*), hibiscus (*Hibiscus* sp.), and scarlet pentapetes grow quickly and strongly. And, scarlet pentapetes doesn't expend all its efforts on the crimson flowers alone. Its serrated glossy foliage is as ornamental as that of any of the commercial tropical foliage plants that have become so popular today. To cap off the accomplishments of an already stellar plant, scarlet pentapetes self-sows readily, the seed germinating when the weather warms in mid-May. A plant of stunning virtues, it is poised to make a dramatic comeback in the gardens of the twenty-first century.

Corn Poppy

(Papaver rhoeas)

FLOWERING ANNUAL

The red corn poppy is the same flower as the immortal Flanders poppy, which has come to symbolize the incalculable loss of life on the blood-soaked fields of Flanders during the trench warfare of World War I. It is the poppy of Great Britain's Remembrance Day, when the monarch places a wreath of poppies at the base of the Cenotaph in London.

This poppy has long held dark associations, having been the emblem of Morpheus, Roman god of death. And the narcotic qualities of its sister species the opium poppy *(Papaver somniferum)* further darken the already murky mythological waters surrounding this flower. The short bloom period and the delicacy of its bloom also signify loss and remorse. So why would we grow a flower of such sadness, so steeped in darkness? Well, its brilliant red has led more than one writer to wax lyrical. John Gerard wrote of its "gallant red" in the sixteenth century, and John Ruskin, the great nineteenth-century aesthete, likened the nearly transparent nature of the flower petals to "painted *glass*."[1]

Untangling the plants called *poppy* by the ancients is a very inexact process. The Greek word for *poppy* was ascribed to a number of similar-looking plants,

but those plants fall into different genera in modern botanical organization. Theophrastus, the Greek botanist, described what sounds like is the corn poppy: "Another kind of poppy is that called *rhoias*, which is like wild chicory, wherefore it is even eaten: it grows in cultivated fields and especially among barley. It has a red flower, and a head as large as a man's finger-nail. It is gathered before the barley-harvest, when it is still somewhat green. It purges downwards [i.e., it evacuates the bowels]."[2]

The sixteenth-century German herbalist Leonhart Fuchs attributed to the corn poppy the same properties as those described by the ancient botanical writers Dioscorides, Galen, and Pliny: "It alleviates erysipelas and suppresses female menstrual hemorrhage. Placed on the liver, it checks nosebleed. When the tongue is washed with a decoction of it, it cures a burning throat. It shrinks tumors of the private parts. Rubbed on the temples, it calms frenzied dreams. Applied on a bandage, it soothes severe pains in the eyes." Gerard, the Elizabethan herbalist, added to this litany of claims and repeated Theophrastus's assertion that the wild red poppy is found in arable fields with wheat, rye, and barley.[3]

Established in British gardens by the seventeenth century, when Alexander Marshal painted it for his flower book, the corn poppy soon became the subject of deliberate as well as inadvertent garden selection. A group of these annual poppies came to be known as Dutch poppies. While the original corn poppy is a bright red color, Dutch poppies developed in other colors. In 1722, Thomas Fairchild, an English nurseryman, extolled these new Dutch poppies:

"One of the most beautiful Flowers that can be imagin'd. They are commonly as double as a Rose of a rich Scarlet striped with white, as fine as a Carnation."[4]

This genetic movement away from the original red color was accelerated by the work of the Reverend W. Wilks of Shirley, his parish in England. In 1880, in his vicarage garden, he wrote, "I noticed, in a waste corner of my garden . . . a patch of the common wild field Poppy (Papaver Rhoeas), one solitary flower of

which had a very narrow edge of white." Over several years, he "at last fixed a strain with petals varying in colour from the brightest scarlet to pure white, with all shades of pink between."

What this means for the gardener intent on using older noncultivar types is that the red corn poppy was, by 1722, and probably earlier, succumbing to genetic drift and suggesting new forms of itself. As a result of genetic drift and the human tendency to tinker with things, seed of pure red corn poppy can be difficult to obtain. When ordering corn poppies, the gardener may well receive Shirley poppies. Indeed, in the trial garden, such a substitution may have occurred, as we saw a variety of colors from red to pink to white that were indeed manifestations of the red poppy.

In 1767, Thomas Jefferson made a fleeting reference to poppies blooming on June 4 and then, on July 5, said, "Larger Poppy has vanished—Dwarf poppy still in bloom but on the decline." It is uncertain to which poppy, annual or perennial, he was referring. In 1771, he again mentioned poppies, this time in a list of "Hardy perennial flowers." A more certain American historical reference to the annual poppy is found in a 1761 plant inventory of a Moravian farm in North Carolina that specifically mentions "corn poppy (Papaver rhoeas)" as well as, in a separate reference, "Seed of red poppy."[6]

As to its growing habit, its common names corn poppy and red weed imply its considerable ease of cultivation and allude to its tendency to widely infest grain fields in England. The experience of growing the corn poppy in the trial garden was nearly textbook in two respects: its simple and easy germination in very cool weather and the very ephemeral nature of the flowers. Sown in middle March in cold ground, the seeds germinated by April 24, and flowering began June 4 but lasted only to June 16, not even two weeks. It seemed that they were there one day, most beautiful, and gone the next, leaving the unexpectant gardener bereft of the glimmering, gallant stands of poppies. To fully appreciate the corn poppy, modern expectations need to be curbed. The old-fashioned flowers bloom and fade in their own time. Finessing that temperament and submitting to its imperative are part and parcel of the art and craft of gardening.

The corn poppy can be a staple in many late fall, winter, and spring gardens in the South. Seed germination requires sowing in cold ground. Given the corn poppy's preference, indeed its insistence, for cool temperatures as well as its tendency to bloom for only a brief period, multiple, successive sowings should be undertaken throughout September and late October, followed by a similar pattern of sowing the following spring, commencing in early March in the South. Though not essential to its sure performance, sowing the seed on the surface of snow as winter is coming to an end and allowing the seed to be introduced into the soil whenever and as the snow melts is a recommended practice. Poppies should never been sown in pots and transplanted; the trademark taproot makes this practice all but impossible.

CORN POPPY, FLANDERS POPPY, RED POPPY, RED WEED
(*Papaver rhoeas*)

TYPE hardy annual
HEIGHT up to 36 inches
SPREAD up to 12 inches

HABIT
• the true corn poppy bears 3-inch crimson, iridescent flowers
• tends to be floppy
• reliably self-sows
• resists most pests

NATURAL RANGE
Europe, including Great Britain, Asia; naturalized in North America

TIPS
• use in the annual, cottage-style, or mixed garden
• provide full sun; partial shade in hot climates
• sow seeds directly in the garden at or near the surface of the soil in March or September
• thin seedlings to 6–8 inches

Mexican Poppy

(Argemone mexicana)
FLOWERING ANNUAL

ARGEMONE. *Mexicana chum 138.*

Upon its discovery by Spanish conquistadors in the early sixteenth century, Mexican poppy was uncharitably named *"Ficus infernalis"* (infernal or hellish fig) because of the sharp thorns that terminate the lobes of the beautifully variegated leaves. It is, however, a member of the poppy family and not a fig; the name *fig* referred to the seed capsule's purported resemblance to the fruit. Native to the West Indies, Central America, and Florida, it earned the reputation of being a troublesome weed in the emerging agriculture of the southern colonies and Caribbean plantations.[1]

Appearing in England in 1592, the Mexican poppy was described by John Gerard, the Elizabethan herbalist, as a plant whose "leaves are divided after the maner of horned poppy, smooth, with white veins & prickly edges: the floure is yellow." He added that it was found only "in the gardens of some prime herbarists," meaning that it was still rare at the time. But, he seemed uncertain as to its origin, inaccurately speculating that it may be one of many poppylike plants mentioned by several ancient Greek botanists, a botanical impulse to this day among classically minded armchair botanists. Gerard was mistaken.[2]

In *Figures of the Most Beautiful, Useful, and Uncommon Plants* (1760), Philip Miller accurately places the origin of the Mexican poppy in the West Indies, where, he said, the seeds were used as a purgative and the orange latex sap was thought good for the eyes. But, Miller said he didn't believe it was used medicinally anywhere in Europe. And, with the caution of a true gardener, he warned of the poppy's infernal seeding habit: "For if a few Plants are suffered to scatter their Seeds, they will sufficiently stock the Ground."[3]

The bold illustration that accompanies Miller's commentary does not do justice to the stiff architectural beauty of the Mexican poppy's foliage; nor does it represent the striking variegation that courses through the venation of the leaves. The leaves, which in the garden have a distinct crispness, are rendered more relaxed in Miller's engraving. In the garden, without fail, the stand of prickly poppy garnered almost rapt attention.

That the Mexican poppy made its way to the English colonies is evidenced by Thomas Jefferson's mention of it by its Latin, Linnaean name. He recorded *Argemone*'s bloom at Shadwell, his birthplace in Virginia, on June 18, 1767.[4]

This heat-tolerant annual thrives in gardens in the South and rewards its growers with lovely pale yellow blooms. Its seed is quite fertile: self-sown seedlings germinate before the parent plants have even begun to finish flowering. Considering the sobering fact that very few antique annuals provide the length of bloom we expect from modern cultivars, Mexican poppy's eight weeks of bloom and its precocity in bearing flowers seven weeks from seeding make this a strong if problematically prolific player to gardeners looking for certain colonial pedigrees and precise attributions. Mexican poppy is a robust vintage annual whose countenance is so bold as to evince immediate notice. Garden experience with Mexican poppy proved it to be effortless; the plant was impervious to pests and heat and very vigorous. Its mottled leaves and perilous thorns are novelty qualities that cause considerable interest among those newly acquainted with it.

MEXICAN POPPY, PRICKLY POPPY
(*Argemone mexicana*)

TYPE nonhardy annual
HEIGHT up to 36 inches
SPREAD 24–36 inches

HABIT
- bears 2-inch yellow flowers
- stiff foliage; variegation of veins
- self-sows prolifically
- resists most pests
- very thorny; care should be taken when handling plant

NATURAL RANGE
West Indies, Central America, Florida

TIPS
- use with caution in the annual, cottage-style, or mixed garden
- provide full sun
- sow seeds, which need light to germinate, directly in the garden at the soil surface when the soil warms
- thin seedlings to 12 inches

Yellow Horned Poppy

(Glaucium flavum)

FLOWERING ANNUAL

Beel Slmagen.   CCXCIIII.

Throughout Western herbal history, yellow horned poppy (*Glaucium flavum*) and its close relation celandine poppy (*Chelidonium majus*) have often been mistaken for each other because their flowers share the same strong, clear yellow. They also share parts of each others' native regions, which overlap in southeastern Europe. In addition, both types of poppy, horned and celandine, are noted by Theophrastus in his *Enquiry into Plants* (ca. 300 BC); both became incorporated into the English gardening vocabulary; and both reached American shores by the eighteenth century. But, yellow horned poppy has the good fortune of bearing bright silvery leaves, deeply lobed, quite unlike the celandine poppy's usual green.[1]

Of the horned poppies (*Glaucium*), two kinds should be of interest to gardeners, the annual scarlet horned poppy (*G. corniculatum*) and the remarkably handsome annual (or biennial) yellow horned poppy (*G. flavum*), a silver beacon when placed in strategic spots in the garden. These close cousins have been companions of humans for millennia. Theophrastus addressed the horned poppy by its most distinguishing characteristic: "The fruit is twisted like a little horn: it is gathered at the time of wheat harvest." In fact, the annual scarlet-flowered species, *G. corniculatum*, is named for this attribute, from the Latin *cornu* meaning "horn." A further identifier is Theophrastus's comparison of the *Glaucium* leaf to common mullein (*Verbascum thapsus*), a well-known plant bearing silver gray foliage. Theophrastus said that horned poppy "has the property of purging the belly, and the leaf is used for removing ulcers on sheep's eyes" and that "it grows by the sea, wherever there is rocky ground."[2]

The Renaissance German herbal of Leonhart Fuchs does little more than repeat the ancient commentaries with respect to horned poppy. It does note, however, that, although wild in some places, "in Germany it grows only where planted." John Gerard, in his 1633 English herbal, was more forthcoming: "The yellow horned Poppie hath whitish leaves very much cut or jagged, somewhat like the leaves of garden Poppie, but rougher and more hairie. . . . The floures be large and yellow, consisting of foure leaves; which being past, there come long huskes or cods, crooked like an horne or cornet."[3]

John Clayton's eighteenth-century

discovery of yellow horned poppy, an Old World native, amongst the flora of Virginia shouldn't strike us as odd. The plant was observed naturalized along the New England coast as early as the seventeenth century. Seeds are among the most gregarious vagabonds, opportunistic stowaways catching a ride on the flow of goods and people to new places. The Royal Horticultural Society's *Dictionary of Gardening* considers the horned poppy's native region to include Britain, and, from there, and other places, it made the transatlantic leap to the colonies prior to 1753, when John Clayton collected his herbarium specimen of it. In the early nineteenth century, Thomas Jefferson noted its use in his garden.[4]

Although a little difficult to start, the yellow horned poppy grows stoutly and rewards its grower with spectacular gray foliage and flowers of a deeper, brighter yellow than the prickly poppy (*Argemone*

mexicana). Horned poppy derives its name from its nearly foot-long signature seedpods that develop very late in the season. *Glaucium* refers to the bluish color of the hairy-textured leaves. Although horned poppy behaves as an annual in the garden, botanists consider it either an annual or biennial when grown under its ideal circumstances.

Seed sown in early March, or as early as the soil can be worked, results in blooming plants by the end of June. In the trial garden, yellow horned poppy was slow to start but grew steadily and remained in flower until August 15 when the plants began to make their elongated seedpods. A spate of very wet weather arrested the drying of the seedpods, and the crop was terminated. The dramatic coloring of the flowers and the cooling effect of icy blue leaves fully warrant the gardener's attempt, likely successful, at establishing horned poppy in the mixed flower garden.

Hormium Sage

(Salvia viridis)

FLOWERING ANNUAL

Hormium, an annual flowering sage, was one of the most exciting finds that Colonial Williamsburg horticulturists came across during the plant trials conducted in the Historic Area. Its superb flowering habit; its ancient English pedigree, introduced from the continent in 995; and its documented use by North Carolina farmers in 1761 make it a highly desirable annual for historically minded gardeners. Although its actual flowers are small, the colored leaf bracts, in shades of purple, pink, and mauve, arranged on plumb-straight stems fifteen inches tall, are showy and long lasting.[1]

William Turner, an English herbalist, wrote in 1562 that hormium sage came in a diversity of colors. John Gerard included it in his 1633 *Herbal* calling it "Horminum sylvestre folys purpureus," or "wilde Clarie," with "leaves somewhat round . . . not much unlike Horehound." In the seventeenth century, Alexander Marshal painted hormium in watercolor and included it in his masterful florilegium (ca. 1653).[2]

Hormium sage's appearance in a 1761 plant list from a Moravian farm in North Carolina makes it a slam dunk for colonial gardens. Later, in the twentieth century, in a passage from *The Cottage Garden* called "Working with Nature," the great gardener and writer Christopher Lloyd advocated adopting into the garden the little wild things of nature, the near-weeds, the self-sowing annuals and biennials that are the flesh and fiber of the cottage garden. A riff on Lloyd's approach would include viper's bugloss (*Echium vulgare*), corn poppies (*Papaver rhoeas*), and clary sage (*Salvia sclarea*). Lloyd particularly extolled the purple hormiums. And one could easily add unkempt ageratums (*Ageratum houstonianum)*, sunflowers (*Helianthus annuus)*, annual candytuft (*Iberis umbellata)*, and love-lies-bleeding (*Amaranthus caudatus)* to a Lloyd-inspired mixture.[3]

Hormium's ease of cultivation is matched by its superb show of color, mixed in shades from light pink to rose to purple. In the trial garden, seed sown in mid-March resulted in seedlings that flowered by June 6. As the flowers began to fade, and as thunderstorms took their toll, the clump of hormium was cut back by a third and managed a rebloom that lasted until late July. The plants were left in the ground to self-sow their seed, and seedlings appeared by mid-October of the same year. Surviving light November

by judicious thinning and weeding, the gardener becomes savvy to the relative competitiveness of different seed armies and can then better lead them.

HORMIUM SAGE, HORMIUM
(*Salvia viridis*)

TYPE hardy annual
HEIGHT 18 inches
SPREAD 12 inches

HABIT
• bears showy rosy to purple bracts
• reblooms if deadheaded
• reliably self-sows

NATURAL RANGE
southern Europe

TIPS
• use in the annual, cottage-style, or mixed garden
• provide full sun
• sow seeds directly in the garden at or near the surface of the soil March–April or August–September
• thin seedlings to 6 inches

and December frosts, they finally succumbed to the worst of winter weather. However, self-sown seedlings sprouted again in the spring and were in bloom by the third week of April. That same spring still more of the self-sown hormium came up amongst nearby Canterbury-bells (*Campanula medium*), sown the previous fall; judicious weeding assured the simultaneous culture of the Canterbury-bells and the hormium that was left in place to bloom amongst them.

Like other reliable annuals such as candytuft, ageratum, Adonis (*Adonis aestivalis*), dragonwort (*Dracocephalum moldavica*), and sweet scabious (*Scabiosa atropurpurea*), hormium played a central role in the mixed trial plantings that arose out of both deliberately sown seed and randomly dispersed seed. What developed was a patchwork of haphazard drifts of flowers that was pleasant, rewarding, and constantly changing. By coordinating different groups of plants

Scabious

(Scabiosa atropurpurea)
FLOWERING ANNUAL

As with so many plants in the Western gardening palette, sweet scabious made its way from the warmer parts of southern Europe to the northern realms where it became part of the greater Renaissance garden vocabulary. In 1613, it appeared in *Hortus Eystettensis*, a sumptuous flower book by the German apothecary, chemist, and botanist printer Basilius Besler. Although the accepted date for its entry into English horticulture is 1629, one source cites Englishman John Goodyer, author of the first Greek-to-English translation of Dioscorides's herbal, as having received seed from William Coys's Essex garden in 1620.[1]

By 1653, scabious was a preferred garden flower, painted meticulously three times by Alexander Marshal for his magical flower book of watercolors on vellum. The fact that all three renderings are red supports an argument that the first scabious to be grown in Europe were red and that blue only subsequently came to be found and used.[2]

In his 1657 herbal, *Adam in Eden*, William Coles classified scabious according to that arcane system of temperatures and degrees that may have had some internal logic at the time but that escapes modern botanists: "Scabious is hot and dry in the second Degree, opening, cleansing, digesting, and making thin." He recommended it for coughs and sundry other complaints and reiterated its primary function as a way to control skin conditions such as scabies, from which the name of the plant is derived. Besler had earlier associated scabious with skin-healing properties, which it shared with related species.[3]

Scabious soon came to occupy a naturalized place among the English meadow flora in the centuries after its introduction there. In *Gardening with Antique Plants* (1997), David Stuart discussed the traditional English meadow, where flowers keep company with selected meadow grasses, and mentioned collecting the seed of scabious, toadflax (*Linaria vulgaris*), viper's bugloss (*Echium vulgare*), and knapweed (*Centaurea* sp.) in order to establish a new meadow planting. Christopher Lloyd, the late, legendary English gardener, wrote that scabious was indelibly part of the cottage garden: "The flower garden at the front of the cottage is laid out in typical cottage-garden style, with many of the old favorites, including peonies, evening primroses and sweet scabious."[4]

Its early presence in the New World is confirmed by an ad placed in a 1760 *Boston Evening-Post* by John Townley for sale of the seed of "sweet scabus." Also, by the last quarter of the eighteenth century, Lady Jean Skipwith had included it in a 1793 inventory of her great garden on the River Dan at Prestwould in Virginia, south of the James River. It is evident from a 1793 receipt from Minton Collins of Richmond that Lady Jean's husband, Sir Peyton Skipwith, abetted his wife's gardening habits with the purchase of "Sweet Scabious" seed.[5]

The scabious in the trial garden proved to be not inordinately vigorous, with slow and sparse germination and slow growth of seedlings. Although always prone to heat stress, the plants over the summer became quite beautiful, flowering profusely from mid-July to the end of August. Grown away from the hottest afternoon sun and provided with a constant and sufficient water source, they are quite worth the effort, flowering in shades of blue, pink, and russet.

The importance of scabious to the colonial garden is its relatively large flowers. Western floriculture since the sixteenth century has selectively bred for larger flowers. Many vintage plants, though, are still small compared to modern cultivars. But, the humble annual scabious was often the most prominent flower in the trial garden, tall, large flowered, deeply colored, and eminently suited as a cut flower. Scabious makes a prolifically flowering clump and is particularly effective when it mingles with scarlet small-flowered zinnia (*Zinnia pauciflora*), China asters (*Callistephus chinensis*), and striped French marigolds (*Tagetes patula* 'Striped').

SCABIOUS, SCABIOSA, SWEET SCABIOUS, PINCUSHION FLOWER, MOURNFUL WIDOW (*Scabiosa atropurpurea*)

TYPE nonhardy annual
HEIGHT 18–36 inches
SPREAD 12–24 inches

HABIT
- bears large, ornamental flowers
- tends to flop and may need staking
- resists most pests

NATURAL RANGE
southern Europe

TIPS
- use in the annual, cottage-style, or cutting garden
- provide full sun; partial shade in hot climates
- sow seeds directly in the garden at or near the surface of the soil after danger of frost
- thin seedlings to 6–12 inches

Sunflower

(Helianthus annuus 'Italian White')
FLOWERING ANNUAL

Though a landmark American native of the Great Plains, the sunflower wound a circuitous path to early American gardens. It was imported into England in 1596 after its discovery by the Spanish roughly eighty years before in Mexico and Peru. John Gerard, the Elizabethan herbalist, commented that "it hath risen up to the height of fourteene foot in my garden, where one floure was in weight three pound and two ounces, and crosse overthwart the floure by measure sixteene inches broad." Although it was initially the subject of great curiosity and sensation by plant lovers, it fell out of favor by the end of the seventeenth century. The eminent early-eighteenth-century botanist John Rea commented, "Heretofore admired, but now grown common, not at all respected." Another writer complained that it was a disagreeable sight and that it "incommode[d] the Flowers growing near it."[1]

Once in Europe the sunflower went through dramatic metamorphisms. The single giant sunflower from the American West and Central America began to yield, through judicious seed selection, varieties that included huge double flowers akin to giant Chinese chrysanthemums (*Chrysanthemum* sp.). Even earlier in Europe, varieties that had multiple and branching stems, much like modern ones, were depicted as early as 1613 with the publication of *Hortus Eystettensis*, Basilius Besler's florilegium.[2]

Besler's florilegium contains an illustration of an annual sunflower displaying a branching habit with multiple flowers per stalk. Besler called this strain *"Flos Solisprolifer,"* or multiflorous sunflower. It may be the precursor to many of the modern multiple-flowered varieties, one of which, *Helianthus annuus* 'Italian White', was planted in the trial garden. The illustrations from the seventeenth century demonstrate that light hues and multiple-headed forms were popular at the time. The 'Italian White' strain, therefore, though modern, has significant historical precedent.[3]

When the annual sunflower made it to the American colonies, probably from the south and west where it was undoubtedly more popular, is not completely clear. The Carolinas and Virginia were rife with perennial sunflowers of the *Helianthus* genus. Botanist John Clayton collected three *Helianthus* specimens, but all perennial species. Thomas Jefferson made a reference in his Garden Book in 1771 to a "Sunflower," but it is

included in a list titled "Hardy perennial flowers." References to an annual sunflower are sparse.[4]

A firsthand narrative account by Thomas Harriot, who was tasked with recording the events of the ill-fated Roanoke Island colony in what is now North Carolina, suggests that natives of that region were cultivating the sunflower by 1588. Harriot wrote, "Another great hearbe in forme of a Marigolde, about six foote in height; the head with the floure is a spanne in breadth. Some take it to bee *Planta Solis* [sunflower]: of the seedes heereof they make both a kinde of bread and broth." Harriot's commentary implies that the diet of the indigenous peoples included sunflower seeds, in addition to the well-known maize, beans, melons, and squash. Considering that these four plants are annuals, we might surmise that the sunflower included in this dietary and agricultural mix was an annual as well.[5]

Also accompanying the Roanoke Island colonists was a man named John White, who complemented Thomas Harriot's narrative records with watercolors. The watercolors, executed at Roanoke Island in 1585–1586, do not include sunflowers. However, an edition of Harriot's *A Briefe and True Report of the New Found Land of Virginia* published in 1590 features engraved illustrations, based on White's original watercolors, that do include sunflowers. Although the watercolors and the engravings are virtually identical, the engraver, Theodor de Bry, added a number of details, including sunflowers, in the engraving done from White's watercolor of an Indian village, *The Towne of Secota*. The engravings show figures that can only be the great sunflower known by generations of Americans. Why John White left out of the original watercolors the sunflowers that Thomas Harriot described so clearly in his narrative is not known.[6]

Much later in the seventeenth century, in the Boston area, John Josselyn, in his *New-Englands Rarities Discovered* (1672), described a "*Marygold of Peru,* of which there are two kinds, one bearing black seeds, the other black and white streak'd, this beareth the fairest flowers, commonly but one upon the very top of the stalk." This was likely the tall annual sunflower possibly imported from Europe by cosmopolitan Boston gardening Brahmins. In his 1633 *Herbal,* Gerard used "*floure of the Sun*" as a synonym for the "*Marigold of Peru.*"[7]

Another intrepid explorer and plant collector, John Lawson, published *A New Voyage to Carolina,* a valuable account of his journey through the Carolinas, in 1709. In a section titled "*Of the Vegetables* of Carolina," he wrote, "We have also the Wood-bind, much the same as in *England*; Princes-feather, very large and beautiful in the Garden; *Tres-Colores,* branch'd Sun-flower, Double Poppies, Lupines, of several pretty sorts . . . the *Sensible* Plant is said to be near the Mountains. . . . Saf-Flower . . . the yellow Jessamin is wild in our Woods, of a pleasant Smell." Because Lawson is discussing a number of European ornamentals, including double poppies (*Papaver* sp.) and "*Tres-Colores*" (i.e., Joseph's-coat, *Amaranthus tricolor*), he may be alluding to a branched, annual sunflower.[8]

Regardless of its popularity in Europe, it is not certain the extent to which the annual American sunflower was formally cultivated in seventeenth- or eighteenth-century colonial gardens. Its sightings by Harriot, Josselyn, and possibly Lawson suggest that it may have been part of the colonial gardening palette as early as the seventeenth century, but whether their testimonials to the annual sunflower constitute a few serendipitous occurrences or are indicative of widespread use is unknown.

In the trial garden, traditional tall, single sunflowers (*H. annuus*) were planted simultaneously with castor bean (*Ricinus communis*), providentially since stem borers destroyed the sunflowers and the castor beans went on to compensate for the loss in height by going on to reach, in one notable case, twenty-two feet. The 'Italian White' multiple-branched sunflower variety flourished, with soft, pale yellow flowers by the dozens decking numerous graceful stems on four-foot plants. Careful deadheading of the spent sunflowers kept them in bloom nearly perpetually for about one month.

As to the traditional, tall sunflower of old? We're still left with its nearly inescapable awkwardness and its ungainly habit. Perhaps like those writers of the late seventeenth century, we are at first entranced by its sheer height and the almost surreal size of the flowers (in some cases up to eighteen inches across), only to later become frustrated with its unquiet boastfulness. Without a doubt, the dazzling array of modern sunflower cultivars and varieties presents opportunities for the modern gardener who can take some comfort in the fact that the multiplicity of sunflower forms began over 450 years ago.

SUNFLOWER
(*Helianthus annuus* 'Italian White')

TYPE nonhardy annual
HEIGHT 4 feet
SPREAD 4 feet

HABIT
• bears 4-inch flowers of pale yellow
• much branched growing habit
• grows a bit leggy
• resists most pests

NATURAL RANGE
United States, southern Canada, northern Mexico

TIPS
• use in the annual, cottage-style, or mixed garden
• provide full sun
• sow seeds directly in the garden ½–1 inch deep in May
• thin seedlings to 24 inches

Small-Flowered Zinnia

(Zinnia pauciflora)
FLOWERING ANNUAL

Though small flowered when viewed through our twenty-first-century eyes, this zinnia, introduced from the tropical Americas to England via Paris in 1753, is nevertheless prominent in the garden due to its vivid color. Its best use in the garden is with other brightly colored, relatively small-flowered annuals like the lovely striped French marigold (*Tagetes patula* 'Striped'). The blend of the zinnia's true red and the marigold's yellow, maroon, and orange petals is simple and delightful. The stems of the zinnia and the marigold both tend to be willowy, and, when planted adjacent to each other, they knit themselves into graceful, billowy combinations of stems and brightly colored flowers that persist sporadically, in Virginia, until the first frosts in early November.[1]

Trial plantings demonstrated that this small-flowered zinnia is also very compatible with other rambunctious, directly sown annuals such as the tall blue ageratum (*Ageratum houstonianum*), scabious (*Scabiosa atropurpurea*), mixed four-o'clocks (*Mirabilis jalapa*), and white bishop's weed (*Ammi majus*), each rangy in their own right but scrappy as well. When the bishop's weed's soft white fades early in the growing season,

the ageratum assumes its place and, along with the zinnias, scabious, and variegated four-o'clocks, persists until frost. When viewed from afar and as the exact nature of each small flower dims, the textures of the combined plants and the various greens and hazy patterns cool the weary eye during hot Virginia days.

The earliest date for this flower's mention is in 1806 when it was included in Philadelphia nurseryman Bernard McMahon's *American Gardener's Calendar*. Other sources, more vague, say that this zinnia was grown in American gardens in the fourth quarter of the eighteenth century. In fact, Arthur Shurcliff, Colonial Williamsburg's first landscape architect, in a memo dated 1936, suggested this zinnia's use in the Historic Area based on its arrival in England in 1753. But, the heyday of the zinnia in American gardens was certainly in the nineteenth century, especially after the advent in America of the *Zinnia peruviana* and the multitude of resulting cultivars. Assiduous gardeners can be certain, however, that this small-flowered, brightly tinted zinnia was known to the gardening cognoscenti of England by the middle of the eighteenth century and the American public early in the nineteenth century.[2]

As with so many of the annuals that were grown in the trial garden, this zinnia is conveniently self-seeding if the gardener is careful to distinguish zinnia seeds from the multitude of weed seeds also sprouting at the same time. In fact, this ability to ascertain the seed leaves of our best-loved annuals from the weeds that impair them is essential to achieve a cottage-garden effect. This small-flowered zinnia has an added bonus in that the seed of spring-blooming plants ripens, sets, and disperses new seed in time for a second generation during a single spring-summer-fall growing season. The small-flowered zinnia is a prime candidate for the cottage-style garden where, with timely interventions on the part of the gardener, it might perpetuate ad infinitum.

SMALL-FLOWERED ZINNIA
(*Zinnia pauciflora*)

TYPE nonhardy annual
HEIGHT 3–4 feet
SPREAD up to 36 inches

HABIT
- bears ¾-inch bright-red flowers
- sports ornamental, delicate foliage somewhat vinelike in nature
- reliably self-sows
- resists most pests

NATURAL RANGE
Arizona, Mexico to Argentina, West Indies

TIPS
- use in the annual, cottage-style, or mixed garden
- provide full sun
- sow seeds directly in the garden ⅛ inch deep after danger of frost and when the soil warms
- thin seedlings to 12 inches

Malva

(Malva sylvestris 'Brave Heart')
FLOWERING BIENNIAL

In the investigation of historic plants, ambitious gardeners sometimes cast far afield to catch those plants that might in time prove to be authentic to their target time period. Discovered by an elderly gardener at his home in Kettering in Britain, 'Brave Heart' was a chance seedling of the common *Malva sylvestris*, which grows in the waste places of Britain. This modern selection is likely a bit better colored, possessed of a deeper hue, but, for all intents and purposes, this is the malva of old.[1]

Malva is a member of the very large mallow family and is often referred to in just that way, as "one of the mallows," typified by their five-petaled flowers. Hollyhocks (*Alcea rosea*), hibiscus (*Hibiscus* sp.), okra (*Abelmoschus esculentus*), and cotton (*Gossypium* sp.) all belong to this family. Most of the *Malvas* proper are undistinguished, not having the punch of the hollyhocks and hibiscus. But, malva, with its "reddish colour mixed with purple strakes," became an essential component in the mix of plants in the trial garden.[2]

Malva provided fodder for humans for millennia. In Hesiod's *Works and Days and Theogony* (ca. 800 BC), the poet spoofed rich landowners and proud nobles by pointing out their alienation from the very ground that fed them:

> Damn fools. Don't know the half
> from the whole,
> Or the real goodness in mallows
> and asphodel.

Later, in *Enquiry into Plants* (ca. 300 BC), Theophrastus, in the section called "Of other uncultivated herbs, which may be classed with pot-herbs," discussed "all those [that] may be included which have a similar appearance, but juices suitable for food whether raw or cooked; for some need the action of fire, as *malakhe* (cheeseflower [Malva])." Almost four hundred years later, Dioscorides concurred with his predecessor and wrote that "Malache . . . that is sown is more fitt to be eaten than that which is wilde." He then attributed many topical healing qualities to the juice of the leaves. Leonhart Fuchs, in 1542, reiterated the ancient wisdom on the plant and mentioned that in Germany it grew "in rich, damp uncultivated places."[3]

John Gerard, in his 1633 herbal, mentioned no less than fifteen "Mallowes," including the cultivated hollyhock and the "wilde Mallowes."

Since Gerard couldn't resort to the Linnaean system of binomial plant names established in 1753, it would ordinarily be difficult to point to one and say with confidence that it is what we know today to be *M. sylvestris*. He did, however, providentially describe one of the "wilde Mallowes" as "*Malva sylvestris*. The field Mallow," saying, "[This] wilde Mallow hath broad leaves somewhat round and cornered, nickt about the edges, smooth, and greene of colour: among which rise up many slender tough stalkes, clad with the like leaves, but smaller. The floures grow upon little footstalkes of a reddish colour mixed with purple strakes, consisting of five leaves, fashioned like a bell." The attribution of a reddish color mixed with purple streaks indicates that Gerard was discussing what has come to be known as *M. sylvestris* and may indeed be the parent of 'Brave Heart'.[4]

Indications of malva's presence in colonial America come from two references in John Josselyn's 1672 *New-Englands Rarities Discovered*, where, in a section called "*Of such Plants as have sprung up since the* English *Planted and kept Cattle in* New-England," he mentioned "*Mallowes*" in a list that includes "*Couch Grass. Shepherds Purse. Dandelion. Groundsel. Sow Thistle. Wild Arrach. Night Shade. . . . Nettlesstinging.*" In another section, "*Of such Garden Herbs (amongst us) as do thrive there,*" he mentioned "*French Mallowes*" in a list that includes "*Cabbidge. Lettice. Sorrel. Parsley. Marygold. . . . Chervel. Burnet. Winter Savory. Summer Savory. Time. Sage. Carrats. Parsnips. . . . Red Beetes. Radishes. Turnips. Purslain. Wheat. Rye. Barley. . . . Oats, Pease.*" Granted, these are vague descriptions,

MALVA, HIGH MALLOW, CHEESES
(*Malva sylvestris* 'Brave Heart')

TYPE biennial, usually treated as an annual
HEIGHT up to 4 feet
SPREAD 24 inches

HABIT
- bears striped flowers of red and purple
- sports ornamental, crisply textured foliage
- reliably self-sows
- resists rust more so than hollyhocks

NATURAL RANGE
Europe, including Great Britain; naturalized in United States

TIPS
- use in the annual or mixed garden
- provide full sun; partial shade in hot climates
- sow seeds, which need light to germinate, directly in the garden at the soil surface in May or August–September
- thin seedlings to 12 inches

but *M. sylvestris* was prevalent in the English countryside at the time and is now considered naturalized in the United States, begging the question of how early America became inoculated with malva.[5]

In John Lawson's account of his journey through the Carolinas in the first decade of the eighteenth century, he mentioned "Mallows several Sorts" in the list "*Of The Herbs of Carolina.*" Their use as a potherb should surprise no one considering the ancient testimony from Theophrastus and Dioscorides. In the nineteenth century, the U. S. Dispensary, whose influence is now wielded by the Food and Drug Administration, included malva on its list of standardized drugs, thus recognizing its medicinal properties.[6]

Though technically a biennial, malva is best thought of as a recurring annual. Plants of seed sown early in the season will bloom the same year as they are planted. In the trial garden, seed planted directly in garden soil on May 1 germinated on May 4; flowering began on July 13 and persisted until September 4. Alternatively, seed sown in the fall and allowed to germinate will form basal rosettes of leaves that will flower the next year at their full height. When grown in this manner, flowering is earlier than with seed sown in the spring, and, once the fall-sown plants have bloomed out, they may be cut down to half their height and allowed to regrow and reflower. Although malva is not a perennial, it does cast its own seed, so it is impelled forward by this fertile habit.

To many observers, malva looks like a small hollyhock, and in many respects it is. In fact, the foliage of malva is superior to hollyhock, and it seems more impervious to the rust that can wreck such havoc among hollyhocks. Malva was one of the easiest and most robust flowers studied in the trial garden—showy, sensational, healthy, and regenerating.

Viper's Bugloss

(Echium vulgare)
FLOWERING BIENNIAL

Hundßzungen.   CCXXIX.

Some modern gardeners consider this large, sprawling, dusty-blue plant of little consequence, just a weed taking up space. But, the spiral arrangement of blooms around tall, but half-floppy stems makes it somewhat fascinating. In antiquity, at least, viper's bugloss was given its due. Theophrastus remarked on a principal merit of it and plants like it: "They do not produce all their bloom at once, [and so] cover a longer season . . . for instance dandelion bugloss chicory plantain." It is this capacity for long bloom and its coarse, mannish appearance that give it acceptance in the mixed garden.[1]

In its native Europe, it was celebrated for healing "ulcers and other ills of the mouth" and "all sores, wounds." It was also prescribed for dysentery and for all diseases involving discharges from the lungs. From John Gerard (1633), we know that Nicander, the Greek, "in his book of Treacles makes Vipers Buglosse to be one of those plants which cure the biting of serpents, and especially of the Viper, and that drive serpents away."[2]

In his 1754 *Gardeners Dictionary,* Philip Miller was more derisive: "The first Sort is found wild upon dry chalky Hills, and gravelly Soils, in divers Parts of *England,* and is sometimes used in

Medicine: but there are none of the Varieties which are cultivated for their Beauty; though I think the first, fifth, and sixth Sorts deserve a Place in some dry abject Part of the Garden, where little else will grow, for the sake of Variety, and the long Continuance of their Flowers." Lys de Bray, amongst the twentieth century's greatest gardeners and authors, wrote more forgivingly of *Echium vulgare* as "a native wild flower with brilliant violet blue flowers from June to August. An annual . . . for . . . the border." The truth is somewhere in between.[3]

Evidence of the presence of viper's bugloss in colonial America is certain. It was collected by John Clayton, the Virginia botanist, and was classified as *Echium vulgare* by Linnaeus when Clayton's herbarium specimen of viper's bugloss was sent to him in Amsterdam in the mid-eighteenth century. Also, in John Lawson's *A New Voyage to Carolina* (1709), bugloss was mentioned as one of "Our Pot-herbs and others of use, which we already possess," though this citation is less certain since another common herb, alkanet *(Anchusa officinalis),* also carries the common name of bugloss.[4]

As if stiffening its pedestrian reputation, bugloss proved recalcitrant in the

extreme in the trial garden. A true biennial and not masquerading as a hardy annual, it took a full year and a quarter to flower from seed sown in April of the previous year. By June of the first year, clumps, twelve inches high, displayed every aspect of health and little sign of blooming. The healthy but unimpressive clumps went through the winter with no injury and, during the next summer, thrust up robust three-foot stalks of dusty blue–green leaves and small blue-purple flowers that spiraled upward.

Alongside the simple viper's bugloss, we also grew the modern cultivar called 'Blue Bedder'. (Horticulturists often sow modern seed with the intention of observing whether it might revert to native forms over three or four generations, a scant four years in the garden.) 'Blue Bedder' proved to be one of the most prolific and satisfying annual-blooming plants encountered during the trial plantings. This modern selection flowered on May 20 from seed sown in late March, with the bloom persisting until very late

July, when it finally succumbed to the heat. The plant proved so stalwart that a light shearing in early June prompted a second bloom later in the month. 'Blue Bedder' bore masses of bluish flowers over a long period of time, and, as the flowers aged, the blue morphed into a light shade of purple, a characteristic of the species first noted by Leonhart Fuchs in his *New Herbal of 1543* and reiterated by Gerard in 1633.[5]

So different in nature are the two plants, so far is the modern from the species, that the modern cultivar, as satisfying as it was, proved too horticulturally "pumped" for the traditional colonial garden. But, both plants proved very versatile in their own ways. 'Blue Bedder' makes an exceptionally attractive, nearly perpetually blooming bedding plant. Viper's bugloss in its natural state has a light grandeur that makes it most welcome.

Somewhere in between these two extremes of the same species is the specimen in a watercolor by Alexander Marshal (ca. 1653). It suggests a distillation of the species with an improvement of the flower size and a more herbaceous, less stout frame than simple viper's bugloss. In its slightly limp habit, it bears more of a resemblance to the 'Blue Bedder' variety. Whether Marshal's selection was more like an early 'Blue Bedder', larger flowered and blooming with vigor quickly the first year from seed, is unknown. But, it does speak of some improvement over the simple species.[6]

Though ungainly, coarse, and pedestrian, viper's bugloss has its charm. Because it is so persistent in reseeding, it satisfies the imperative of easy fertil-ity, with the plants doing the seeding for you. It is only its vigor that presents any problem at all, but still a leg up on the garden aristocrats that are coddled and pampered only to disappoint the gardener in the end. Not a plant of refinement, perhaps, but a plant with an extremely favorable crude presence. In volume and mass, the species is quite lovely in its own right and exudes a soft, smoky blue haze. It well warrants use in colonial-style gardens.

VIPER'S BUGLOSS, BLUEWEED, BLUE-DEVIL
(Echium vulgare)

TYPE biennial
HEIGHT 12–36 inches
SPREAD up to 36 inches

HABIT
- bears small blue flowers, turning to pink, on long stems
- sports hairy, dusty-blue foliage
- introduces a casual element into the garden

NATURAL RANGE
continental Europe, Asia; naturalized in North America

TIPS
- use in the annual or mixed garden
- provide full sun
- sow seeds directly in the garden near the surface of the soil in the spring for bloom the next year
- thin seedlings to 6 inches

All-Heal

(Prunella grandiflora 'Pagoda')
FLOWERING PERENNIAL

While the medicinal all-heal *(Prunella vulgaris)* is well-known by its therapeutic reputation, it is the large-flowered *P. grandiflora* that is welcome in any flower garden. In the trial garden, it flowered stunningly at six inches tall in the front of the border. Prolific, its large blossoms, each as large as one and a half to two inches, soon scatter seed, and the pink-purple, large-flowered all-heal becomes a movable feast. As it is prone to migrating, the gardener ought to be aware of its wandering nature and deftly work it into a seed-driven garden.

Large-flowered all-heal was introduced into Europe by 1596. By the late eighteenth century, it appeared in William Curtis's London *Botanical Magazine* with the following commentary: "In July and August, it puts forth its large shewy blossoms, of a fine purple colour. Such as are partial to hardy herbaceous plants, of ready growth, which are ornamental, take up but little room, and are not apt to entrench on their neighbours, will be induced to add this to their collection." In the nineteenth century, William Robinson, in *The English Flower Garden*, wrote, "This handsome and vigorous plant *P. grandiflora* is readily distinguished by its large flowers. There is a white and a purple variety, both handsome plants, thriving in almost any soil."[1]

Like any two cousins, plant species often shine in their own individuality. On the one hand, *P. grandiflora*, the large-flowered all-heal, is a colossus in the flower garden; on the other, its smaller and less showy cousin, *P. vulgaris*, common all-heal, is a well-known powerhouse among healing herbs. It is as a result of the medicinal properties of this species that *Prunella* gets its common name of *all-heal*.

P. vulgaris, also a perennial, has long been written about. Maud Grieve, the late dean of modern English herbalists, wrote, "The Self-Heal holds an equal place with Bugle *[Ajuga reptans]* in the esteem of herbalists." This is not a new attribution. John Gerard, the Elizabethan herbalist, spoke of "the decoction of Prunell made with wine and water, doth ioine together and make whole and sound all wounds, both inward and outward, even as Bugle doth."[2]

Herbal medical testimony has it that all-heal's healing properties are profound, not only for external wounds, burns, bruises, and sores but also for throat and

eye infections and complications involving liver function. Leonhart Fuchs, the sixteenth-century German herbalist, was specific in this: "It is evident that the plant is a vulnerary. Its juice, mixed with vinegar and rose oil, is claimed by later authorities, unanimously, to soothe violent headaches, if the temples are anointed with it. Its juice cures white spots and ulcers in the mouth, and sore throat."[3]

Philip Miller, in the commentary of his 1760 illustrated opus, only added to all-heal's fame: "This is the Species which is used in Medicine. . . . It is much used as a vulnerary Herb, and is brought from *Switzerland,* with several others, under the general Appellation of Wound-Herbs. The Leaves and Flowers of this Plant are used. . . . It is prescribed . . . for Spitting of Blood, and for the Bloody-flux, and for all Sorts of *Hæmorrhages,* or *Fluxes of Blood.* It is used by way of *Injection* in deep Wounds, and by way of *Clyster* in the Bloody-flux." Modern Chinese medicine considers it antibiotic against a broad range of bacterial infections.[4]

Although sources differ as to the natural range of common all-heal, the National Plant Data Center, part of the United States Department of Agriculture (USDA) and the American arbiter of all things botanical, considers it a native to the continental United States. Interestingly, three different painted herbals testify to common all-heal's wide geographical distribution. In *The Frampton Flora,* a work of nearly three hundred watercolors executed between 1828 and 1851 by eight women of the Clifford family living at Frampton Court, all-heal appears as an inhabitant of the waysides and grassy places of their area of Gloucestershire,

England, in the Cotswolds. In 1902, Schuyler Mathews, a botanist and watercolorist, described in his book *Fieldbook of American Wild Flowers* all-heal as "very common along roadsides, and on the borders of woods and fields. Across the continent." And, in 1940, Bessie Niemeyer Marshall completed a watercolor florilegium of the plant species found in a wildflower sanctuary in Petersburg, Virginia. Her exquisite work not only depicts beautifully the blue fringed petals of all-heal but also documents its presence in a natural setting in Virginia.[5]

But, was it known by colonial Virginians? The online John Clayton Herbarium database, a project of the Natural History Museum in London, reveals that a specimen of *P. vulgaris* was gathered by John Clayton himself sometime towards the middle of the eighteenth century, putting *Prunella* squarely on the map in colonial Virginia.[6]

In behavior and habit, both all-heals are much like the aforementioned bugle, or ajuga, diminutive overall and migratory. *P. vulgaris* is not more than four inches tall in leaf and about ten inches tall in flower. The flower, more ornamental in the large-flowered species, is itself much like that of ajuga, not surprisingly since both are members of the Labiatae family. They are creepers like ajuga, and plant encyclopedias are quite explicit about the cautions as to their use. Indeed, their spread is quick, mostly via their own self-sown seed and, to a lesser extent, a result of their creeping tendency. But, when happy, both all-heals will soon delight.

All-heal typically prefers damp soil and light shade. Despite its location in direct sun and at the base of a

height is generally twenty-four inches, and taller cultivars of large-flowered all-heal are also available, such as 'Alba' and 'Carminea', as well as other low-growing cultivars such as 'White Loveliness' and 'Pink Loveliness'.

When considering showy small-statured plants for the front of the garden flower border, look no farther than the large-flowered all-heal. The enlarged flowers on the dwarf plants of this 'Pagoda' cultivar are startling, and sufficient water and persistent deadheading keep the patch fresh and in flower for many months.

ALL-HEAL, PRUNELLA, LARGE-FLOWERED ALL-HEAL
(*Prunella grandiflora* 'Pagoda')

TYPE hardy perennial
HEIGHT 6 inches
SPREAD 10 inches

HABIT
- bears 1–1½-inch pink flowers
- forms mats of subsets
- reliably self-sows
- resists most pests
- blooms first year from seed

NATURAL RANGE
continental Europe, except Portugal and southwest Spain

TIPS
- use in the annual, cottage-style, or herb garden
- provide full or partial sun
- sow seeds, which need light to germinate, directly in the garden at the soil surface in early spring
- water regularly

vitex shrub (*Vitex agnus-castus*), which robbed the surrounding planting bed of much moisture, the all-heal in the trial garden thrived as a result of adequate irrigation. In optimum situations with more reliable moisture, it spreads with predictable alacrity. Blooming the first year from seed was not much of a trick,

the legendary rampancy of its self-sown seedlings only too apparent. Its leaves provide a crisp texture to the garden, and its overall fitness makes it an excellent ornamental groundcover. There is a great variety of height among the cultivars of large-flowered all-heal. Though 'Pagoda' grew to only six inches, this species'

Anise Hyssop

(Agastache foeniculum)
FLOWERING PERENNIAL

Gardeners who are familiar with native North American plants likely know the genus *Agastache* well and are probably most familiar with the anise hyssop in particular. Of the nine species of *Agastache*, eight are North American in origin; the ninth, *A. rugosa*, is Asian. They are all noted for their abundant, erect, four- to twelve-inch spikes of flowers and for having the typical square stems of members of the Mint family. In the case of the anise hyssop, also known as the blue giant hyssop, the flower spikes are blue and are produced in such quantity as to qualify it as amongst the showiest plants raised in the trial garden. However, its precise provenance is a stumbling block for Colonial Williamsburg horticulturists.[1]

Although it is thought to be native to the north and central plains of North America, its range in the United States, according to the U. S. Department of Agriculture (USDA), also now includes Delaware, Pennsylvania, and Kentucky, though not Virginia. In addition, it now occurs from New York to Oregon, along the upper tier of states. But, whether any colonial American husbandman or English trekker became aware of this plant during Virginia's colonial period is un-

known and considered unlikely.[2]

A staple of native peoples in those places where the plant occurred, it was used as a tea, cough medicine, and respiratory tonic. Use by Americans began in the first quarter of the nineteenth century, after its native range of the northern and central plains were open to American settlement, and by 1826 it appeared in English horticulture. The anise hyssop's habit of attracting bees made it a particularly important and popular plant from which European and American beekeepers to this day make a light, fragrant honey.[3]

An effective herbal remedy and a recognized "honey plant," the anise hyssop has become a subject of interest to plant breeders eager to exploit the myriad ornamental qualities of this hardy perennial. In the trial garden, its pronounced bloom immediately drew the attention of guests who not only noticed its vibrant bloom and sturdy habit but also remarked on the plant's attractiveness to insects. Bees, wasps, and moths are so eager for nectar that they ignore entirely the pushy gardener intent on grooming and removing spent flowers.

With regret, Colonial Williamsburg's horticulturists hold the anise hyssop at arm's length due to its late entry into the

emerging American gardening lexicon. Nevertheless, Virginia can lay claim to two other *Agastaches: A. nepetoides*, the yellow giant hyssop, and *A. scrophulariifolia*, the purple giant hyssop, both gathered and documented by the colonial Virginia plant collector John Clayton sometime prior to the middle of the eighteenth century. Clayton's two *Agastache* herbarium specimens are preserved at the Natural History Museum in London as part of a collection of 710 original Clayton dried herbarium specimens.[4]

Often, when one member of a genus does well, horticulturists experiment with other species within that genus. The yellow giant hyssop, having been collected in Virginia by John Clayton himself, seemed a good place to start. It has pale yellow flowers scattered thinly over the green five-inch flowering spikes held aloft above four to six feet of catmintlike foliage. This gigantism makes the plant a liability in any ornamental garden. But, one of Colonial Williamsburg's floral designers saw a heap of drastic clippings from a patch of yellow hyssops left on a compost pile and noticed that, though the ephemeral yellow flowers had long gone, the green flesh of the flower spikes themselves persisted, neither yellowed nor browning. She later used the still-green spikes in arrestingly lovely Christmas decorations.

The anise hyssop is possessed of an edible flower that can be used as a colorful garnish on fruit salads, iced teas, and desserts. Its dried leaves have long been used as a tea for respiratory complaints, and, as its common name implies, it is used as a seasoning that imparts an anise flavor. Its many practical uses; its spectacular, long bloom (nearly two months); and the perfect, stout, and purple-tinted foliage make this an enormously appealing plant. The number of modern selections, such as 'Alabaster', 'Album', 'Senior', 'Camphorata', and 'Blue Fortune', indicates the high regard plant breeders hold for this unique ornamental from the American high plains. Although these modern cultivars diversify the color range of *A. foeniculum*, gardeners shouldn't disregard the true species. It is easily raised from seed sown directly in the garden, and its spontaneity with regard to its germination in subsequent years can be prodigious. As neither the species nor the cultivars are inordinately long-lived, an investment in seed-sown anise hyssop in comparison to the purchase price of the named cultivars argues for the former.[5]

ANISE HYSSOP, BLUE GIANT HYSSOP, LICORICE MINT, LAVENDER HYSSOP
(*Agastache foeniculum*)

TYPE hardy perennial
HEIGHT 36–40 inches
SPREAD 24 inches

HABIT
- bears 4-inch spikes of blue flowers
- sports attractive, crisp foliage
- reliably self-sows
- flowers the same year as seed is sown

NATURAL RANGE
northern and central plains of North America

TIPS
- use in the annual, cottage-style, or mixed garden
- provide full sun
- sow seeds directly in the garden at or near the surface of the soil March–April or August–September
- thin seedlings to 6 inches

Blue Pimpernel

(Anagallis monelli)
FLOWERING PERENNIAL

There are two pillars of English-language botanical encyclopedias. The first is the American *Hortus Third: A Concise Dictionary of Plants Cultivated in the United States and Canada*. The second is British, the Royal Horticultural Society's *Dictionary of Gardening: A Practical and Scientific Encyclopaedia of Horticulture*. It is not uncommon for them to differ in their opinions about the correct naming of plants and their relations to other species within a genus. A case in point is the pair of blue pimpernels best known to some gardeners as an indispensable source of saturated blue in the garden.

Both American and British botanical sources aver that there is a blue variety, called *caerulea*, of the famous scarlet pimpernel (*Anagallis arvensis*), an annual known best from the novel *The Scarlet Pimpernel*. But, the sources disagree about a particular short-lived blue perennial pimpernel. The Americans consider it its own species, *A. monelli*; the British consider it a variety of *A. linifolia*.[1]

Both blue pimpernels, the annual and the perennial, are nearly indistinguishable in appearance. The perennial *A. monelli*, very often used as an annual in seasonal ornamental plantings, has been prized for centuries. It features a small but showy blue flower set on a delicate nest of shiny foliage. It has been a favorite in European gardens for over three hundred years. Though distinct from the *caerulea*, it is so similar that the differences would be lost to the casual observer. Both pimpernels make a very attractive subject and so fascinated Alexander Marshal that he painted the *monelli* three times in his great florilegium. The *monelli* is playing a role again at the restored late-seventeenth-century garden at Het Loo, the Dutch palace favored by William of Orange, where plants of that period are being used in the restored, intricately patterned parterres.[2]

The blue pimpernel first comes to light in Theophrastus's ancient Greek herbal, *Enquiry into Plants*, dated to about 300 BC. We don't know whether Theophrastus addressed the *monelli* or the *caerulea*, but what is curious is that he included the blue pimpernel in the section he titled, *"Of other uncultivated herbs, which may be classed with the pot-herbs,"* in other words, those edible plants useful as a salad or cooked green. In this class of plants, he included chicory (*Cichorium intybus*), dandelion (*Taraxacum officinale*), cat's ear (*Hypochoeris* sp.), groundsel (*Senecio vulgaris*), chervil (*Anthriscus*

cerefolium), green mint (Mentha viridis), "and in general all those that are called 'chicory-like' because of the resemblance in the leaves." "Some," he noted, "need the action of fire, as *malakhe* (cheese-flower) beet monk's rhubarb nettle and bachelor's buttons. . . . There are also many more, including the plant which has become proverbial for its bitterness, blue pimpernel, which has a leaf like basil."[3]

Throughout the ancient literature concerning the pimpernels, the speculation that the scarlet pimpernel was male and the blue pimpernel was female was a persistent theme until modern times. This legend seems to have had its birth in the text of Dioscorides, a first-century physician. He said quite simply, "There are two kinds of *anagallis,* differing in the flower, for that which has an azure [blue] flower is called the female, but that of a Phoenician [red] colour is called the male." With this simple statement, millennia of skewed judgment were birthed.[4]

Dioscorides also laid the foundation for the medicinal use of the pimpernels saying, "They are both lessening in strength, drive away inflammation, extract [draw out] splinters or thorns that were run into the body, and repress gangrenous ulcers. The juice gargled purges the head of mucus, and poured into the nostrils it stops toothache. It is put in the opposing nostril to the sore tooth. With Attic [Athenian] honey it mends *argemae* [small white ulcers on the cornea] and helps moisture of the eyes. It is good . . . for those bitten by vipers, as well as for kidney and liver ailments, and for dropsy."[5]

The task in the trial garden was to ascertain the relative habits and vigor of the annual and perennial pimpernels. In comparing the two blue pimpernels, the annual *caerulea* outperformed the perennial *monelli.* Experience with both plants demonstrated that the annual was superior to the perennial. The color was stronger and the entire plant was more vigorous than the perennial. The *caerulea* annual variety is a very, very redoubtable plant, with very good bloom, good heat resistance, and a long flowering period. Climatic differences may account for the better performance of the annual over the perennial in light of the preference for the *monelli* in older testimony.

Although the scarlet and the blue pimpernels were well-known in England during the seventeenth and eighteenth centuries, appearing in Philip Miller's *Gardeners Dictionary* (1754), their American entry date is uncertain. Rudy Favretti, the well-known landscape historian, cites the scarlet pimpernel as suitable for American gardens in the 1776–1850 range, and one could assume that the blue, whether *monelli* or *cerulea,* was not faster in making its way to the New World. This realization comes with some regret. As a garden plant, the *caerulea* performed well, and the small flowers were numerous and so deeply hued and the leaves so lustrous as to cause the plants to have an effect even from a small distance. Indeed, Arthur Shurcliff, Colonial Williamsburg's illustrious first landscape architect, left notes to the effect that the scarlet pimpernel was a well-known garden plant in England and was particularly adept as an edging plant, a use to which the blue could be

put as well. That use and as a diminutive bedding plant for small, intimate situations would suit the blue pimpernels to their best advantage.[6]

BLUE PIMPERNEL, POOR-MAN'S-LOOKING GLASS (*Anagallis monelli*)

TYPE short-lived perennial
HEIGHT up to 10 inches
SPREAD 12 inches

HABIT
- bears ½-inch deep-blue flowers
- sports glossy, delicate leaves
- stays compact

NATURAL RANGE
Mediterranean region

TIPS
- use in the annual, cottage-style, or mixed garden
- provide full sun
- sow seeds directly in the garden ⅛ inch deep after danger of frost
- thin seedlings to 6 inches

Boneset

(Eupatorium perfoliatum)

FLOWERING PERENNIAL

It is as a long-blooming white perennial that boneset should be used in the American historical garden. Growing to five feet tall and bearing flat, white flower heads from June into August, it can be effective as a background filler behind other native American plants such as swamp milkweed *(Asclepias incarnata)*, wild quinine *(Parthenium integrifolium)*, and blue vervain *(Verbena hastata)*. Too many gardeners assume that the use of white is a surrender of some other, more impressive color. But, as most artists know, white needs to be part of the palette in order to illuminate other colors. In the words of the late, well-known English landscape gardener Russell Page: "I had just planted a long bed with orange-scarlet, crimson, vermilion, salmon and magenta geraniums spiced with enough white to make these clashing reds vibrate together."[1]

To our North American forebears, boneset was a well-used native herb. Its Native American name roughly translates to "ague weed," indicating its effectiveness against what can best be identified as a flu or fever. No other plant probably had more extensive and frequent use among popular remedies in the United States where it was once official in the U. S. Pharmacopoeia and is now part of herbal medicine, wherein it is used to reduce fever. It is considered a diaphoretic, an agent to induce sweating and, in so doing, "break" a fever. In large doses, it is an emetic and purgative. According to Maud Grieve, author of *A Modern Herbal* (1931), it was largely used by the African-American population of the old rural South to treat all fevers but was thought less effective for typhoid and yellow fevers. Boneset derived its name from the attribution of its curative effects on break-bone fever, the very painful dengue fever once endemic to the Deep South. Modern attributions also include its purported use as a stimulant to the immune system, what was called in the past a *tonic*.[2]

Though no specimen exists in the John Clayton Herbarium in the Natural History Museum in London, Linnaeus's inclusion of boneset in *Species Plantarum* (1753) suggests that it was collected in Virginia by John Clayton, the eighteenth-century botanist, some years earlier. Linnaeus would have brought the plant to the attention of the Latin-literate, horticulturally inclined public in Europe, but this plant was probably elusive to the majority of Europeans and colonial

for other, flashier plants. Given its attractiveness, usefulness, and long history in the folk tradition, and given the public's renewed interest in herbal cures, boneset ought to have a higher profile in the gardens of the moderns.

BONESET, COMMON THOROUGHWORT, INDIAN SAGE (*Eupatorium perfoliatum*)

TYPE hardy perennial
HEIGHT up to 5 feet
SPREAD up to 4 feet

HABIT
- bears flat corymbs of white flowers
- sports crisp, textured leaves
- long blooming
- resists most pests

NATURAL RANGE
eastern North America

TIPS
- use in the annual, cottage-style, or mixed garden
- provide full sun
- sow seeds directly in the garden 1/8 inch deep in March

Americans alike, save for those few who were privy to Native American healing traditions. An entry on boneset in Jacob Bigelow's *American Medical Botany, Being a Collection of the Native Medicinal Plants of the United States* (1817–1820) appears to be the first American printed reference to it.[3]

This immensely useful native perennial was also inordinately helpful in contributing to the successful mix of annual and perennial plants that gave the trial garden both a variability and a permanence over many seasons. The very robust, even crisp foliage is pleasantly crinkled and, though one could want better of the somewhat wan, white flowers, the plant was nevertheless a great asset to the garden overall. With its tendency to seed and reseed, boneset can become a weed in some situations, but it quickly develops mature leaves, and unwanted

plants are but a pull away. In the meantime, its long flowering period and stout nature make it a nonfussy ingredient in a mixed garden setting. Its relative height, five feet, and its long blooming period recommend its use with blue vervain, purple coneflowers (*Echinacea purpurea*), and the large-flowered blue asters (*Aster grandiflorus*) in perennial beds featuring primarily native American plants.

Seed sown directly in the ground in late March yielded thirty-inch flowering plants by July 12. By August 22, after careful deadheading and prodding, they flowered again and were sturdy enough to be transplanted to other places in the garden where they could adequately fill out their reputed, optimal five-foot height. When used in mixed plantings, the bold foliage provides a pleasing texture while the innocuous white flowers can be an especially understated foil

Cardoon

(Cynara cardunculus)
FLOWERING PERENNIAL

Native to the Mediterranean region, it is no wonder that the cardoon and its cousin artichoke (*Cynara scolymus*) came to the attention of Theophrastus twenty-three hundred years ago. The cardoon and the artichoke are alike in many respects. In fact, many encyclopedias postulate that the artichoke was derived from the cardoon. Both bear striking silver leaves, sometimes as long as three feet, that are heavily serrated and veined. Both sport four- to six-foot-tall stalks of three-inch-wide purple thistle flowers. The cardoon is often used as a strong decorative plant in modern perennial flower schemes; the artichoke is as well, but less often.[1]

In Theophrastus's discussion of "spinous under-shrubs" and thistles, he discussed the cardoon and the artichoke: "But the plant called *kaktos* (cardoon) grows only in Sicily, and not in Hellas. It is a plant quite different from any other; for it sends up straight from the root stems which creep on the ground, and its leaf is broad and spinous: these stems are called *kaktoi*; they are edible, if peeled, and are slightly bitter, and men preserve them in brine." Cardoon is eaten just in this manner today in some parts of the world. "There is another kind [artichoke] which sends up an erect stem, called the *pternix*. This too is edible, but cannot be preserved. The fruit-vessel, which contains the seed, is in shape like a thistle-head: and when the downy seeds are taken off, this too is edible and resembles the 'brain' of the palm; and it is called *skalias*."[2]

Dioscorides addressed either the cardoon or the artichoke nearly four hundred years later. He too said "it puts out a long stalk full of leaves on which is a prickly head. The root lies underneath—black, thick, its strength good for those with a bad smell in the armpits and the rest of the body . . . and taken as a drink as it draws out much stinking urine. The new growth of the herb boiled like asparagus is eaten instead of a vegetable." Although he mentioned the terminal bud, he made no comment regarding eating it, instead referring to the new herbage, making this seem more like a discussion of the cardoon than the artichoke.[3]

In John Gerard's early-seventeenth-century herbal, both the cardoon and the artichoke are mentioned: "Two tame or of the garden; and one wilde, which the Italian esteemth greatly of, as the best to be eaten raw, which he calleth *Cardune*. . . . The Artichoke is to be

Cinnamon Vine

(Apios americana)
FLOWERING PERENNIAL VINE

The cinnamon vine, which has no connection with the spice, gets its name from the color of its flowers. The plant is of particular ornamental interest because of its unusual cinnamon-colored flowers of complicated architecture. As with other members of the Pea family, the flowers of the cinnamon vine seem to curl into themselves with great complexity, resulting in a three dimensionality that enhances the odd ruddy color of the bloom.

Also known as the American groundnut, the cinnamon vine was once an important food crop for Native Americans, who cooked and consumed the nearly spherical tubers of the plant. With the gradual growth in the Williamsburg area over the past four hundred years, many native plants, such as the cinnamon vine, that were common in the seventeenth century are now rare in the local environment. Colonial Williamsburg horticulturists endeavor to recover not only imported cultivated species used in the eighteenth century but also native plants that were not intensively cultivated but would nevertheless have been abundant prior to the settling of Jamestown.[1]

Fortunately for garden historians, the historical literature is replete with mention of the groundnut. John Lawson referred to "Ground-Nuts, or wild Potato's" in his *New Voyage to Carolina* (1709), and John Clayton, eighteenth-century Virginian botanist, enumerated it among the plants he found in Virginia. It is this groundnut that Carolus Linnaeus named *Glycine apios* and that he included in his *Species Plantarum* (1753).[2]

Thomas Harriot, in his 1588 account of the lost Roanoke Island colony in what is now North Carolina, in a section he titled *"Of Rootes,"* said, "OPENAUK are a kind of roots of round forme, some of the bignes of walnuts, some far greater, which are found in moist & marish grounds growing many together one by another in ropes, or as thogh they were fastened with a string. Being boiled or sodden they are very good meate." The spherical tubers "fastened with a string" distinguish the "openauk" as cinnamon vine.[3]

In his *New-Englands Rarities Discovered* (1672), John Josselyn made note of *"Earth-Nut,* which are of divers kinds, one bearing very beautiful Flowers." Josselyn's insistence on the "earth-nut's" beauty puts one in mind of the beautiful, curvilinear form of the American groundnut, or cinnamon vine. As the

native region of the cinnamon vine is the entire eastern United States, it would certainly have been found in New England.[4]

In a seminal work on edible plants, the nineteenth-century botanist E. Lewis Sturtevant discussed the written records of the traveling naturalist Peter Kalm (1772): "Kalm says . . . the Indians on the Delaware . . . ate the roots; that the Swedes ate them for want of bread, and that in 1749 some of the English ate them instead of potatoes."[5]

But, it was its beauty that led Robert Furber to include the cinnamon vine in his famous *The Flower-Garden Display'd* (1732), his twelve compositions of flowers set into elaborate arrangements. In the commentary, he said of the *"Apios of America,"* "This has Roots like the Potatoe, and loves a light Soil. It is a twining Plant, rising out of the Ground in *April,* and decaying at the End of the Summer."[6]

By the end of the nineteenth century, Americans had embraced this curious native plant, and Denise Adams, in her book *Restoring American Gardens,*

documented the profusion of vines that were then recommended as a way to romanticize and ornament the Queen Anne–style houses of the time. In one case, the American groundnut was one of two dozen such vines that could be combined to ornament a single dwelling.[7]

The cinnamon vine was introduced into the trial garden in a corner that had also become seeded with cypress vine *(Ipomoea quamoclit),* an annual morning glory. Although the cinnamon vine has a reputation as rambunctious, the sheer rampant weight of hundreds of cypress vine seedlings inhibited the establishment of the groundnut during the course of two summers. Even as the gardener weeded considerably more than halfheartedly, cypress vine's infernal onslaught choked the better-behaved groundnut. On a fence and in a situation with less competition, the American groundnut provides a curiousness and novelty to any garden it occupies.

Given the groundnut's American nativity, its reputation in Britain as a

"graceful tuberous-rooted perennial of twining habit," and a plant of such unusual beauty, this charming plant is likely adaptable to many situations. Part of the great charm of Colonial Williamsburg's Historic Area are the small oases of ravines and woodlands that lay tucked within the city grid, natural pockets nestled amongst the level, rectilinear baroque plan imposed on a countryside of abrupt dips and steep ridges. Somewhere within that hybrid landscape, horticulturists hope to reestablish the groundnut to a habitable clime.[8]

CINNAMON VINE, AMERICAN GROUNDNUT
(*Apios americana*)

TYPE hardy, tuberous-rooted
   perennial vine
HEIGHT up to 8 feet
SPREAD 8 feet

HABIT
• bears dense, convoluted racemes of chocolate-colored flowers
• bears strings of edible tubers, 1–2 inches long
• propagates via underground tubers
• prefers trellis support

NATURAL RANGE
New Brunswick to Florida, west to Minnesota and Texas

TIPS
• use in a wild part of the garden
• provide full sun
• plant 2–4 tubers in the garden 3–4 inches deep in spring
• provide climbing support

Columbine

(Aquilegia canadensis)

FLOWERING PERENNIAL

A staple of spring, columbine sports elongated bicolored flowers held well above clover-shaped, bluish gray leaves. When in bloom, a large patch of columbine appears from a distance as a rosy mist suspended over the garden. Despite the dainty spring flowers and elegant foliage of the columbine, it is a short-lived perennial. Nevertheless, if time is allowed for the seed heads to mature, prodigious amounts of columbine seed self-scatter with the subsequent effect of shimmering masses of red and yellow flowers again the next year.

In very sunny conditions, columbine can typically grow quite tall, up to twenty-four inches, and sometimes taller with the benefit of full sun, fertilizer, and abundant water. When given sufficient water, it blooms spectacularly from mid-April to early May in Tidewater Virginia. In Williamsburg gardens, columbine blooms at the same time as basket-of-gold (*Aurinia saxatilis*). In one planting, beds edged in yellow-flowering basket-of-gold set off the alternating red and yellow petals of the flowers of the columbine, which, with much water, fertilizer, and sun, bloomed at its full two feet of height. In the South, columbine will eventually succumb to sunscald in sunny areas and retreat underground for the summer. In semishady conditions, its blue-gray lobed foliage develops over the summer to a fuller extent. Although its habitat is moist to dry rocky woods and ledges in the eastern United States, columbine will prosper in almost any situation given adequate moisture.

This eastern columbine has become the parent to many crosses involving other species, especially the American *Aquilegia caerulea* and *A. chrysantha,* from the Rocky Mountains and California, respectively. It was from these American species that the modern long-spurred varieties were developed. Many times, gardeners growing several kinds of columbine will notice spontaneous crosses among the progeny of self-sown parent plants. Garden writers recommend that new plants of fancy hybrids be obtained from a fresh source of seed or stock in order to maintain finer flowers and prevent a degeneracy of flower size and color. For some gardeners, though, there's an excitement as species cross and rogue seedlings pop up amongst their more cultivated cousins.[1]

An Englishman, John Tradescant the Younger, collected columbine and took it to England by the time that John Parkinson

published his 1640 *Theatrum Botanicum*. By 1653, Alexander Marshal had painted it in watercolor for his stupendous florilegium. Despite its subtle beauty, it was not highly regarded in England: in the eighteenth century, it was observed as having "no great beauty in the flowers." The English were content with their own species, the blue *A. vulgaris*, and the double and multicolored flowers derived from it that can be seen in the illustrations of Basilius Besler's florilegium (ca. 1613). The English columbine also made its own transatlantic jump, with evidence of its use found amongst old seed lists of the Moravian settlers of North Carolina in the mid-eighteenth century.[2]

Columbine, being a native, is not hard to pin down in the historical record. The Reverend John Banister, a naturalist, plant explorer, and protégé of the plant-mad Bishop of London, Henry Compton, in his late-seventeenth-century trek through Virginia, recorded columbine, calling it "Aquilegia Virginiana Park.," a botanical nod to its first mention in Parkinson's *Theatrum Botanicum* where it is called *"Aquilegia Virginiana flore rubessente precox*. The early red Columbine of *Virginia."* Later, in the middle of the eighteenth century, John Clayton, the Virginian botanist, collected a specimen. Perhaps as a result of that specimen, columbine appears in Carolus Linnaeus's *Species Plantarum* (1753). In 1791, Thomas Jefferson noted its bloom on April 30, along with fringe tree (*Chionanthus virginicus),* red mulberry (*Morus rubra),* and three species of magnolia (*Magnolia* spp.), unnamed.[3]

In the South, columbine is a fixture of the spring garden, rarely persisting beyond the first of June. As prolific seeders, they perpetuate themselves with abandon and embody the carefree nature that true inhabitants of cottage gardens possess, a certain happenstance about where they'll seed, but determined to do so. To start or to expand a patch, the gardener needs no more than to cultivate the surrounding soil with a hand cultivator, which some people call a "claw," and scatter or allow the seed to fall. Columbine's bluish gray leaves, which resemble the shape of clover leaves, should alert the gardener when seedlings arise.

COLUMBINE
(*Aquilegia canadensis*)

TYPE hardy, short-lived perennial, although it reseeds heavily
HEIGHT 12–24 inches
SPREAD 12 inches

HABIT
- bears pendulous flowers in red and yellow
- sports ornamental blue-gray lobed foliage
- reliably self-sows
- can be ephemeral in hot climates

NATURAL RANGE
eastern United States

TIPS
- use in the annual, cottage-style, or mixed garden
- provide full sun; partial shade in hot climates
- sow seeds, which need light to germinate, directly in the garden at the soil surface in April when the soil warms to 70°F or in August–September
- provide a light, sandy soil
- thin seedlings to 6 inches

Orange Coneflower

(Rudbeckia fulgida 'Goldsturm')
FLOWERING PERENNIAL

The orange coneflower and its sister black-eyed Susan (*Rudbeckia hirta*) exemplify quintessential American flora. The difference between the two is slight. The former is reliably a perennial while the latter can be variable and behave like an annual, biennial, or perennial. The great *raison d'être* of these flowers, and there are as many as twenty-five species of *Rudbeckia*, is that they are part of the floral backbone of the American summer garden. They represent that classic, indispensable midseason trio of black-eyed Susans or orange coneflowers, summer phlox (*Phlox paniculata*), and tawny daylilies (*Hemerocallis fulva*) that provide needed bloom in late June/early July. In an unkempt field, rather than a garden setting, that combination could be expanded to include Queen Anne's lace (*Daucus carota*), horsemint (*Monarda punctata*), and bee balm (*M. didyma*).

Considered native to the entire eastern United States, the orange coneflower is recorded as having entered Britain rather late in the Anglo–colonial American botanical conversation. The Royal Horticultural Society places its date of entry into Britain in 1760. It eluded Clayton's collection of American plants as well as Linnaeus's groundbreaking *Species Plantarum* (1753). Its sister, the more annual-behaving black-eyed Susan, was more familiar to colonial Americans and Europeans alike, arriving in Britain in 1714. Its later collection is documented by its presence in the John Clayton Herbarium as an original element, around 1750, and its inclusion in Carolus Linnaeus's *Species Plantarum* (1753).[1]

In the trial garden, we sowed an improved cultivar of *R. fulgida* called 'Goldsturm', and, after a slow start, the results were heartening. Although the seed failed to take root the first year, hibernating seed germinated during the subsequent year, and pockets of orange coneflower popped up among the other crops. During its bloom, the thick, textured leaves and stout, strong flowers were nearly impervious to Virginia's strong summer sun, and its long bloom was a boon. 'Goldsturm' is considered one of the showiest cultivars, and, used lightly, it can add dramatic points of color at a time when the garden might be failing in color and brawn.

Perhaps the orange coneflower and the black-eyed Susan present that problem of over-familiarity. But, a garden completely bereft of them, and one without summer phlox and tawny daylily, is

one that may have a famine of color after the spring things have gone and before the autumn perennials begin to bloom in late August and September. The orange coneflower is a tough perennial, resistant to drought, and long blooming. Nothing more recollects the historic American garden than orange daises with brown cones and the mix of other traditional perennials that have been the mainstay of many a home place for many years.

ORANGE CONEFLOWER
(*Rudbeckia fulgida* 'Goldsturm')

TYPE hardy perennial
HEIGHT up to 36 inches
SPREAD up to 24 inches

HABIT
- a stout perennial bearing black-eyed Susan–like flowers
- sports crisp, slightly hairy foliage impervious to heat
- long and late blooming
- resists most pests

NATURAL RANGE
eastern United States

TIPS
- use in the annual, cottage-style, or mixed garden
- provide full sun
- sow seeds directly in the garden ¼ inch deep in early September

Purple Coneflower

(Echinacea purpurea)
FLOWERING PERENNIAL

Purple coneflower is known today by its botanical name, *Echinacea,* to much of the American public, who have become aware of its possible stimulating effect on the human immune system. Sold in the forms of teas and capsules, it is touted primarily as a remedy to reduce the symptoms and duration of colds and flu-like illnesses. It is also being investigated for treating immunodeficiency diseases. Aside from its medicinal application, its value as a garden plant, with its large bright-purple flowers and beautiful dark-green foliage, is not to be outdone.

Purple coneflower was much appreciated by eighteenth-century English horticultural cognoscenti. The Reverend John Banister, an early English plant explorer sent to the English colonies by Bishop Compton in 1678, included this plant in his catalog of Virginia plants. Purple coneflower was collected in eighteenth-century Virginia by John Clayton, colonial America's most important plant collector and botanist, and was included in the dried herbarium specimens that he sent to Europe that later led to the publication *Flora Virginica* (1739–1743). Purple coneflower also appeared in Linnaeus's *Species Plantarum* (1753) bearing the name *Rudbeckia purpurea*.[1]

As a garden plant, not only does purple coneflower boast large, attractive flowers, but it also has the fortunate habit of blooming the first year from seed, if sown early enough. In trials, seed sown in March germinated by the middle of April with flowering commencing by the second week in July. The plants remained in flower through the third week of August. But, purple coneflower offers more than just its bright-purple flowers. The foliage is a beautiful dark-green, and the plant as a whole never needs staking. Experience with it proved that purple coneflower is as drought tolerant as most perennials come. Its ability to bloom the first year and the sensational seed heads it produces as the flowers go by should ensure its place in any flower garden. With its solid American pedigree and its durable nature, it is a natural in combinations with other American natives such as the blue lobelia (*Lobelia siphilitica*), joe-pye weed (*Eupatorium purpureum*), and swamp milkweed (*Asclepias incarnata*) among others.

In the herbal arena, purple coneflower's reputation is emerging as a powerfully effective natural healing herb. Both Andrew Chevallier, in his *Encyclopedia of Medicinal Plants* (1996), and Deni

Bown, in the Herb Society of America's *New Encyclopedia of Herbs and Their Uses* (2001), consider purple coneflower the most important immune stimulant in Western herbal medicine. Chevallier explained that the polysaccharides in the plant inhibit the ability of viruses to enter and take cells; other molecules called *alkamides* are antibacterial and antifungal. He wrote that purple coneflower also has a general stimulating effect on the body's immune defenses and is being investigated for a treatment for HIV.

Deni Bown, in her commentary on the plant, mentioned that it stimulates interferon production, which inhibits viral replication as well. Like elecampane (*Inula helenium*), purple coneflower contains the molecule inulin, which destroys free radicals. Bown also cited polyacetylenes in purple coneflower, which are antibacterial and antifungal, and caffeoyl derivatives, which are strongly antioxidant, "preventing skin photodamage." She reported that Plains Indians regarded purple coneflower as a cure-all and that currently it is "considered the most effective detoxicant in Western medicine for the circulatory, lymphatic, and respiratory systems." It is used for infections of all kinds and is particularly helpful for chronic infections such as post-viral fatigue syndrome. Modern herbal and scientific research is beginning to corroborate purple coneflower's beneficial properties related to colds, flu, skin disorders, and respiratory problems and as a gargle for throat infections.[2]

Purple coneflower, it would seem, is a minor botanical miracle. It is a vigorous and floriferous native American plant with an enormous, genetically important herbal inheritance that is just now being tapped. That, and its enormous aesthetic merits, would argue strongly that it, and its many cultivars, should find wide-scale application in emerging American gardens and landscapes.

PURPLE CONEFLOWER
(*Echinacea purpurea*)

TYPE hardy perennial
HEIGHT 3–4 feet
SPREAD 24 inches

HABIT
- sports purple florets surrounding an orange cone
- dark-green leaves susceptible to drought
- flowers first year from seed
- resists most pests

NATURAL RANGE
Ohio to Iowa, south to Louisiana and Georgia

TIPS
- use in the cottage-style or mixed garden
- provide full sun
- sow seeds directly in the garden ¼ inch deep after danger of frost
- thin seedlings to 6–12 inches

Indian-Shot

(Canna indica)

FLOWERING PERENNIAL

Perhaps no other plant suggests to so many people true, lush tropicality. Indian-shot, or canna lily as it is also called, is almost cliché in our culture for the torpid sensuality of the South. Though its size can make a bold statement, the unimproved species has a certain elegant simplicity: pristine red flowers on simple, green, bladelike leaves. Its popularity and breeding have resulted in cultivars with yellow, pink-orange, and glaring red flowers, many having variegated or dark-bronze foliage, some of them awkwardly showy.

A strong presence in any garden, Indian-shot can often overpower a planting, and careful thought should be given to its use. Single, small plantings might be an option. Gardeners should be even more careful with the modern cultivars. In addition, Indian-shot is too often planted in landscape schemes where its complicated flowers are never afforded the grooming they need. To avoid the appearance of a disheveled clump with spent flowers strewn on torn leaves, a stand of Indian-shot entails the daily removal of spent petals, the weekly removal of whole sprays of spent flowers, and the monthly removal of entire spent three- to six-foot stalks. This can be

tedious work, but, if it becomes part of a near-daily gardening cycle, the Indian-shot will deliver that burst of pure red color like almost nothing else amongst its old-fashioned brethren.

Such tropicality seems so out of character in the colonial past. With respect to climate, Virginia only flirts with the tropics. With respect to trade, she is more committed. Perhaps through maritime intercourse, John Custis of Williamsburg was able to acquire and send to Peter Collinson in London seed of "Indian frill," a plant specific to tropical America. Collinson, in a letter back to Custis, wrote, "The seed you Call Indian frill Wee call Cana Indica or Wild Plaintain or Bonana from some Resemblance in the Leafe. With us it is perannuall by secureing the Roots from the Frost & Comes up Ev'ry Spring."[1]

Canna indica also appears in *Flora Caroliniana*, a catalog of plants collected in the Carolinas and compiled in Charleston in 1788 by Thomas Walter, a British botanist who immigrated to South Carolina in 1768. Indian-shot is now naturalized in some southeastern states but is considered indigenous only to the tropical West Indies, and the circumstances of its presence in Charleston, as

print in Leonhart Fuchs's unpublished *Vienna Codex* (1566), although scholars maintain that the first literary reference was by Andrea Cesalpino, an Italian botanist, in his work *De Plantis Libri XVI* (1583). It entered England by 1570 but eluded Gerard's herbal (1633). Unsuited in the extreme to even cool soils, it likely caused more frustration than admiration when grown in clammy England. At the time of its discovery, a sister species, *C. edulis*, was a widely used food root crop in the American tropics. The two species are often confused, the latter arriving in England by only 1820.[3]

The seeds of Indian-shot are famously and uniformly round and hard and are drilled, strung, and used as beads in cultures throughout the tropics. So satisfactory are the density and roundness of the seeds that the common name *Indian-shot* describes its purported use in firearms that scatter a blast of multiple small-caliber shot, such as a blunderbuss or shotgun. The effectiveness of their use in this application has been demonstrated, and romantics speculate on Indian-shot's use among pirates plying the West Indian islands.[4]

To have recourse to a plant of such tropical pretensions dated so early in Virginia is itself a minor miracle, and Indian-shot adds a welcome schizophrenic and seemingly unlikely presence in colonial gardens dominated by simple Elizabethan herbs. It and castor bean (*Ricinus communis*), an African herb of treelike dimensions, when surrounded by England's herbal legacy and amended by Virginian flora, make for a cluster of species representing four continents, an early whisper of the accelerating globalization of species that would ensue.

well as its route to Williamsburg, are as yet unknown.[2]

Encountered first by the Hispanic explorers in the West Indies and tropical South America, Indian-shot was known in Europe well before Custis gifted it to Collinson in 1736. It is thought that an image of it appeared for the first time in

INDIAN-SHOT, INDIAN FRILL, CANNA LILY, SAKA SIRI, BANDERA
(*Canna indica*)

TYPE tropical perennial rhizome, hardy to zone 7a with protection
HEIGHT 3–6 feet
SPREAD 24 inches

HABIT
- bears ornamental sprays of brilliant red flowers
- provides a source of bold texture in the garden
- adds verticality in a design

NATURAL RANGE
American tropics

TIPS
- use in the annual, cottage-style, or mixed garden
- provide full sun
- plant rhizomes in the garden with the tops of the crowns set just below the surface when the soil warms

Maltese Cross

(Lychnis chalcedonica)
FLOWERING PERENNIAL

Lychnis hirsuta flore coccineo major.
Greater hairy Campion with a Scarlet Flower.

John Parkinson, royal botanist to Charles I, heralded the arrival of the Maltese cross in England because of its bold coloring. In his *Paradisi in Sole* (1629), Parkinson listed several varieties of the "Single Nonesuch," as he called the Maltese cross, and described its "tuft or umbell . . . of a bright red orenge colour." He also mentioned varieties of "pure white. . . . Another is of a blush colour wholly, without variation. And a third is very variable; for at first it is of a pale red, and after a while groweth paler." Still more elaborate is the double Maltese cross whose flower is as rare as it is beautiful, said Parkinson, whose "every flower consisting of three or foure rowes of leaves, of a deeper orenge colour then it, which addeth the more grace unto it."[1]

Incorporating the somewhat chaotic color of the fiery orange red into gardens seeking chromatic harmony can present a challenge. Iconoclasts might cope with orange reds by throwing them in with the purples. But, in a vintage garden, with dozens of different species seeding themselves and migrating around the garden, confining them to a specific area may not be realistic. Also, a small infusion of the Maltese cross will accent the more subtle colors without overwhelming the whole. It certainly makes sense, however, to counter the vibrant Maltese cross with a cool blue perennial such as speedwell (*Veronica officinalis*). A smattering of blue ageratum (*Ageratum houstonianum*) in front of the Maltese cross sets it off as well, with the Maltese cross generally growing taller than the ageratum in front of it.

The Maltese cross is one of those plants blessed with a plethora of botanical and common names, which in small number can be charming and in large number tedious. It was given its common name *Maltese cross* because the arrangement of the petals of the individual flowers resembles a Maltese cross, an elaborate cross with flared, equal arms. Its botanical genus *Lychnis* simply means that it is a catchfly, or a campion, and a member of the pink family (with *Dianthus*, *Silene*, and *Saponaria*). *Chalcedonica*, a weighty word, is from an ancient Greek city of Asia Minor on the Bosporus Sea, founded opposite Byzantium in 685 BC. Though not native to Chalcedon, it was introduced to English gardens from there by 1596. Garden historians place its native region in eastern and northern Russia.[2]

Continental gardeners seem to have had a step up on English gardeners where this plant is concerned. Leonhart Fuchs featured it in his unpublished Vienna Codex (1566), saying, "This flower was first sent to me by Johann Schmidlapp, who lives in Schorndorf, near Stuttgart, a very enthusiastic botanist, with a garden planted with most beautiful plants." In England by 1633, it received ample description in Gerard's herbal of that year, where he called the Maltese cross the "Campion of Constantinople. . . . The floures grow at the top like Sweet-Williams, or rather like Dames violets, of the colour of red lead, or Orenge tawny." Gerard said that several varieties were available, such as with "blush coloured floures, as also a double kinde with vary large, double and beautiful floures of a Vermelion colour." In addition, although the Maltese cross is possessed of "that grace and beauty which it hath in gardens and garlands," it has "no [herbal] use, the vertues thereof being not as yet found out."[3]

Alexander Marshal painted the single and double Maltese cross twice in his florilegium, completed around 1653. Another English gentleman, John Evelyn, writing in the middle of the seventeenth century, addressed the Maltese cross in his supremely specific guidelines as to what he considered a proper gentleman's garden of "Coronary" (ornamental) plants should include. In his *Elysium Britannicum, or The Royal Gardens*, he recommended *"Lichnis Constantinop"* as a coronary plant for the middling height of a flower border along with *"Bulbous Violets, Star-flower, Crow foote, . . . Cyclamen, Martagon, Fritillaria, Hyacinth, None-such* [another common name for the Maltese cross], *Rose-Campion, Winter-Wolfe bane, Bee-flo:, Snow flo:, Carnations, Corne flo:, Sweete William, Peony, etc.*" Evelyn was aware of several kinds as well: "*Lychnis is of severall kinds: The rarest is the {dubble} Chalcedonica to us an admirable flo: both for colour & shape.*"[4]

One American writer places the Maltese cross in colonial American gardens in the first century of the American experiment, 1600–1699, while another historian cites the earliest American reference as the Goldthwaite & Moore seed company, Philadelphia, 1796. An advertising broadsheet demonstrates that the Maltese cross was offered commercially by Bernard McMahon in 1802 or 1803, and Monticello historians date Thomas Jefferson's use of the Maltese cross as part of his plan for the winding "*Round-about*

Walk" to the rear of the house to 1807.[5]

Monticello and Colonial Williamsburg horticulturists both experimented with growing the Maltese cross in their respective regions of Virginia. The plant's performance suggests that it prefers the cooler temperatures at Monticello in the Virginia Piedmont where it reliably grows to four feet. In the sand or clay of Williamsburg's Tidewater coastal plain, it must be watered and coddled if it is going to have any place in the garden at all. In the trial garden, the Maltese cross that began in April had flowering plants by June 12 of the same year. With care, they grew to two feet and were still flowering on July 22. The plant's origins in northern Russia should indicate that the plant prefers a more temperate climate than is found in regions of the American South.

So, why go to the effort if the color is awkward in the first place? Because there's no other like it, and, in a truly mixed-color floral border or garden, not to have an orange would risk losing some intensity in the scheme. The orange of the Maltese cross serves the same function of the red of the small-flowered zinnia (*Zinnia pauciflora*): punctuating the garden with small bursts of strong color that make the whole harmonic.

MALTESE CROSS, JERUSALEM-CROSS, SCARLET-LIGHTNING, NONESUCH, LONDON-PRIDE
(*Lychnis chalcedonica*)

TYPE hardy perennial
HEIGHT up to 4 feet in ideal
  circumstances
SPREAD 18 inches

HABIT
- bears umbels with many orange-red flowers in the shape of a Maltese cross
- can be lanky and may need support

NATURAL RANGE
northern and eastern Russia

TIPS
- use in the annual, cottage-style, or mixed garden
- provide full sun; partial shade in hot climates
- sow seeds directly in the garden at or near the surface of the soil late April–May
- thin seedlings to 12 inches

Common Milkweed

(Asclepias syriaca)
FLOWERING PERENNIAL

The milkweeds come with a noble pedigree. They fall into the plant family named for the Greco-Roman deity Asclepius, a son of Apollo. In the classical world, Asclepius was revered for his beneficence and his healing powers and had a reputation for affording solace to the afflicted. The healing centers and temples named on his behalf, asclepions, were the first of their kind and were the hospitals of ancient times.[1]

The common milkweed, though, bears few elements of refinement. Perhaps one of the more inelegant perennials, looking almost prehistoric in its ungainliness, this native American wildflower is, however, inextricably linked to the life cycle of the monarch butterfly, being a host plant during that butterfly's larval phase. In fact, due to its heavy sweet scent, it attracts a wide variety of flying insects in addition to the monarch and other butterflies. The plant's odd appearance makes it best suited to the wild meadow, where large swathes of it will easily colonize amongst competing grasses and native weeds. If used in a more ornamental, formal planting, it would be a sharp and effective contrast to just about any other plant because of its large, flat-bladed leaves and its

statuesque height (to six feet), both attributes making for a bold, if not entirely graceful, statement.[2]

A native to most of North America east of the Mississippi, common milkweed was certainly one of the first plants encountered by English settlers landing in Virginia, where it grows in abundance. Sent to England early in the colonial era, where it was documented in 1629, it quickly became naturalized and spread throughout the European continent. Common milkweed turns up again in the historical record when it was collected by John Clayton in the eighteenth century and sent as an herbarium specimen to London. From London it went to Amsterdam, where it was most likely viewed by Linnaeus himself and used in the compilation of his *Species Plantarum* (1753).[3]

Had they known, the colonial American settlers could have fattened themselves on the flowers of common milkweed. Some modern gourmets liken the flowers to broccoli florets. Peter Kalm, traveling in North America in the late eighteenth century, said the French in Canada regarded common milkweed as a type of asparagus and prepared it in the same way. Because the sap of the

plant is milky, an indication of toxicity, the flowers, young fruits, and young stems must be thoroughly boiled (three times) to remove toxins. Such excessive preparation little warrants its use in modern kitchens.[4]

Seeds begun in late March sprouted robustly by the third week of April. Although vigorous in its first year, common milkweed blooms only in the second year and afterwards. The clusters of honey-scented dull-rose and white flowers are borne from mid-May to mid-June and give way to a distinctive seed-pod, which upon bursting reveals the silky threads for which this plant is also named. Be aware that the plant, because of its underground runners, can become invasive.

Although odd and coarse in appearance, a combination of it and the delicate, ferny-leaved, floriferous larkspur (*Consolida orientalis*) proved very rewarding. Because of its American nativity, its effectiveness in attracting insects to the garden, and its funny, even odd, appearance, common milkweed deserves a place in the well-diversified garden.

COMMON MILKWEED, SILKWEED, WILD COTTON
(*Asclepias syriaca*)

TYPE hardy perennial
HEIGHT up to 6 feet
SPREAD 24 inches

HABIT
- bears clusters of white and dull-rose flowers
- foliage is coarse with waxy blue-gray leaves
- multiplies by underground runners
- attracts insects, especially the monarch butterfly

NATURAL RANGE
eastern North America

TIPS
- use in the wild or meadow garden
- provide full sun
- sow seeds directly in the garden ¼ inch deep in March–April or August–September
- thin seedlings to 6 inches

Pilewort

(Ranunculus ficaria)
FLOWERING PERENNIAL

Buttercups range in form from the common buttercups *(Ranunculus acris, R. bulbosus, R. repens)*, which any American would recognize and which are the bane of lawn custodians everywhere, to the similarly simple but more impressive pilewort to the grotesquely enlarged, colorful varieties of the Persian buttercup *(R. asiaticus)*, bearing flowers up to four inches across. In fact, *R. asiaticus* flowers became so large and colorful that they became "florist flowers," in the eighteenth-century usage of the term, and remain popular in the floral trade today.

Colonial Williamsburg's nurserymen grow the small, tuberous pilewort amongst other period plants at the Colonial Nursery, an interpretive site in the Historic Area that is especially exciting for gardeners. In this intimate setting, pilewort's humble one-inch, bright-yellow flowers set on nests of shiny foliage show to their best advantage, forming a slowly growing clump of this nearly imperishable perennial.

Pilewort is a common sight to most European gardeners and was well-known to both Dioscorides and Galen, authors of two of the earliest surviving herbals. Dioscorides, ever the physician, recom-

mended pilewort for many things: "It takes away both the Psoras, and scabrous nayles. But ye rootes being iuiced are good with hony to be put into the nosthrills for the purging of the head [as likewise the decoction thereof with Hony, being gargarized, doth powerfully purge ye head, & all thinges out of the Thorax."[1]

Pilewort was later included in the major European herbals that proliferated during the Renaissance. Leonhart Fuchs, the great sixteenth-century German herbalist, said, "It grows in swamps, near water, and in damp areas, in all soggy places, and in gardens everywhere." Its habitat, according to modern writers Ippolito Pizzetti and Henry Cocker, is not only by ponds and stagnant water but also in "cool, moist fields and meadowlands. They grow side by side with white field daisies and blue hepaticas."[2]

Fuchs also mentioned what the ancient writers once said about this small buttercup and what was well-known to practical herbalists at the time: that it was a well-known remedy for what the polite called "piles," or hemorrhoids; thus, its common name. John Gerard, the Elizabethan herbalist, said that, in addition to curing piles,

it maketh rough and corrupt
nailes to fall away.

The juice of the roots
mixed with honie, and drawne
up into the nosthrils, purgeth
the head of foule and filthie
humours.

The similarity of the language suggests
that Gerard relied heavily on Dioscorides
for his commentary. Modern authorities
warn against any internal use of any part
of pilewort but discuss its use in oint-
ments for external application.[3]

Pilewort became attractive to gardeners for reasons beyond its medicinal
claims. In 1737, John Custis of Williamsburg received word from Peter Collinson
of London of his satisfaction with "double
yellow pile Wort." That Collinson specifically mentioned the doubled nature of the
flower suggests that he was more interested
in the ornamental value of the flower than
its more practical virtues. So iffy was the
transatlantic shipping of bulbs that Collinson wrote Custis detailed instructions for
the handling of them: "When You Receive

the box of Bulbs Turn them all out at once
& seperate them as well as you can for I
apprehend the Roots are pretty Much Mat-
ted, there is no safe Way of sending these
sorts of Roots but in Earth."[4]

Native to Europe and western Asia,
pilewort was introduced into America at
least by 1737. It has since escaped cultivation and has become established in the
northeastern and Ohio River Valley states
as well as in Washington and Oregon. In
the home, mixed garden, where its tendency to spread can be restrained, it is a
pretty flower indeed in the single form.
Prolific where happy, it blooms in early
April in a deeply saturated yellow. The
flowers are set off by highly glossy green
leaves, extremely ornamental in themselves, leaves that John Gerard described
as "greene round . . . smooth, slipperie,
and shining."[5]

Because of its exuberantly glossy
foliage and somewhat larger flowers, this
buttercup stands a notch higher than the
ubiquitous but beloved *R. acris,* which so
vexes the modern homeowner intent on
the weed-free lawn. In fact, it deserves a

place in the select garden, set among other
delicate, woodland items, where its small
stature isn't imperiled by the great rush of
other plants. In the modern garden or the
period garden, in the single form or the
double form, pilewort can quietly colonize out-of-the-way places and provide
points of interest in the first, ground-level
tier of the multilayered garden.

PILEWORT, LESSER CELANDINE, LITTLE CELANDINE, FIGGEWOORT
(*Ranunculus ficaria*)

TYPE hardy tuberous perennial
HEIGHT 6 inches
SPREAD 12 inches

HABIT
- bears 1-inch glossy yellow flowers
- sports heart-shaped leaves
- can be invasive in shade
- resists most pests
- goes dormant in summer

NATURAL RANGE
continental Europe, western Asia;
   naturalized in North America

TIPS
- use in the annual, cottage-style, or mixed garden
- provide dappled sunlight
- plant tubers in the garden 1–2 inches deep in the fall
- thin bulbils assiduously as they form
- consider using less-invasive modern cultivars such as 'Brazen Hussy', a double form, or 'Albus'
- use to underplant and accent other plants

Ragged Robin

(Lychnis flos-cuculi)
FLOWERING PERENNIAL

Ragged robin is one of those flowers that might first appeal because of the alliteration of its name; or because it hints at Edwardian plant lore and animated landscapes like the River Bank, that place in *The Wind in the Willows* where Mr. Mole, Water Rat, and friends pass their time amidst the grassy swales and lazy waters of the "full-fed river." Craving moisture, ragged robin would have been patently part of that watery realm. Jessica Kerr, author of *Shakespeare's Flowers* (1969), affirmed that the plant would have been common along the River Avon and was no doubt known by Shakespeare, who made it a choice for mad Ophelia's handiwork in *Hamlet*.

> There with fantastic
> > garlands did she make
> Of crow-flowers, nettles,
> > daisies, and long purples.

Crowflower, another common name for ragged robin, describes the footprint found in the quirky arrangement of the flower, perhaps reflective of Ophelia's disordered mind.[1]

The commentary on ragged robin in John Gerard's 1633 herbal is devoted mostly to its classification, ever the botanist's delight. He considered it kin to the wild gillyflower, of "a degenerate kinde,"

meaning he thought of it as an errant member of the sweet-scented pinks (*Dianthus* sp.). He said that some considered ragged robin to be a sweet William (*D. barbatus*), which he thought incorrect. The campions, he thought, might be a truer relation. In this, he struck pay dirt. Modern taxonomists have placed ragged robin, along with the other campions, in their own genus, *Lychnis*, whose most well-known species is the rose campion (*L. coronaria*), that gray-leaved plant with almost indescribable cerise-magenta flowers familiar to almost everyone who has seen it even once.[2]

Ragged robin's common name presents something of a misnomer as it bears no resemblance to a robin. The other half of its name, however, clearly alludes to the dissection of the flower petals. Twentieth-century writers Ippolito Pizzetti and Henry Cocker described their arrangement beautifully: "flowers pink . . . in loose panicles, the petals divided for half their length into four narrow segments, giving the blooms their typical 'ragged' appearance." Gerard commented that, unlike so many plants in the old herbals, ragged robin has only simple charm to strike the fancy as "these are not used either in medicine or in

Rue Anemone

(Thalictrum thalictroides)

FLOWERING PERENNIAL

This small-flowered rue anemone, a native of eastern North America, is one of the more obscure wildflowers in the region but recognizable to, and immensely appreciated by, all native plant enthusiasts. Its preference for rich woods presupposes an undisturbed site with an intact humus layer of decayed leaves and the colonies of fungi that decompose it. This type of woodland ecosystem is difficult to install over reclaimed land. Many gardeners who lament their lack of sunlight because of too many trees, however, might turn to this kind of woodland native that lives in that black, friable layer above the topsoil itself.

Throughout its history of interest to early European plant explorers and later American taxonomists, the rue anemone has borne three genus names. Upon discovering it in Virginia, John Clayton, the great eighteenth-century Virginian botanist, named it a *Thalictrum*. When Carolus Linnaeus included it in his groundbreaking *Species Plantarum* (1753), he gave it the name *Anemone thalictroides*, perhaps as a nod to Clayton. In the twentieth century, its name was changed to *Anemonella thalictroides*, only to be changed back once again to John Clayton's original *Thalictrum*, the genus name the United States Department of Agriculture (USDA) now recognizes as correct, although other agencies differ.[1]

Although this is seemingly so much effort for so small a plant, the rue anemone is a small jewel for the woodland garden. Resembling a small anemone, the delicate white flower sits atop foliage that in different habitats can be either green or reddish. Said to prefer dry, open or rocky woods and upland slopes and ridges, it will nevertheless happily inhabit the average, undisturbed woodland garden given enough shade. One source, in fact, describes the plant as tolerating full shade.[2]

Because of the plant's dormancy throughout the summer, it should be planted adjacent to other plants that will subsume the space left vacant when it goes dormant. Ferns are well suited to this purpose, and a festival of woodland plants could be its neighbors: the aptly named foamflower (*Tiarella cordifolia*), the scented lily of the valley (*Convallaria majalis*), the much-loved bloodroot (*Sanguinaria canadensis*), the witty jack-in-the-pulpit (*Arisaema triphyllum*), our native, glossy wild ginger (*Asarum canadense*), and the edible scarlet partridgeberry (*Mitchella repens*) with its white-veined leaves.

The rue anemone could as well be a lovely addition to another potential habitat: the shaded rocky garden, one replete with drifts of native columbine (*Aquilegia canadensis*), naturalized bluebell (*Endymion non-scriptus*), and miniature daffodils (*Narcissus* ssp.) amidst clumps of native plum-leaved azalea (*Rhododendron prunifolium*), an understory element between the ground planting and the high forest canopy above.

RUE ANEMONE
(*Thalictrum thalictroides*)

TYPE hardy tuberous perennial
HEIGHT 9 inches
SPREAD 9 inches

HABIT
- white flowers above whorls of three-lobed leaves
- tuberous rooted
- dormant in summer
- resists most pests

NATURAL RANGE
eastern North America

TIPS
- use in the woodland garden
- purchase tubers from specialized bulb retailers and plant directly in the garden 1 inch deep in the fall
- provide a woody setting with humus
- provide other plants as fill during dormancy

Spring
Beauty

(Claytonia virginica)

FLOWERING PERENNIAL

The story of *Claytonia virginica*, or spring beauty, is the story of the man for whom it was named: John Clayton (1694–1773). In the annals of American history, John Clayton is considered the foremost botanist of the eighteenth century. In fact, Thomas Jefferson remarked about Clayton, "[He] is supposed to have enlarged the botanical catalogue as much as almost any man who has lived."[1]

While carrying out his fifty-three-year career as clerk of court for Gloucester County, Virginia, Clayton also donned his botanist's hat and collected and assembled 710 herbarium specimens that he sent to Europe via Mark Catesby, his mentor when the latter resided in Virginia in the early eighteenth century. Catesby in turn passed them to a Dutch senator named Johannes Fredericus Gronovius, who, without Clayton's permission or knowledge but admitting to and admiring Clayton's phenomenal field work, used Clayton's specimens and much of his commentary to publish *Flora Virginica* (1739–1743). Gronovius allowed the revolutionary new botanist Carolus Linnaeus access to Clayton's herbarium specimens, and, when Linnaeus published his groundbreaking *Species Plantarum* (1753), many of the North American species were based on Clayton's specimens. In honor of Clayton's botanical achievements, Linnaeus named the genus *Claytonia*. Linnaeus also nominated John Clayton to the Swedish Academy of Sciences at the University of Uppsala.[2]

Following the John Claytons through English and early American history can be daunting because John Clayton of Virginia was the third in a line so named. As far back as the early 1600s, the Claytons were well established in Yorkshire, England, and practiced law as barristers. Sir John Clayton, the botanist's grandfather, and Sir Jasper Clayton, the botanist's great-grandfather, were graduates of Eton and Cambridge, and both were knighted by Charles II in 1660 and 1664 respectively. Sir John Clayton was also an original fellow of the Royal Society in London and became a gentleman of the private chamber to William III of England.[3]

The botanist's father, another John Clayton, came to Virginia around 1705 as secretary to Lt. Gov. Edward Nott, who died a year later. That John Clayton remained in Virginia to pursue his political career, becoming attorney general from 1711 to 1737 as well as serving as a private attorney to William Byrd II,

John Custis, Robert "King" Carter, and Benjamin Harrison. It is thought that the botanist John Clayton came to Virginia after his father, arriving about 1715. He probably attended Eton and Cambridge, but no specific record exists. There is no doubt, though, that the botanist's Latin was exemplary.[4]

It is clear that John Clayton the botanist did not come from humble roots. His great-aunt was the dowager countess of Yarmouth; his uncle Gen. Jasper Clayton was governor of Gibraltar in the eighteenth century; another uncle, Henry Symonds, was a great-nephew of Sir Christopher Wren and was clerk of works at Wren's redesign of Hampton Court; and the botanist's first cousin Martha Lovelace was married to Lord Henry Beauclerk, a grandson of Charles II and Nell Gwyn, his mistress.[5]

Once in America, Clayton's social status was confirmed by his marriage to Elizabeth Whiting, whose father, Maj. Henry Whiting, and grandfather Peter Beverley were members of the Virginia Council. Clayton's brother, Dr. Thomas Clayton, was a graduate of Eton and Cambridge and was married to Isabella Lewis of Warner Hall, whose father, John Lewis, was also a councillor.[6]

The Claytons of England and John Clayton the botanist of Virginia had illustrious histories. But, the flower named for the botanist, spring beauty, is a small, rarely seen wildflower that blooms early in the spring for a brief period of time. The plant is seldom even twelve inches tall. The small, one-inch flowers bloom in a range from very pale pink to deep pink. In Nancy Kober's beautiful book *With Paintbrush & Shovel,* she wrote, "The ephemeral flowers are often white with fine pink pinstripes but can range to a deep pink with darker pinstripes." This lack of consistency in the coloration of the flowers of spring beauty is attributable to its having an "instability of chromosome numbers, with about 50 different chromosomal combinations."[7]

John Banister recorded spring beauty during his travels through Virginia from 1678 to 1692 while acting as a plant explorer for Bishop Compton of London, one of that century's greatest botanical patrons. Of course, Banister called it by a different name since Linnaeus hadn't yet named it according to his new binomial classification of plants into genus and species. Clayton also collected and sent to London the plant that would ultimately be named for him. The curators of the John Clayton Herbarium at the Natural History Museum in London speculate that this very dried herbarium specimen sent by Clayton was possibly seen by Linnaeus at Hartekamp, home of George Clifford, who hired Linnaeus in 1737 to write his *Hortus Cliffortianus*, and, if so, would be an original element (type specimen) for *Claytonia virginica*.[8]

Spring beauty's native habitat is open, rich, moist woodlands, clearings, and wood borders. It would be at home in a woodland planting with rue anemone (*Thalictrum thalictroides*), bloodroot (*Sanguinaria canadensis*), pilewort (*Ranunculus ficaria*), and all the other delicate things of the open forest floor. The plant develops from a small underground corm, which Native Americans used for food and is said to have a chestnutlike flavor. The culture of spring beauty is the same as with the rue anemone. Provide moist, humus-rich soil and light shade, and plan for the eventual disappearance of the foliage by early summer, the trait that gives the ephemerals their name. Corms should be planted in fall when dormant, within one inch of the soil surface. Once established in a suitable situation, it reseeds readily.[9]

Because it is so associated with Virginia and so well commemorates one of Virginia's and the nation's leading early scientists, spring beauty, or Claytonia, will always have a place in the hearts of those who know the botanist's story and appreciate the delicate drifts of this rare, ephemeral, and native species during the cooler days of spring.

SPRING BEAUTY, CLAYTONIA
(*Claytonia virginica*)

TYPE hardy perennial corm
HEIGHT 12 inches
SPREAD 10 inches

HABIT
- bears 1-inch flowers in shades of pink and white, sometimes with venation
- tends to be ephemeral in hot weather
- corms will colonize if left undisturbed
- foliage disappears by early summer

NATURAL RANGE
eastern North America

TIPS
- use in the mixed woodland garden
- provide dappled sunlight
- purchase corms from specialized bulb retailers and plant directly in the garden 1 inch deep in the fall
- provide light, humus-rich woodland soil

Blue Vervain

(Verbena hastata)
FLOWERING PERENNIAL

A four-to-seven-foot native perennial that prefers damp soil and sports long blue and violet spikes in June and July, blue vervain was one of the most surprising and valuable finds in the field trials. It performed splendidly in the trial garden and was a significant perennial plant addition to a garden predominately composed of annuals and biennials. Schuyler Mathews, a turn-of-the-century field botanist, artist, and American Brahmin, wrote in his charming 1902 field guide, "One of the handsomest . . . members of the genus."[1]

Forming strong stalks typically four to five feet tall, blue vervain bloomed easily the first year from seed sown in April, which germinated in early May. By June 13, the plants began flowering and were still flowering profusely on July 12 when it became obvious that this is an immensely satisfying plant. Deadheading the stand in mid-July resulted in reflowering through the third week of August. Mature seed heads, if left in place, can result in aggressive self-seeding in moist areas of the garden. The resulting seedlings grow quickly and can easily be moved to other locations. Though it does self-seed and germinate easily, it can be finicky and give up the ghost if it is crowded or if the soil becomes too dry. Nevertheless, its seeds' fecundity is such that it isn't a terrible loss. Blue vervain should be seen as somewhat of an intermittent, but persistent and nice, presence in the garden.

Another variety, an annual, *Verbena officinalis*, hails from Europe and is shorter and bears less intense blue flowers than its American cousin. *V. officinalis*, however, has a longer documented history as a healing herb. In Dioscorides's first-century herbal, *De materia medica*, he discussed this European vervain as a panacea for a number of gory afflictions that he enumerated at length, including putrefied ulcers and fistulas.[2]

In later times, vervain was also highly regarded. As revealed in any of the sixteenth- or seventeenth-century English herbals, vervain was held by our European ancestors to be a potent healing herb. From headaches and toothaches to rotting wounds, vervain seems to have been the prescription of the day. Its use as a treatment for nervous complaints, depression, and headaches was also noted by John Gerard, the Elizabethan herbalist, who recommended it as a garland worn round the head for relief from headaches and wrote that, if a

decoction is made of it and sprinkled in the dining room, the guests will be the merrier for it. Later in England, Philip Miller, curator of the Chelsea Physic Garden from 1722 to 1771, described it as nearly ubiquitous in Britain, used by physicians for medical purposes and often found close to home.[3]

Maud Grieve, the dean of twentieth-century English herbal writers, maintained that it is useful for up to thirty of life's complaints, including afflictions of the eyes and the bladder. Its early reputation as a tonic for nervous exhaustion and depression is repeated by many modern herbal writers who also endorse its use for various internal conditions. The American blue vervain is said by the Herb Society of America to have effects in the relief of liver disorders, respiratory weaknesses, and menstrual complaints.[4]

Various ancient authors mentioned European vervain's use as a sacramental herb. Specific references to vervain in the Roman era are found in at least three different translations of the *Aeneid*, Virgil's account of the founding of Rome. A temporary truce between the emerging Romans and a local tribe was solemnized by "priests these, in their ritual robes and wreathed with vervain." These accounts were repeated by English herbalists. In his reference to vervain in his 1657 herbal, *Adam in Eden*, William Coles wrote that, in addition to its

acquaintance by the Greeks, it was known "also amongst the Romans; for with it they purged their houses and made clean the Table of *Jupiter* before the Sacrificiall Banquets were set there on." In John Gerard's Elizabethan herbal, he recounted the history of vervain's use as a sacred herb employed by the Roman consuls and praetors in their roles as state priests. Mrs. Grieve reiterates vervain's long history of sacramental use saying that "the druids included it in their lustral water, and magicians and sorcerers employed it largely," and she repeated a legend that vervain was used to staunch the wounds of Jesus Christ. So consistent were its sacred attributions that a host of names was generated, such as herba sacra, holy wort, and herb of grace.[5]

Despite European vervain's usefulness, it is the American vervain that makes the better perennial garden plant for distinguished height and form and sustained color. Taller than its squat, three-foot European cousin and distinctly more ornamental, blue vervain only asks for adequate, even copious moisture, and, given that and deadheading, it provides sustained blue through the middle of the summer. As gardeners look for more native perennials that provide sustained color and resistance to pest predation, they should surely be cognizant of the virtues of this native perennial whose only demand is adequate water.

BLUE VERVAIN, SIMPLER'S-JOY
(*Verbena hastata*)

TYPE hardy perennial
HEIGHT 4–7 feet
SPREAD 36 inches

HABIT
- produces strong vertical stems sporting blue and purple flowers
- seldom needs staking
- self-sows at a frantic pace
- resists most pests

NATURAL RANGE
North America

TIPS
- use in the perennial or mixed garden
- provide partial shade
- sow seeds directly in the garden on the soil surface, barely covering the seeds, in early April; allow for a seven-day cool period (40°F–50°F) followed by warmer temperatures
- gradually thin seedlings to 15–20 inches
- provide copious water

Wallflower

(Erysimum cheiri)

FLOWERING PERENNIAL

Famous for bearing brightly colored, fragrant flowers, wallflower has been used for floral decoration from time immemorial. Many cultures have used and still today use blooms and greens to mark observances, special days, and ceremonies. Floral garlands, crowns, and wreaths festooned the altars, homes, and festival grounds of the ancient world, not to mention the Anglican Church. When the ancient Theophrastus addressed the "coronary plants" and their serviceable nature as decorative flowers, he said that wallflower, "of all the flowers that the garland-makers use, far outrun the others." Another clue to its early use is one writer's assertion that "the word Cheiranthus [its former Latin name] means 'hand-flower' because bunches of the flowers were carried in processions and pageants."[1]

Twentieth-century gardeners Ippolito Pizzetti and Henry Cocker wrote that in medieval times wallflower was worn as a boutonniere by troubadours and minstrels because of its associations with good fortune and luck. In 1542, Leonhart Fuchs noted wallflower's intentional presence in Renaissance Germany, saying it was planted in gardens and never occurred spontaneously.[2]

Wallflower's exact legacy in Britain is hidden by the mists of time. Some say wallflowers followed the Romans into Britain while others see the Normans as the route by which wallflower crossed the Channel from the Continent. It was, however, well introduced into England by the time John Gerard, the Elizabethan herbalist, recorded that the double form could be found growing "in most gardens of England," a trend that continued after the Stuart succession and even until today.[3]

Throughout the history of horticulture, multiple common names were afforded most every flower. Wallflower, however, is nearly singular in the consistency of one most frequently used common name. The name reflects its habit of growing amongst the cracks between the large stones of cathedrals and along the tops and sides of stone walls that divide the countryside. In the nineteenth century, when English gardening flourished during the Pax Britannia of Queen Victoria and her son Edward, drywall gardening became a specialty in the ever-widening British horticultural tableau. Wallflower is so suited to this use, as well as to England's climate in general, that William Robinson, a late nineteenth-century garden writer, asserted that

wallflower is capable of becoming "a dwarf enduring bush on an old wall if planted in mortar." Furthermore, he said that no variety is unworthy of cultivation and all "are worthy of a place among the finest border plants." Because of its tenacity among rocks and dry places, it came to symbolize the constancy of love in the face of trial.[4]

Still extensively grown in England and on the Continent, wallflower continues to enjoy accolades. In the twentieth century, Christopher Lloyd, ever the articulate champion of the cottage garden, recommended that another closely related wallflower species, *Erysimum hieraciifolium*, which Lloyd identified as *Cheiranthus allionii*, be grown in particular because of its merry tendency to self-sow. One eloquent author described his delight in "an endless variety of lovely tints of russet, gold, dull crimson, orange, and pale yellow which blend so satisfactorily into a country garden."[5]

Wallflower was among the earliest of European flowers brought to the colonies. Rudy Favretti, the dean of plant introduction dates, places it in the 1600–1699 range. Lady Jean Skipwith of Virginia referred to blood red wallflowers in her 1793 garden diary, her husband bought seed from Minton Collins of Richmond the same year, and the plant was widely available commercially as per Bernard McMahon's seed catalog broadsheet published in Philadelphia in 1802 or 1803.[6]

Resentful of Tidewater Virginia's humid summers, wallflowers are best

effective. When assiduously cultivated with water, fertilizer, and attention, these scrappy plants from the Mediterranean, with a reputation for mean tenacity, will fulfill the highest expectations for floral impact.

WALLFLOWER
(*Erysimum cheiri*)

TYPE short-lived perennial
HEIGHT up to 30 inches
SPREAD 30 inches

HABIT
- small, sub-shrublike appearance
- produces stems of intensely colored flowers
- prefers dry soil

NATURAL RANGE
southern Europe

TIPS
- use in the annual or mixed garden
- provide full sun
- sow seeds directly in the garden ¼ inch deep in early September in the South or after danger of frost in the North
- thin seedlings to 6–12 inches

used in the South as a fall to spring bedding plant, although they will settle themselves into a situation for several years running given moderate winters. Seeding should take place in September, so that plants are well established prior to winter, with flowers expected by late November. Wallflowers can assume the character of small shrubs, producing a clump of semievergreen, grayish foliage. In the Tidewater Virginia climate, fully grown plants can be impervious to cold and snow and bloom throughout the cold first quarter of the next year.

In the trial garden, seed planted on September 12 germinated on September 16. The seedlings went through a twenty-nine-degree night on November 12. By November 28, they were sixteen inches high and mingling with the white candytuft (*Iberis umbellata*) nearby. They bloomed on December 17. The blooms, so late in the season, after strong steady growth, emerged in orange with budded red flowers beginning to appear. The crop proved to be very strong, and very

Herbs

For what can be more convenient & full of diversion, then the contemplation of the infinite varieties, & wonderfull effects of those Plants which are best known by the names of Simples & of which our Botanists have filled such prodigeous volumes, & the shops of the Apothecarius are almost entirely furnished.

—John Evelyn (1620–1706)

How long have we been collecting pieces of plants in order to ensure some therapeutic benefit? Once again, in Western literature, the story starts with Theophrastus. In his *Enquiry into Plants* (ca. 300 BC), he discussed "medicinal things of all kinds, as fruit, extracted juice, leaves, roots, 'herbs'; for the herb-diggers call some medicinal things by this name."[1]

His use of the word "herb-diggers" implies some specialty, perhaps a caste, or an inherited occupation. It, along with his use of "garland-makers" when referring to ornamental plants, represents an identification of horticultural vocations. How long this tradition preceded Theophrastus's recording of it is impossible to know.[2]

By the second century AD, Western knowledge regarding plants and their properties had been codified by four luminaries in Western civilization: Theophrastus; Pliny the Elder, a Roman statesman and natural history writer; Dioscorides, a Greek physician who served in the Roman army; and Galen, court physician to the emperor Marcus Aurelius.

The title of Galen's primary work, *De simplicium medicamentorum temperamentis ac facultatibus* (Of the Temperaments and Faculties of Medical Specimens), provided the historical term for what we today call herbs. The title, shortened to *De simplicibus* (Of Medical Specimens), lended itself, in English translation, to the word *simples*. *Simples* became the accepted common word for medicinal plants during the seventeenth century. In 1657, William Coles published *The Art of Simpling* and defined its intent: "Simpling is an Art which teacheth the knowledge of all Druggs and Physicall Ingredients, but especially of Plants." The use of the word occurred in the colonies in 1668. A correspondent wrote of getting lost in the woods near Urbanna, Virginia, while "simpling."[3]

Coles described herbs as "those whose footstalkes cannot be reckoned to be wood, but doe for the most part consist of Leaves, as Fennel, Everlasting, Baume, Mints, & c." Our use of the word *herb* comes from the corruption of *herbaceous*, meaning made up of only green matter and having no real wood. Coles classified herbs as "1. Potherbs [greens and root crops], 2. Breadcorne [cereal grains], 3. Pulse [peas], 4. Physicall Herbes [simples], 5. Flowers, 6. Grasse, and 7. those which we in England call weeds."[4]

It is the potherbs and "Physicall" herbs that we are primarily concerned with here. By potherbs, Coles meant culinary greens and seasoning herbs. He was very specific: "those we boyle, or eat raw, whether roots, fruits, or tender stalks, and leaves, as Turneps, Carrets, Radishes, Leeks, Onyons, Cives, Cucumbers, Melons, Pompions, Lettice, Parsley, Sorrel, & c."[5]

Several of the flowering plants discussed earlier, such as the nasturtium (*Tropaeolum majus*), the balsam pear (*Momordica charantia*), and Job's tears (*Coix lacryma-jobi*), could just as well have been incorporated into this section as potherbs. Nature makes no fine line in this regard, though some plants are lethal to specific species of animals and taste and custom impel our food choices.

Likewise, some of the ornamentals, such as boneset (*Eupatorium perfoliatum*) and purple coneflower (*Echinacea purpurea*), might well have been classed with the "physick" herbs, or the simples, those medicinal herbaceous plants and sub-shrubs from which humankind has extracted chemicals that we are only now becoming able to understand. Coles embarks on a hasty list of "some of the chiefest Simples that England affords":

The best Elecampane grows in England, the roots of which being candied with Sugar, helps the Cough, shortnesse of breath, and wheesing in the Lungs. . . . Our Angelica is as good as that of Norway and Ireland: It is very Soveraigne against Potson and the Plague. . . . Pimpernill drawes thornes and splinters out of the flesh. Smallage provokes the Termes. . . . Fennell increaseth Milke in Nurses. . . . The lesser Centaury, Wormwood, Garlick, Lavender Cotton, and all Plants that have a bitter juice kill the wormes.[6]

The point of this narrative is not to endorse the use of herbs but to report on their use in the historical sense. But, can we not consider the following: If we allow for the fact that plants can kill—Jane Percy, the duchess of Northumberland, and her poison garden at Alnwick Castle will tell you that—then why should we find it impossible that they can heal? It behooves us to determine the exact nature of plants and how they really work within the human body. That is the work of esteemed others and the road into the future.[7]

Blessed Thistle

(Cnicus benedictus)
ANNUAL HERB

Thistles of many kinds make up a bonanza among plants in the dry Mediterranean region, and the ancient herbalists expended a lot of commentary on distinguishing their types. Theophrastus, in his *Enquiry into Plants* (ca. 300 BC), discussed blessed thistle in passing, as a contrast to a number of other thistles such as the milk thistle (*Silybum marianum*), safflower (*Carthamus tinctorius*), distaff thistle (*C. lanatus*), golden thistle (*Scolymus hispanicus*), yellow star-thistle (*Centaurea solstitialis*), and globe thistle (*Echinops* sp.). Centuries later, Dioscorides's reference to *Cnicus*, in his first-century *De materia medica*, was more specific and discussed its ancient uses:

> The leaves, filaments, and fruit of this plant (pounded into small pieces and taken as a drink with pepper and wine) help those touched by scorpions. Some relate that those touched this way are without pain as long as they hold the herb, and taking it away are in pain again. It is also called *amyron, cnicus sylvestris,* or *aspidium*.[1]

Medieval herbalists also addressed the healing properties of *Cnicus*. Writing in sixteenth-century Germany, Leonhart Fuchs said it was "planted everywhere in gardens" and that it was known in England as blessed thistle, or *"Carduus-benedictus,"* a name he attributed to Dioscorides. Fuchs maintained that Dioscorides and Galen, the classical herbalists, reported it to have been used to remove obstructions of the internal viscera, stimulate urine, break up stones, and heal ulcers, especially of the lungs. It alleviated violent headaches, resolved vertigo, reversed loss of memory, and dried suppurating ulcers if applied as a powder.[2]

John Gerard, the Elizabethan herbalist, commenting on its origins, said, *"Carduus Benedictus* is found every where in Lemnos, an Island of the Midland Sea, in Champion grounds . . . it is diligently cherished in Gardens in these Northerne parts." Gerard also related that the leaves, as spiny as they are, were added to salads and the greens boiled down to a bitter tonic, whence its reputation as a health elixir. Indeed, if Gerard's account can be believed, plague could be averted, serpent bites abated, and poisons disarmed. Among the most esteemed healing herbs of Old Europe, blessed thistle was so prized as to earn the ultimate

Borage

(Borago officinalis)

ANNUAL HERB

Although known primarily as an herb, borage is too ornamental to be thought of in only that way. Its three-quarter-inch flowers of a pure blue, described by John Gerard as "gallant," and its large, coarse, and hairy leaves give borage a voluminous character, something akin to clary sage *(Salvia sclarea)* but with flowers of a much deeper saturation. It is, however, one of the most ephemeral crops, quickly sprouting, attaining its three-foot potential, and flowering briefly with brilliant blue flowers that dangle downward. Thereupon, borage is history, and something must be found to take its place.[1]

The first-century Greek doctor Dioscorides, a surgeon who traveled with the Roman army, included borage in his medical commentary, *De materia medica*: "It has leaves laying on the ground, both rougher and darker (like the tongue of an ox) which, put into wine, is thought to be a cause of mirth." His commentary recommends it for abscesses, the chills of acute fevers, and fevers with paroxysms.[2]

Borage continued as a staple in the Western pharmacopoeia. Gerard, in his 1633 herbal, said, "Those of our time do use the floures in sallads, to exhilerate and make the mind glad. There be also many things made of them, used every where for the comfort of the heart, for the driving away of sorrow, and encreasing the ioy of the minde." By far, the most salient property attributed to borage was that it gave men mirth, that a syrup made of the flowers comforted the heart, purged melancholy, and quieted the frantic and the lunatic. In fact, Gerard affirmed borage's seemingly antidepressant properties four times.[3]

Modern investigation of borage has concentrated on the composition of its seed oil, which, along with flaxseed oil and evening primrose oil, has a high concentration of the essential fatty acid GLA (gamma-linolenic acid), an omega-6 fatty acid, which the human body does not manufacture. It has also been suggested that borage oil plays a role in regulating and balancing the endocrine system.[4]

Essential fatty acids were not on John Lawson's mind when he recorded borage during the period prior to his publication, in 1709, of *A New Voyage to Carolina*, where borage appears as one of the herbs used there at that time. Borage was also exploited by Moravian-German farmers in the piedmont of North Carolina, as evidenced by a 1761 seed and crops inventory.[5]

BORAGE, TALEWORT, COOL-TANKARD
(*Borago officinalis*)

TYPE annual
HEIGHT 36 inches
SPREAD 36 inches

HABIT
- bears ¾-inch piercingly blue flowers
- sports bold-textured leaves
- assumes a casual pose in the garden
- susceptible to stem borers

NATURAL RANGE
continental Europe, northern Africa

TIPS
- use in the cottage-style, herb, or vegetable garden
- provide full sun; partial shade in hot climates
- sow seeds directly in the garden ½ inch deep after danger of frost
- thin seedlings to 12–24 inches

Easy to germinate and grow, borage provides almost instant gratification to the novice gardener. The flowers possess a unique charm, and its coarse leaves contribute a strong textural addition to a garden scheme. It is best grown in part of a large herb garden or small vegetable garden, where its tendency to slump to one side on its hollow stems, like squash, can be accommodated.

An experiment involving the simultaneous and interspersed sowing of the seeds of borage and cardoon (*Cynara cardunculus*) was surprisingly successful. The borage germinated with brilliant ease, and its growth was swift given water and warmth. In the meantime, cardoon seedlings of the most pleasing silver quietly germinated in the shade of the borage leaves. And, just when the borage was removed, its haunting blue flowers spent, the silver cardoons, free of competition, bolted and filled the naked space with silver mettle reaching six feet in flower.

To believe the chroniclers of borage, we would add whole flowers and chopped leaves to mixed salads, giving them a cucumber essence. Leaf stalks could be used like celery in Sunday brunch Bloody Marys, and borage is traditionally included in Pimm's Cup, a punch popular in the South but of English origin. Although modern herbalists caution against its overuse, a little borage can be delightful. Whether as flowers in a salad, an herbal note in a leafy soup, or an oil used as a skin ointment, borage can be a subtle culinary curiosity or a quick "physick" remedy.

Calendula

(Calendula officinalis)

Most modern gardeners regard calendula, or pot marigold, its older name, as one of the first flowers of spring, a hardy annual capable of surviving temperate winters in the mid-Atlantic states. The many uses calendula has as an herb are not as ubiquitous as they once were, but modern herbalists are reintroducing calendula's medicinal purposes back into popular herb culture.

Surprisingly, this eminently recognizable plant is not found in the earliest written herbal, that of Theophrastus (ca. 300 BC). It first appears in the Roman Pliny's *Natural History* in the first century AD. But, not until the sixteenth century is calendula given full scrutiny. Leonhart Fuchs, a renowned German doctor of the time, said, "The green plant itself is used in seasonings and salads. Its flowers, drunk with wine, stimulate the menses; likewise the juice of the plant used as a mouthwash is a ready remedy for toothache. Also, its flowers are quite good for dyeing the hair blonde. Likewise, just like the green plant, it (the flowers) is very effective for drawing out the afterbirth."[1]

As well as having for centuries been a well-loved and extensively used garden flower and herbal remedy on the Continent and in England, pot marigold, our calendula, was extensively grown in the kitchen garden for use as a potherb in soups and stews, as one might use spinach and celery leaf. This penchant for pot marigold in soups was so prevalent as to have evoked this lament from Charles Lamb, the English essayist, in referring to the food at his school Christ's Hospital: "Boiled beef on Thursdays . . . with detestable marigolds floating in the pail to poison the broth."[2]

Recognized modern uses of calendula are legion. Culinary artists use the flower petals lightly in green salads and as an alternative to saffron to color and flavor rice and soup. Its use as a colorant extends to milk, butter, and cheese products, and it can be a coloring component in breads and cakes. Modern herbal writers consider calendula to be a key healing plant and to have antibacterial, antifungal, and antiviral properties. Calendula oil is often an ingredient in modern, high-quality skin creams, an echo of its early use as an emollient and wound herb. Its internal uses are considered equally credible, with some holding that it can play a role in alleviating gastric complications.[3]

For a plant so well-known in continental Europe, it arrived in England

relatively late, 1573. John Gerard, the herbalist, soon after extolled its visual delight: "The floures in the top are beautifull, round, very large and double, something sweet, with a certaine strong smell, of a light saffron colour, or like pure gold." Double flowers, that is, a doubling or tripling of the number of petals on the flower, and variability of color were evidently common given Gerard's *Herbal* commentary (1633) and Alexander Marshal's depictions of both the yellow and orange, single and double calendulas in his remarkable flower book (ca. 1653).[4]

Conveniently for plant historians, all four varieties were included in Basilius Besler's 1613 florilegium. The flower book also depicts a number of cultivars of calendula, including one called 'Prolifica', whose single or double flowers erupt with a second set of flowers, like satellites, subsets of the mother flower. The tendency for calendulas to behave this way is noted by many people who grow them, and Colonial Williamsburg

horticulturists collected seed from 'Prolifica' calendulas to propagate our own proprietary strain.[5]

Calendula's early repute, its near ubiquity as an antique potherb, its documented ornamental use, and its colonial American attestations by Thomas Jefferson recommend it for all early gardens. Calendula is one of those hale and hearty annuals that are the backbone of the fall and early spring planting schemes throughout colonial gardens. Preferring cool weather, an autumn sowing in the trial garden in early September resulted in a blooming clump well before frost, one that went on to flower through an eight-inch snowfall in January and into the spring. Not unlike most plants, dedicated fertilizing results in lush foliage and tremendous flowering, and, by keeping spent flowers picked, leaves groomed, and plants generously watered, a spot of calendulas, away from the hottest sun of the day, can laze into early July when seed heads yield large, easily handled seed. Stored in a paper bag in a cool and dry place, they are the genesis of new green sprigs in the fall, greens in winter, and flowers in the spring.[6]

As either an ornamental or an herb, calendula insinuates itself into other plantings with extreme ease. It is a natural in a mix with other annual and perennial herbs, and, in the flower garden, it would coordinate with other flower crops that share calendula's adeptness at navigating Virginia's winter: Adonis (*Adonis aestivalis*), the wallflower (*Erysimum cheiri*), sweet William (*Dianthus barbatus*), larkspur (*Consolida orientalis*), corn poppy (*Papaver rhoeas*), prickly poppy (*Argemone mexicana*), and

others that constitute a palette of self-seeding hardy annual flowers. Calendula is the archetypal cottage garden flower, one that the venerable, late dean of English gardening, Christopher Lloyd, a master in this art, said everyone prefers in the double form and one that, with genetic drift, can quickly revert to single form, which is pretty nonetheless.[7]

CALENDULA, POT MARIGOLD, MARYGOLD
(*Calendula officinalis*)

TYPE hardy annual
HEIGHT up to 24 inches
SPREAD up to 24 inches

HABIT
- tolerant of all but the coldest winters
- bears flowers from pale yellow to vivid orange, up to 4 inches across
- long blooming if plants are kept deadheaded
- can self-sow if time is given for seed heads to mature

NATURAL RANGE
southern Europe

TIPS
- use in the annual, cottage-style, or mixed garden
- provide full sun; partial shade in hot climates
- sow seeds directly in the garden 1/8 inch deep in the fall for spring bloom or sow seeds very early indoors in spring and set out as soon as the soil can be worked

Dark-Leaved Orach

(Atriplex hortensis 'Cupreata')
ANNUAL HERB

In hard times, some plants become identified as starvation food, those edible weeds that stave off hunger and deter the Reaper. Orach has played that role in many places and times. A member of the Chenopodium family, orach is one of dozens of species within that family that provide fodder for humans. Another of those species, lamb's-quarters (*Chenopodium album*), a very close cousin to orach, is one of the most prevalent weeds in Eastern Virginia. A letter I received as the garden columnist of the *Newport News (VA) Daily Press* in 1992 demonstrates the usefulness of the plant:

> I find that not many people know what L[amb's] Q[uarter]s are and even fewer respect them. I first learned about them in my grandfather's Victory Garden, where he proclaimed them his favorite "potherb." He also told me that during the disastrous times of the Great Depression and the Civil War, L[amb's] Q[uarter]s were a literal Godsend to many malnourished people.
>
> I always plant spinach for its nice texture in salads, but for my year's supply of "cooking spinach," I rely on L[amb's] Q[uarter]s. We enjoyed it in a stir-fry last night and I'm making a "spinach" casserole today. Of course, we freeze it for the winter, but I never knew about harvesting the seeds until I read Ewell Gibbon's *Stalking the Wild Asparagus*. Now I use small amount [seeds] in oatmeal cookies & other baked goods, and share some with the cockatiels (who also love the fresh stalks of "overgrown" L[amb's] Q[uarter]s).[1]

The fact that Chenopodium family greens have provided nourishment for millennia is illustrated by orach's mention in ancient Greece literature. Theophrastus (ca. 300 BC) broke down the potherbs into the seasons in which they were sown, saying that orach was sown in the second period of cultivation, which began after the winter solstice. Dioscorides, the Roman doctor of the first century, included orach in his *De materia medica*, indicating that there were two types of *Atriplex*: "one wild, the other sown in gardens. The latter is eaten

St. Mary's Thistle

(Silybum marianum)

ANNUAL HERB

Were the cures attributed to St. Mary's thistle not so multiple, the herb would not be so well tolerated for all the trouble it causes in the garden. Charming it is, with purple thistle flowers and leaves described by John Gerard in 1633 as "light green and speckled, with white and milky spots and lines drawne divers waies." But, the seed of this thistle is preposterously fertile, and its thorns are nasty and particularly irksome and fester when embedded in the gardener's hand. Optimistically described as a biennial, due to its ability to withstand winters, St. Mary's thistle flowers in a mere ten weeks after seeding, a ferocity that doesn't bode well for the inattentive gardener.[1]

Its great aesthetic charm, the main reason we tolerate its presence, flows from its boldly variegated, white-veined leaves (attributed to the Virgin's lactation) and the purple starburst with its aureole of thorns. And, if myth can be believed, Mary's munificence imbued this plant with powerful properties, now called flavolignans, compounds that protect the liver against toxins. Poor liver function was once thought to be the cause of depression, and St. Mary's thistle was an early Prozac.[2]

Modern herbal writers report progress in demonstrating that the active ingredient in St. Mary's thistle, silymarin, shows great promise as a powerful liver cleanser, and some consider it an essential element in Western medicine's crusade to protect the liver and its metabolic processes. It is also thought highly beneficial for gall bladder diseases, hepatitis, and cirrhosis and to alleviate the effects of chemotherapy.[3]

It is ultimately to Dioscorides, the Greek, that its name is attributed. Coming from a Greek word meaning "thistle," *Silybum* was one of the wild, herbaceous herbs whose young leaves, spines shorn, were eaten raw as a salad or cooked like spinach. The immature flower buds were treated much like an artichoke (*Cynara scolymus*), another edible thistle when timely harvested. European Renaissance sources also testify that this thistle was considered an edible green.[4]

That St. Mary's thistle was brought to the New World is demonstrated by a reference to it in a 1761 Moravian farm inventory from North Carolina. Whether the Moravian farmers considered it a potherb, a food crop, or a medicinal plant is unknown.[5]

While its efficacy in treating certain disorders awaits the study of biochemists,

it is even now part of our popular herbal culture as milk thistle extract, extolled by millions of people seeking herbal alternatives. And, while its aggressive handsomeness and reputed utility are a boon to many a garden, beginning gardeners are warned to prevent wholesale reseeding by promptly removing the beautiful, full, purple thistle flowers just as they begin to fade.

ST. MARY'S THISTLE, MILK THISTLE, HOLY THISTLE
(Silybum marianum)

TYPE hardy annual
HEIGHT up to 4 feet
SPREAD up to 36 inches

HABIT
- bears spiny, variegated foliage
- bears large purple thistle flowers
- self-sows with abandon

NATURAL RANGE
Mediterranean region

TIPS
- use in the cottage-style or herb garden
- provide full sun
- sow seeds directly in the garden at or near the surface of the soil during cool weather March–April or August–September
- thin seedlings to 18 inches
- prevent proliferation of self-sown seedlings

Strawberry Blite

(*Chenopodium foliosum* 'Strawberry Sticks')

<small>ANNUAL HERB</small>

In the curious world of plants, there are few so curious as strawberry blite, whose daring, edible, strawberry-like fruits begin to flaunt themselves a mere two months after seed is sown. Its various English names—atriplex, berry-bearing orach, red spinach, and strawberry blite—allude to its membership in a broad category of plants that constitute edible greens, variants on collards (*Brassica oleracea*), mustards (*Spinacia* spp. and *Brassica* spp.), and cresses (*Barbarea* spp.).

This particular green was of interest to Stuart-era gardeners because of the exaggeration of the fruit. In his 1633 herbal, John Gerard commented, "This elegant Orach hath a single and small root, putting forth a few fibers, the stalkes are some foot high[;] . . . about the stalke . . . grow as it were little berries, somewhat like a little mulberry, and when these come to ripenesse, they are of an elegant red colour, and make a fine shew." Gerard mentioned that it grew only in choice gardens in England, including that of John Parkinson, botanist to Charles I.[1]

In another work dating from the seventeenth century, Alexander Marshal captioned his watercolor of strawberry blite thusly: "atriplex baxcifera rubrum, / the read [red] spinnage [spinach]," suggestive of its culinary origins but so ornamental as to be included in Marshal's flower book of the prettiest flowers of his time. Its reputation as a curious ornamental persisted into the nineteenth century with William Robinson including it in *The English Flower Garden* and saying it was one of three *Chenopodium* suitable for use in the garden.[2]

In a genus known for its general usefulness and weediness, strawberry blite is one of several species bearing something of interest to the inquisitive gardener. Another, Good-King-Henry (*C. bonus-henricus*), also called English mercurie, is an Old World perennial and was used extensively as a potherb in England. The leaves were "boiled with other pot herbes and eaten" and were thought to have a cleansing and scouring effect, much like garden orach (*Atriplex hortensis*), edible if not delectable. A third species most Americans know all too well is lamb's-quarters (*C. album*), the ubiquitous weed stretching across the northern hemisphere that is used by many cultures as a potherb and known to some as starvation food, those weeds, greens, and herbs readily at hand to boil at the first sign of real hunger. A handful of North

Americans continue to eat lamb's-quarters to this day.[3]

Another New World *Chenopodium* species, wormseed (*C. ambrosioides*), known also as Mexican tea or epazote and used extensively in Mexican cooking, was found by the Reverend John Banister traveling in Virginia around 1680–1690. It had already become an exotic invasive in the Virginia landscape, a thousand miles from its home in the West Indies. John Lawson also included wormseed in his 1709 *New Voyage to Carolina*, where he classed it as a pot-herb. Aside from its use as a culinary ingredient, this aromatic annual was held to possess insecticidal and fumigant properties and was known as an effective wormer. Wormseed was likely part of health maintenance as the Virginia colonists knew it.[4]

Preferring warmer starting temperatures than other greens, blite is best begun in May when the soil warms. In the trial garden, seed was sown in earliest May with germination occurring approximately two weeks later. By the middle of June, the fruits had matured to the point where they became noticeable, later becoming greatly enlarged and very ornamental. The effect was quite dramatic.

Although strawberry blite's traditional venue has been the kitchen garden, given the modern penchant for controverting outdated rules, its place could properly be in any situation where the novelty fruits are likely to catch the eye of a passerby. Without exception, this plant in the trial garden attracted the attention of anyone who strayed close enough to catch sight of the clump of perfunctory foliage and smashingly funny fruits. Seed firms recommend strawberry blite for patio containers and borders. Whether in a row or along a path in the kitchen garden, or as a patch scattered in the mixed garden, "read spinnage" is a novel plant with noble fruit, a fit, bright embellishment for twenty-first-century garden salads.

**STRAWBERRY BLITE,
RED SPINACH, ATRIPLEX,
BERRY-BEARING ORACH**
(*Chenopodium foliosum* 'Strawberry Sticks')

TYPE nonhardy annual green
HEIGHT 16 inches
SPREAD 18 inches

HABIT
- bears edible strawberry-like fruits
- useful as an edging to a border
- potential patio plant

NATURAL RANGE
continental Europe

TIPS
- use in the annual, cottage-style, or mixed garden
- provide full sun; partial shade in hot climates
- sow seeds directly in the garden near the surface of the soil when the soil warms
- do not allow to dry out
- thin seedlings to 12 inches

Moth Mullein

(Verbascum blattaria)

BIENNIAL HERB

BLATTARIA *alba C. B. P. 244.*

Although it is often derided as an invasive, nonnative weed, moth mullein, also known as blattaria, became an indispensable ingredient in the combinations of annual and biennial species grown in the trial garden. When in full bloom, the multiple willowy wands of yellow, or frequently white, flowers articulate graceful arabesques when set in front of plants of coarser textures. Its long flowering period is also a considerable asset. The esteemed Philip Miller, in his 1760 publication, commented on this virtue: "The Flowers are produced almost the whole Length of the Stem, at every Joint . . . and these succeed each other, so that the same Stem will be garnished with Flowers upwards of Two Months." In the trial garden, flowering commenced in early May and persisted into very late June. Because the seed capsules are slow to ripen, it is necessary to leave the plants in place for quite a long time, up to two months, until they brown, yet, even at this stage, they provide decorative, vertical accents in the garden.[1]

Moth mullein is a true biennial by nature. The same Mr. Miller gives us a succinct description of its life cycle: "These are biennial Plants, which per-ish soon after they have perfected their Seeds. The Plants very rarely shoot up their Flower-stems the First Year, but spread their Leaves close upon the Surface of the Ground . . . and the Spring following the Flower-stem is put forth from the Center of the Plant." It takes but a season or two with a plant like moth mullein for even the first-time gardener to seize upon the opportunities afforded by plants that span one winter and then wither after blooming.[2]

Moth mullein may have gained its reputation as a pedestrian weed because it favors dry, poor soils. Plants perceived as "growing anywhere" seem prone to that label. Of moth mullein, Miller explained, "All the Species of this Genus are hardy; and if they are sown upon poor Land, and in Rubbish, or happen to grow upon old Walls, they will resist the greatest Cold of this Country; but in a rich moist Soil they often rot in Winter." But, tenacity in the face of poor conditions doesn't have to preclude beauty.[3]

A garden once inoculated with its seed, given the plant's prolific seeding nature, will never be without moth mullein again. Even if the industrious gardener were to weed away the majority of seedlings in the spring and strategically

leave a smattering of randomly placed self-sown seedlings, the result would still be robust germination the second spring and glimmers of yellow, or white, dancing among the more studied masses of "finer" plants. This dappling effect is the gift of many of the insistent, self-seeding annuals, and this stubborn resolve to infest the garden is really the nature of the game with this Old World moth mullein.

The German Leonhart Fuchs clearly identified the plant as blattaria in 1542. He ascribed no medicinal uses to the plant but said, "When thrown away, it attracts moths to itself." The Englishman John Gerard concurred, saying in his 1633 herbal, "I find nothing written of them, saving that moths, butterflies, and all manner of small flies and bats do resort to the place where these herbs are laied or strewed." Oddly, other authors attributed moth *repellent* properties to this mullein, claiming that it was a general custom in New England to pack these plants and flowers with clothing and furs.[4]

By the nineteenth century, garden writers were beginning to extol the ornamental virtues of moth mullein. William Robinson, writing in *The English Flower Garden* around 1883, called blattaria another one of the *Verbascums* "of interest." Ippolito Pizzetti and Henry Cocker, writing in *Flowers: A Guide for Your Garden* in 1968, suggested moth mullein as "a fine plant for the herbaceous border" where a relaxed and naturalistic effect is wanted.[5]

Moth mullein is now naturalized throughout most of North America. In other words, it is a pernicious "weed." When this species made that fateful transatlantic jump is unknown. As recorded in *Flora Virginica* (1739–1743), John Clayton identified a *"BLATTARIA floribus plurimis albis, foliis odoratis villosis,"* as well as eight other *Verbascums*. Unfortunately, the vagaries of plant taxonomy at that time conceal from us the actual identities of the species. John Lawson, in his 1709 *New Voyage to Carolina*, included a "Mullein" among his list of *"Herbs of* Carolina," but it was probably the tall, common, felty-leaved European Aaron's rod, or common mullein (*V. thapsus*), to which he referred, for good reason. The reputation that common mullein had sterile wound dressing properties began in ancient times and was later repeated by Gerard: "The report goeth, saith *Pliny,* that figges do not putrifie at all that are wrapped in the leaves of Mullein: which thing *Dioscorides* also maketh mention of," demonstrating, in Gerard's mind, mullein's antiseptic capacity. It was also regarded as a beneficial tobacco for respiratory complaints. Rest assured, however, that moth mullein, like common mullein, would have been

familiar to English and colonial American gardeners from time immemorial, and both became part of the North American landscape long ago.[6]

Because of moth mullein's carelessly easy nature and the extended season of color it brings to the garden, the gardener should consider muzzling it and making it an integral element in the mixed garden, where thirty, forty, or fifty species of fertile, seed-bearing plants are selected, juggled, and managed.

MOTH MULLEIN, BLATTARIA (*Verbascum blattaria*)

TYPE biennial
HEIGHT up to 6 feet; more
   commonly 4 feet
SPREAD 24–30 inches

HABIT
- bears graceful vertical stems yielding yellow or white flowers
- reliably self-sows
- resists most pests

NATURAL RANGE
continental Europe, Asia; naturalized in North America

TIPS
- use in the cottage-style or mixed garden
- provide full sun
- sow seeds directly in the garden at or near the surface of the soil in late August or early September
- thin seedlings aggressively in the fall and the following spring

Elecampane

(Inula helenium)

PERENNIAL HERB

Alant.
CXXXIIII.

Elecampane has been a part of the West's pharmacopoeia for twenty-five hundred years. Cited first by Theophrastus the Greek around 300 BC, all-heal of Chaeronea, as he called it, has large, rough leaves, golden flowers, and large, fleshy roots. He thought it beneficial in treating animal bites and in healing wounds or sores when mixed with wine and olive oil and applied as a plaster. Dioscorides, a first-century Roman army doctor, wrote that elecampane was endemic to hilly, shady, and moist places and that its meaty root was prepared as a syrup for coughs and asthma, being primarily a respiratory balm. He mentioned that the root, when preserved in raisin wine, was good for the stomach and gaseousness and that confectioners dried the root, boiled it, and made a decoction out of it that was stored in jars.[1]

Elecampane's traditional role as an expectorant and as a treatment for coughs and other respiratory complaints is legendary. Modern botanists and biochemists sometimes concur with herbal remedies. Arthur Tucker and Thomas DeBaggio, in *The Big Book of Herbs* (2000), described elecampane oil as "bacteriostatic and fungistatic," having the ability to impede the growth of bacteria and fungi.[2]

Elecampane remained prominent in the major medieval and Renaissance herbals. Leonhart Fuchs, a sixteenth-century herbalist and a professor of medicine at Tübingen University in Germany, included elecampane in his great herbal of 1542. Meticulous in his scholarship, Fuchs always cited earlier academic commentary about the plants gathered into his botanical purview. Regarding elecampane, he drew from Dioscorides when describing its preferred habitat: "In shady, dry places in mountains." He also commented that it is "planted almost everywhere in gardens."[3]

Amongst the earliest herbs to be imported into colonial America, elecampane appears as *"Enula Campana"* in the 1672 tract *New-Englands Rarities Discovered* by John Josselyn. It also appears in a later publication, John Lawson's 1709 *A New Voyage to Carolina,* among a list of *"Herbs of* Carolina," herbs both culinary and medicinal. More than fifty-six plants are enumerated in this invaluable passage from an early journey to colonial America.[4]

Growing elecampane presents no real hurdles other than having enough available space to accommodate the sprawling perennial. Seed begun in March germinated in two weeks and

produced plants two feet in diameter by June 3. The leaves can be described only as tremendous, and their huge blades have a decidedly ornamental appeal in the garden, given the space. During the second year, flowering stems were produced in late summer, August to September, and rose up quickly from the basal rosette of huge leaves. Unlike other tall perennials that progressively grow taller as the season progresses, the flower stalks of elecampane make a sudden jump to their eventual six- to eight-foot height. While this makes the incorporation of elecampane in a purely ornamental flower border problematic, one or two or three of these enormous plants could be placed in a large mixed or herb garden so that they may achieve their greatest proportions in relative isolation.

Elecampane is a pleasing, if vast, presence in the household garden, where the huge leaves provide opportunities for sunlight to be captured and filtered through them. The merits of elecampane, the deliciously luminous leaves and the fine elixir drawn from the roots, recommend it for the inquiring, historically minded gardener.

ELECAMPANE, SCABWORT, ALANT, HORSEHEAL, YELLOW STARWORT
(*Inula helenium*)

TYPE hardy perennial
HEIGHT 6–8 feet, rarely to 10 feet
SPREAD 4–5 feet

HABIT
- produces large basal leaves
- bolts to flowering height quickly
- sprawls and can be floppy

NATURAL RANGE
Asia; naturalized in Europe, including Great Britain

TIPS
- use in the annual, cottage-style, or mixed garden
- provide full sun; partial shade in hot climates
- sow seeds, which need light to germinate, directly in the garden at the soil surface March–April or August–September
- thin seedlings to 18 inches

Motherwort

(Leonurus cardiaca)

PERENNIAL HERB

Rated penultimate among ancient, medieval, and modern herbalists, motherwort's properties are reputedly potent. In ancient Greece, motherwort was used for anxiety in pregnant women, hence its name. But, demonstrating chasms between herbalism then and now, motherwort is now contraindicated for pregnant women because of its reputation for inducing menstruation. Long considered a heart remedy (hence *cardiaca*), today motherwort is used generally as a sedative as well as an agent to stimulate menstruation.[1]

Along established lines, the sixteenth-century German herbalist Leonhart Fuchs thought the herb to be an antispasmotic and a sedative under certain circumstances as well as a stimulant of urination and menstruation, a theory repeated up to the present day. As a tonic and a palliative, it was especially thought to allay anxiety and was held by some moderns, such as Maud Grieve, to strengthen and "gladden" the heart. Its properties were held to be legion and strong. The medieval herbalist Macer said, "Yf a man bere this herbe upon hym, there shal no venymous beast greve hym." Nicholas Culpeper, seventeenth-century herbalist and popularizer, said, "There is no better herb to take melancholy vapours from the heart, to strengthen it, and make a merry, chearful blithe soul than this herb." According to John Gerard's 1633 herbal, husbandmen also eagerly sought it out as a remedy for diseases among cattle.[2]

Although not listed among the potherbs included in John Lawson's 1709 *A New Voyage to Carolina*, motherwort is included in a plagiarized, 1737 German translation by Samuel Jenner. Jenner, a land speculator, was trying to tout the merits of planting a community of Swiss immigrants in the southern colonies. It was boosterism that led Jenner to publish Lawson's *New Voyage to Carolina* as *Neu-gefundenes Eden*, which Jenner altered slightly to paint a rosy picture for his potential buyers. Jenner might have been playing to his Swiss audience by slipping motherwort into Lawson's list of potherbs. Philip Miller, commenting on motherwort in 1760, thought it native to continental Europe and wild in, but not native to, England. If motherwort was more an herb of the Continental herbal tradition, it would have been familiar to Swiss immigrants, Samuel Jenner's target audience.[3]

When it definitively arrived in America is uncertain, but motherwort soon colonized large swathes of the

American countryside, where it is now considered a wild, introduced species. Part of its rapid spread through America may be attributable to Johnny Appleseed, who, according to Michael Pollan in *The Botany of Desire* (2001), carried motherwort and other medicinal seed with him and dispensed it to the Indians with whom he regularly dealt. It has now become endemic in the Midwest especially.[4]

In Philip Miller's *Figures of the Most Beautiful* (1760), motherwort is shown in its most charming aspect, the delicacy of the leaves and flowers, arranged in whorls, arrayed on stems that can exceed six feet. The flowers are a pale purple or pink-purple and bear in midsummer. Miller also noted its weedy nature: "When once planted in a Garden, will soon multiply, especially if the Seeds are permitted to scatter; for these will grow where-ever they fall, and become troublesome Weeds."[5]

Sown as a perennial in the fall,

motherwort's first appeal as a garden plant was its vigorous, crisp, palmate leaves, well textured with veins. Blooming the next May, the sagelike arrangement of pink flowers combined with the handsome, dentate foliage made the motherwort more than a medicinal novelty. The clump, in fact, was distinctly ornamental; the flowers though not large were numerous, and the foliage had a long, attenuated, elegant cast to it. It could, in fact, be a premier plant in a catchall garden, one that spans the ornamental and the herbal, with the caveat that seed heads should not be allowed to form. In this effort to keep the plants deadheaded, many wheelbarrows of motherwort herbage were cut in the trial garden. These prunings, along with those of the anise hyssop (*Agastache foeniculum*) and boneset (*Eupatorium perfoliatum*), provided bushels of leaves, stems, and flowers that could have kept any local apothecary busy.

MOTHERWORT, CARDIACA
(*Leonurus cardiaca*)

TYPE hardy perennial
HEIGHT up to 6 feet
SPREAD 36 inches

HABIT
- bears pink sagelike flowers
- provides a fine-textured leaf
- self-sows abundantly
- resists most pests

NATURAL RANGE
continental Europe, the Mediterranean region

TIPS
- use in the mixed or medicinal garden
- provide full sun
- sow seeds, which need light to germinate, directly in the garden at the soil surface March–April or August–September
- thin seedlings to 12 inches
- prevent reseeding

Passionflower

(Passiflora incarnata)

PERENNIAL HERB

An insidious weed of near unsurpassed beauty, the passionflower vine is best kept in mass meadow plantings capable of being mown yearly with a large tractor. The alluring complexity of the passionflower must have come to the instant attention of the earliest Jamestown colonists because it is rampant in the fields and thickets of Virginia. William Strachey arrived in 1610 and, as secretary of the colony, wrote about Jamestown and included a description of the *"maracock,"* which he said was "of the bigness of a queen-apple, and hath many azurine, or blue, kernels, like as a pomegranate . . . a good summer cooling fruit."[1]

Somewhat later, also in colonial America, the Reverend John Banister, the English plant explorer, included the native passionflower in his plant catalog, calling it a *Clematis.* John Lawson gave an account of the plant in his 1709 *New Voyage to Carolina,* saying, "The Maycock bears a glorious Flower, and Apple of an agreeable Sweet, mixt with an acid Taste. This is also a Summer-Vine." The passionflower also came to the attention of Virginia's greatest eighteenth-century botanist, John Clayton, whose dried herbarium specimen survives in the Natural History Museum in London.[2]

The advent of the passionflower in Europe is said to date to 1610 when an Augustine friar brought to the attention of a Roman theologian a drawing of a remarkable flower found in Mexico. It was our *Passiflora incarnata.* The devout immediately saw in the parts of the flower representations of the Passion of Christ: the stigmata in its five stamens, the three nails used to crucify the Christ in the three styles, and the crown of thorns in the seventy-two filaments that surround the center.[3]

It is not without some wonder that persons who having never seen a passionflower before might remark on the complexity of form that nature can conceive from soil and water. Nowadays, one might ask how the complicated parts of the flower enhance the ability of the species to propagate itself. With some sentimentality, we could also remember the story of the passionflower as "the most extraordinary representation of the Cross Triumphant ever discovered in field or forest."[4]

By 1629, the native Virginian passionflower had made its way to England. John Parkinson, royal botanist to King Charles I, noted that it was part of the "surpassing delight of all flowers came

from Virginia. Wee preserve them all in our Gardens." Being Catholic, Parkinson may have had popish affection for the passionflower. Later, the watercolorist Alexander Marshal, long a houseguest of Bishop Compton (the premier botanical patron of his time), included the passionflower in his burgeoning vellum florilegium probably no later than 1653 when it is thought that he finished the bulk of the work.[5]

Strong evidence suggests that an infusion of the passionflower's leaves and flowers acts as a sedative, an antispasmodic, and a tranquilizer, and these properties have led to its commercial use for insomnia, anxiety, and pain relief. Native Americans have long considered it a wound herb to treat bruises, boils, cuts, and inflamed wounds and have also endorsed its use to induce a calming effect. Because of its New World provenance and the claims made on its behalf by Native Americans, its use as a physic herb may speak to an earlier date of origin than those of some European herbal remedies.[6]

Though it bears a beautiful blue flower and might be thought a coronary plant, the passionflower is not a plant suited to the garden proper. In trials, the seed, which can take up to six months to germinate, took forty days to come up. Within the first warm season, its underground stems infiltrated a nearby clump of peonies (*Paeonia officinalis*) and other plantings and gave every indication of becoming an insidious weed. The state of Kentucky and the Southern Weed Science Society consider it an invasive weed. Should one choose to adopt this vigorous native, it should be the inhabitant of a field that is mowed occasionally, every year or two, where grasses, tree saplings, large herbaceous weeds, and the rampant vines of the Virginia countryside bound over endless acres: Virginia creeper (*Parthenocissus quinquefolia*), trumpet creeper (*Campsis radicans*), woodbine (*Lonicera sempervirens*), yellow jessamine (*Gelsemium sempervirens*), and passionflower. The fruit of the passionflower is hollow, and much childhood fun is derived from popping it: hence, the maypop.[7]

PASSIONFLOWER, MAYPOP, MARACOCK
(*Passiflora incarnata*)

TYPE hardy perennial vine
HEIGHT 15 feet with support
SPREAD 20 feet

HABIT
- bears flowers 2–3 inches across of uncommon beauty
- aggressively vining, weedy
- reproduces via underground stems

NATURAL RANGE
Virginia to Florida, west to Missouri and Texas

TIPS
- use in a wild meadow or semiwild area
- provide full sun
- sow seeds ½ inch deep in appropriate wild areas when the soil warms to 80°F

Pennyroyal

(Mentha pulegium)

PERENNIAL HERB

The story of pennyroyal is darkened by its historical use as an abortifacient, an agent that induces abortion. Modern herbalists, obviously, warn against its use during pregnancy. But, commentators, both ancient and modern, recommend it as a way to soothe nausea in general. In this capacity, it is used as a digestive tonic and, in larger concentrations, as a wormer. External applications can mitigate the itchiness inherent in chronic skin disorders and relieve the pain of rheumatic conditions. Once a staple of cottage and kitchen gardens, it was kept within easy reach for use in pennyroyal tea, an old-fashioned remedy for colds and tummy aches. Modern herbal authorities recommend caution when using pennyroyal because of its many active constituents.[1]

Interest in pennyroyal is thousands of years old. In the third-century BC herbal of Theophrastus, the leaves of pennyroyal and dittany (*Origanum dictamnus*) are compared. Pennyroyal received its Latin name, *pulegium*, in the first century from Pliny, who so named it because of its pungent aroma and its use as a fumigant against fleas. Other classical authors considered it a uterine stimulant, and the later Elizabethans thought a garland of pennyroyal "is of great force against the swimming in the head, the paines and giddinesse thereof."[2]

Listed in *New-Englands Rarities Discovered* (1672) by John Josselyn, an intrepid English naturalist who ventured twice to the American colonies, pennyroyal was present in the Massachusetts Bay Colony of that time. In a section called "*Of such Garden Herbs (amongst us) as do thrive there, and of such as do not,*" Josselyn clearly made reference to "*Penny Royal.*" In a different section of the book, "*Of such Plants as are common with us in* ENGLAND," he referred to "*Upright Peniroyal,*" though we do not know if this is the same plant. Maud Grieve, in her book *A Modern Herbal* (1931), discussed two varieties of *Mentha pulegium:* she referred to the smallish, prostrate pennyroyal as "*decumbens*" and another variety as "*erecta,*" perhaps alluding to the double citation found in Josselyn's early writing. Further confirmation of pennyroyal's use in the American colonies is a Williamsburg published tract, *Every Man His Own Doctor: or, The Poor Planter's Physician,* wherein pennyroyal water is recommended for pleurisy, pennyroyal plaster as an application for the chest, and decoction of pennyroyal to raise a sweat.[3]

Seed was sown in the trial garden in mid-April, and flowering plants were obtained by July 16 with bloom continuing sporadically through August. The overall effect was soft and pretty, and the crushed leaves emitted a very lovely scent when tread on, suggesting its use as an alternative to the turf lawn. In addition, pennyroyal has gained a reputation as one of the best tick deterrents available and as a prime candidate for hanging baskets.

PENNYROYAL, GIBRALTAR MINT, RUN-BY-THE-GROUND, PUDDING GRASS
(*Mentha pulegium*)

TYPE hardy perennial
HEIGHT 12 inches
SPREAD 12 inches

HABIT
- bears 8-inch spikes of lavender whirled flowers
- grows in prostrate mats of ornamental grayish foliage
- self-sows
- resists most pests

NATURAL RANGE
Europe, including Great Britain, northern and western Asia, northern Africa

TIPS
- use in the annual, kitchen, cottage-style, or mixed garden
- provide full sun; partial shade in hot climates
- sow seeds, which need light to germinate, directly in the garden at the soil surface in midspring
- keep moderately moist
- thin seedlings to 6 inches

In the garden, pennyroyal is a very attractive presence. Said to prefer moist soil, it thrived in the poor but irrigated soil under a vitex shrub (*Vitex agnus-castus*) that had been trained into a small tree. The pennyroyal produced a thick mat of soft grayish foliage laced with its characteristic lavender whirled flowers, suggesting that this might be its optimal use, as a sufficiently interesting underplanting to other woody things. As a famous creeper, pennyroyal requires diligence of its keeper to limit its thick mats to where one wants them. At the same time, that reassuring gumption allowed it to withstand with little blemish the considerable amount of radiant heat from a nearby brick walk and from the bright, reflective white clapboard of a nearby privy. This versatility, however, doesn't extend to its being able to climb the woody trunks of the multistemmed vitex, a pretty trick accomplished by the insidious English ivy (*Hedera helix*), which so likes to parasitize the trunks of larger things.

General Planting Information

The owner or Gardener ought to remember, that before he committeth seeds to the earth, the beds be disposed and troden out, into such a breadth and length, as best answereth to every plant and root.

—Thomas Hill, 1577

The sowing of seed is nearly primal, yet also intricate and complex. The planting of bulbs, for instance, is a one-stage process; the planting and growing of seed involves many steps.

In an area free of shade and tree roots, establish a bed with stake and string, or with a rubber hose for an organically shaped bed. Measure the dimensions of the proposed bed. Precisely or not, transfer the outline on the ground to a piece of paper roughly to scale (e.g., 1 inch = 1 foot). You can now design your garden on paper, and, at the time of planting, this plan will allow you to transmit your design to the piece of ground allotted.

With the ground allotted and a map of sorts created, choose your seeds with their hardiness in mind. Cool crops such as wallflower (*Erysimum cheiri*), love-in-a-mist (*Nigella damascena*), and calendula (*Calendula officinalis*) can be sown in the mid-Atlantic in mid-March, before the last frost. Others such as marigold (*Tagetes erecta* and *T. patula*) require completely frost-free conditions and mild heat to germinate. Plan your garden accordingly. When selecting seeds, pay attention to the year of release. Always use the current season's seed.

The first task in laying out any new garden is to break up the sod with a twelve-inch spade and shovel. Cubes of sod are cut with a square-bladed spade and turned once so that the turf falls into the hole and the roots are exposed, topsy turvy. The soil must be broken down enough to be able to incorporate compost, or humus (rotted organic matter), into the beds at a ratio of about 1:1. In addition to the humus, appropriate amounts of organic fertilizer (dehydrated poultry manure, for instance) must be added to assure soil fertility. The compost and fertilizer are mixed into the soil by turning the beds three times with a round point shovel. Each time you turn the soil, it breaks apart a bit more, allowing for the incorporation of the compost and fertilizer.

A soil test should be conducted before and after you've incorporated the humus and fertilizer. A pH of 6.5 is the target. If your soil does not have a pH of 6.5, the results of the soil test will include instructions for obtaining it.

Seeds need a friendly and conducive environment in which to germinate, and the soil needs to be fine textured and well drained. You can continue working with spade and shovel to achieve a fine texture, or a two-cycle micro-tiller (the most common is sold under the brand name Mantis) can be hugely instrumental in further breaking down the soil into a finer substance. In fact, a micro-tiller macerates the soil.

The secret of the two-cycle tillers is the sharpness of the tines and the speed at which they rotate. They make fine work of heavy soil. Light and easy to maneuver, they can prepare soil to a depth of fourteen to sixteen inches if the sod is broken first. They will not, and cannot, however, break open sod.

Once the soil is the proper consistency, seeding can begin. Abide by the directions pertaining to soil depth and season of sowing on the seed packet. Larger seeds lend themselves to individual placement in discreet holes at the proper depth. Smaller seeds can be scattered with the fingertips into shallow, narrow furrows. After setting the seed, always firm the soil by tamping the surface with the back edge of a steel rake. Water immediately with a sprinkler or watering can so that the soil is wet to the depth of one inch.

During the germination process, adequate and consistent watering is paramount. The majority of seeds germinate in the top quarter inch of soil, and that quarter inch of well-drained soil can dry out in a day. Daily watering is optimal during the first week of seeding prior to germination, with the caveat that excessive watering is counterproductive.

Nonhardy annuals, such as cypress vine (*Ipomoea quamoclit*), zinnia (*Zinnia pauciflora*), and marigold, need the benefit of warm mid- to late-spring heat to germinate. By this time, the sun is higher in the sky, the temperatures are warming, and seedbeds are more prone to drying out. To compensate for the sun's zenith, more attention should be paid to watering. There is no more crucial time in the life of the seed-generated garden than during the seeding phase.

A challenge to the gardener naive to the practice of sowing large amounts of flower seed is distinguishing their cotyledon (primary seed leaves) from ubiquitous weed seedlings that will inevitably proliferate. If the gardener sows discreet plots, each plot should have its specific set of flower seedlings as well as a set of weed seedlings common to all beds. With time, the gardener recognizes the consistency of weed seedlings throughout all beds and the singular natures of the desired flower seedlings.

Another task awaits the gardener. Due to the tiny size of most seeds and the difficulty sometimes of sowing evenly and sparsely enough, more seedlings inevitably emerge than is desired or healthy, and the thinning of seedlings becomes crucial if one is to obtain premium plants. This can be a painstaking process, usually conducted on one's hands and knees carefully teasing one plant from another. This procedure is a challenge to patience more than to the back but one that will result in stronger, more robust plants down the road.

Care of a garden extends beyond the seeding and germination process. Weeding and watering continue on a daily basis (every other day is enough in some climates). As plants flower, deadheading, removing spent blossoms, is important especially for annuals. Deadheading can often elongate the flowering period.

Annuals and biennials give up the ghost after the production of seed. The gardener can either wait for the seed to mature and ripen and collect it or rogue out the plant and begin anew. Should the gardener await the completion of the full cycle and the production of seed, very often plants yellow and dry, leaving the gardener with an artistic conundrum.

Many gardeners who deliberately collect seed conduct their activities away from the display garden.

The gardener intent on establishing a self-perpetuating seed-driven garden must allow the floral crops to yellow, ripen, and disperse seed. This natural dispersal of seed, and the way it inevitably weaves itself into the seed zones of other plants, creates the multilayered, complex, and abundant garden possible with a few dozen types of seed.

Should the gardener wish to augment his or her garden with plants such as Indian-shot (*Canna indica*) and sweet flag (*Acorus calamus*), more immediate satisfaction can be had by purchasing and planting tubers rather than starting from seed, avoiding years of wait and arcane germination processes.

SEEDS

Finding sources of seed is but a Google away, and the Web-savvy gardener should have no problem at all finding sources of all the plants mentioned in this book, and a great deal more. For your convenience, I've listed below a number of seed outlets with which I am familiar (see p. 272). Additionally, visitors to Williamsburg are encouraged to stop

by Colonial Williamsburg's Colonial Nursery on Duke of Gloucester Street where they can purchase a wide variety of colonial-era seed.

Very often, historically minded gardeners are hampered by the difficulty in finding seed that is true to the period species and that has not been improved or modified. By avoiding seed packs labeled "hybrid," "cultivar," and "F1," you can almost ensure purchasing plant seeds representing the original species. However, some specific cultivars from the past may not be available. Highly bred flowers such as larkspur (*Consolida orientalis*), marigold (*Tagetes patula* and *T. erecta*), and even calendula (*Calendula officinalis*) experienced vast transformations in as little as fifty years of their discovery. Such cultivars are sadly lost to us. We can, however, still produce varieties that mimic those characteristics.

In some cases, it can be rewarding to grow some of the improved varieties, as long as the species, or closely related species, is held to. Often, these improved varieties, after a few generations of self-sowing, will revert to their more distant traits in a process that is called *back breeding*. It is satisfying to observe this process by growing modern selections of older plants to see what traits have been optimized and then letting them literally go to seed and see what characteristics they shed or adopt.

In addition to the plants featured in this book, I successfully grew a number of others. The following plants are accurate to the colonial and early Federal periods, and I highly recommend their use:

Flowering plants:

- BACHELOR'S BUTTON (*Centaurea cyanus*): for instant gratification and for the use of the blue in cosmetics
- CANTERBURY-BELLS (*Campanula medium*): because they're sentimental
- CHICORY (*Cichorium intybus*): because of the blue
- CORN COCKLE (*Agrostemma githago*): weedy, insubstantial but bearing a brilliantly carmine flower
- DRAGONWORT (*Dracocephalum moldavica*): for the blue flower and for John Bartram's mention of it
- GARDEN IMPATIENS (*Impatiens balsamina*): because it's so easy and so tropical
- GLOBE AMARANTH (*Gomphrena globosa*): because Martha Washington's father-in-law grew it

- HELIOTROPE (*Heliotropium arborescens*): because of the unforgettable scent
- HONEYWORT (*Cerinthe major*)*: because Virgil said it attracts a swarming hive of bees to alight and nest
- HORSEMINT (*Monarda punctata*): for the unforgettable three-tiered flower
- JOSEPH'S-COAT (*Amaranthus tricolor*): because it's old, bold, and gaudy
- MIGNONETTE (*Reseda odorata*): dull but famous for the aroma
- ROCKET CANDYTUFT (*Iberis amara* 'Coronaria')*: for the eighteen inches of vertical white flower
- SNAPDRAGON (*Antirrhinum majus*): the Greeks thought it attracted fame
- SWEET-EVENING-STOCK (*Matthiola incana*): because it's so historical
- SWEET FLAG (*Acorus calamus*): an ancient perfume fixative [grown from tubers rather than from seed]
- SWEET-SULTAN (*Centaurea moschata*): the name derived from a sultan's turban
- YELLOW GIANT HYSSOP (*Agastache nepetoides*): because it was collected by John Clayton

Herbs:

- ALKANET (*Anchusa officinalis*): which yields a red dye
- ANGELICA (*Angelica archangelica*): a finicky biennial of hilarious dimensions
- BLACK CUMIN (*Nigella sativa*): a nondescript annual producing a seed ubiquitous in Hindu cuisine
- CHERVIL (*Anthriscus cerefolium*): the finest in *fines herbes;* so subtle that it doesn't bear the heat of the stove
- FALSE SAFFRON (*Carthamus tinctorius*): for its seeds, which are oiled, roasted, salted, and nibbled; the start of a bridge mix
- LOVAGE (*Levisticum officinale*): for its six-foot presence and seeds that are roasted and chewed
- SORREL (*Rumex acetosella*): for its perfect lemon zest
- SPEEDWELL (*Veronica officinalis*): which turned out to be a good blue perennial
- WOAD (*Isatis tinctoria*): from whence the blue dye of the Celts comes after a smelly fermentation

*Honeywort (*Cerinthe major*) and rocket candytuft (*Iberis amara* 'Coronaria') appear in print in America in 1802 or 1803. All of the other plants on these lists appear prior to 1800.

Seed Outlets

ALCHEMY WORKS
643 Newtown Street
Elmira, NY 14904
607-737-9250
www.alchemy-works.com

BOTANICAL INTERESTS, INC.
660 Compton Street
Broomfield, CO 80020
303-410-1677
www.botanicalinterests.com

BROTHER NATURE ORGANIC SEEDS
1159 Wychbury Avenue
Victoria, BC V9A 5L1
Canada
www.brothernature.ca

W. ATLEE BURPEE & CO.
300 Park Avenue
Warminster, PA 18974
800-333-5808
www.burpee.com

CHILTERN SEEDS
Bortree Stile
Ulverston
Cumbria, LA12 7PB
England
+44 (0) 1229 581137
info@chilternseeds.co.uk

COMPANION PLANTS
7247 North Coolville Ridge Road
Athens, OH 45701
740-592-4643
www.companionplants.com

EDEN ORGANIC NURSERY SERVICES, INC.
PO Box 4604
Hallandale, FL 33008
954-382-8281
www.eonseed.com

THOMAS ETTY ESQ.
Seedsman's Cottage
Puddlebridge
Horton
Ilminster
Somerset, TA19 9RL
United Kingdom
+44 (0) 1460 57934
www.thomasetty.co.uk

THE FRAGRANT PATH
PO Box 328
Fort Calhoun, NE 68023
www.fragrantpathseeds.com

GARDENMAKERS
PO Box 65
Rowley, MA 01969-0165
978-948-8481
www.gardenmakers.com

GERMANIA SEED COMPANY
5978 North Northwest Highway
PO Box 31787
Chicago, IL 60631
800-380-4721
www.germaniaseed.com

NICHOLS GARDEN NURSERY
1190 Old Salem Road, NE
Albany, OR 97321-4580
800-422-3985
www.nicholsgardennursery.com

SAND MOUNTAIN HERBS
321 County Road 18
Fyffe, AL 35971
www.sandmountainherbs.com

SEEDMAN.COM
3421 Bream Street
Gautier, MS 39553
www.seedman.com

SELECT SEEDS
180 Stickney Hill Road
Union, CT 06076
800-684-0395, 860-684-9310
www.selectseeds.com

THOMAS JEFFERSON CENTER FOR HISTORIC
PLANTS
PO Box 316
Charlottesville, VA 22902
800-243-1743, 800-243-0743
http://monticellostore.stores.yahoo.net

THOMPSON & MORGAN
220 Faraday Avenue
Jackson, NJ 08527-5073
800-274-7333, 732-363-2225
www.tmseeds.com

THOMPSON & MORGAN
Poplar Lane
Ipswich
Suffolk, IP8 3BU
England
+44 (0) 1473 688821
www.thompson-morgan.com

TROPILAB, INC.
PO Box 48164
St. Petersburg, FL 33743-8164
727-344-7608
www.tropilab.com

UNDERWOOD GARDENS
1250 Galloway Drive
Woodstock, IL 60098
815-338-6279
www.underwoodgardens.com

VANDUSEN BOTANICAL GARDEN
5251 Oak Street
Vancouver, BC V6M 4H1
Canada
http://vandusen.plantexplorers.com

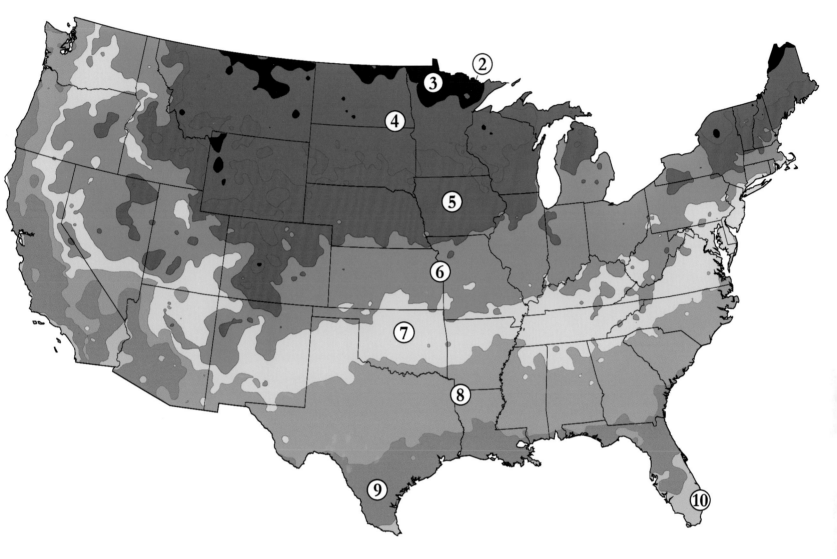

Zones

Both anecdotal observation and scientific research have established the reality of climate change, with the probable attendant rise in summer temperatures. With that scenario in mind, I have included the ArborDay.org 2006 Hardiness Zone Map, which takes into account "zone creep," the slow warming of the climate that may now have put Williamsburg into zone 8 territory, along with the other easternmost parts of Virginia, the Norfolk and Southside regions. While summer temperatures might be creeping up, cold snaps occur, and mid-Atlantic gardeners should observe the traditional cold hardiness map that puts Williamsburg in zone 7B and parts west in 7A. Virginia's mean temperature is 55.7°F, with summer highs in the nineties and winter lows in the teens. Annual mean precipitation is 42.70 inches.

Acknowledgments

I would like to thank the Colonial Williamsburg Foundation and the Mars Foundation of McLean, Virginia, for their generosity and support of this horticultural and research project. These visionary foundations enable us to more clearly understand the past so that we may prepare for the future. I'm indebted to the Mars Foundation for their financial support and to the Colonial Williamsburg Foundation for allowing me the space and the resources to fully pursue the potentialities of this arcane field and for the privilege and honor of working for such an august organization.

Colonial Williamsburg has always had the good fortune to have the philanthropy of its donors to enhance its mission. I'd like to thank Janet and Fred Brubaker of Somerset, Pennsylvania, and Teresa and Ken Wood of Chester Springs, Pennsylvania, for their foresight and generosity in assisting with the publication of this project.

The landscape department at Colonial Williamsburg has been my home for twenty-five years. And during that time, I had the great good fortune to work with people for whom landscape and plants are a visceral enjoyment. I've been blessed to work shoulder to shoulder with generations of professional gardeners. In some cases, Colonial Williamsburg has employed three generations of the same family, and those ties, very strong in the landscape department, imbue the department with family. Being part of that family has been a grounding and rewarding experience, and I've grown as a gardener and a person from my friendships with Colonial Williamsburg's best gardeners who work so hard to beautify the city. I miss those gardeners of the old tradition—Bernard Wright, Tyrone Wallace, William Taliaferro, Hank and James Gaither—and am excited by the enthusiasm as new gardeners fill their large gardening boots.

Orlando Moses Armistead was my first foreman and Denise Greene my first gardening partner, ensuring two years of utopia. I am fortunate to have for my colleagues Wesley Greene and Don McKelvey, garden historians and interpreters, who live and breathe historic plants with a particular intensity and who garden with equal utter enthusiasm. Much of their advice and thoughts were incorporated into this book. In the office, I was mothered by Linda Manogue and Mary Morris, our secretaries. Dorean Neisner kept my files straight and in order, and Diane Schaffe covered my backside while the book progressed. I'd like to acknowledge Suzy Woodall who plucked me from obscurity and Annette Williams Clark who gardened with me for many years and who kept me sane; and Magnolia Mandeville and Galium Woodruff, and Bea and Caro, their heroes.

I am blessed to be part of the landscape administrative staff who, by their collective stewardship, guard the gardens of the Historic Area that we treasure. Gordon Chappell, Laura Viancour, Bob Scott, Susan Dippre, Rollin Woolley, and the impressive work they do collectively to maintain and beautify the eight hundred acres maintained by the Colonial Williamsburg Landscape and Facilities Services Department are deeply respected. Their love for the gardens of Colonial Williamsburg is real, deep, and daily.

I want to thank the Colonial Williamsburg Publications Department for undertaking this task and the Publications Committee for endorsing it, especially Joseph Rountree, whose midwifery of the project assured its success; Helen Olds, whose keen eye for design resulted in a stunning and elegant book; and my editor, Amy Watson. I was especially fortunate in having a crack editor, uncompromising in her standards while maintaining true geniality.

Part of the production of a book are the readers who critique it prior to publication. Frank Robinson, executive director of the Lewis Ginter Botanical Garden in Richmond, Virginia, and Dean Norton, director of horticulture at Mount Vernon Estate, Mount Vernon, Virginia, generously agreed to review the manuscript and offered crucial suggestions. I am indebted to them for their involvement. I would also like to acknowledge Peggy Cornett, director of the Thomas Jefferson Center for Historic Plants, and Peter Hatch, director of Buildings and Grounds, both at Monticello in Charlottesville, Virginia, for the outstanding leadership in this field that has made it so much more rewarding for the rest of us.

It was a privilege to have available the staff at Colonial Williamsburg's John D. Rockefeller, Jr. Library, particularly George Yetter for bringing to the plant curatorial staff the jewels of the rare books collection and Marianne Martin and her patience with "one more request." I'd also like to thank Juleigh Clark, Del Moore, Susan Shames, Doug Mayo, and Joann Proper, who have been so patient with my inconceivably silly questions.

I'd like to acknowledge the audio-visual staff, Dave Doody, Tom Austin, Kathy Rose, Tom Green, Lael White, Kelly Mihalcoe, and Barbara Lombardi, who go out of their way to make what they do happen for everybody else. Barbara Lombardi in particular had the vision for this book, for it was through her eyes that we were brought to appreciate the especial beauty that arose out of a handful of seed and a plot of ground.

Volunteers make up a crucial element in Colonial Williamsburg's operations. Gardening with Sandra Rogers was the highlight of my week for six years. I'd also like to thank Leanne DuBois, who meticulously transcribed many, many pages of eighteenth-century text for me and yet remained a friend. It's been my good fortune to have had such superb support. And thanks goes to Sarah Annunziato at the College of William and Mary for translating the Italian documents from the Uffizi Gallery.

The generous contributions of graphic images from various institutions around the globe have been seminal to the richness of this work. I'd like to thank the representatives of the following institutions for their collegiality and cordiality: the Uffizi Gallery, Florence, Italy; the Jagiellonian Library, Krakow, Poland; the Collections of the Prince of Liechtenstein; the Austrian National Library, Vienna; the City Library of Ulm, Germany; Frampton Court Estate, Gloucester, England; the Petersburg Garden Club, Virginia; and the National Arbor Day Foundation, Nebraska City, Nebraska.

Notes

INTRODUCTION (pages 1–13)

Epigraph. W[illiam] Coles, *The Art of Simpling: An Introduction to the Knowledge and Gathering of Plants* (London, 1657; repr., Falls Village, CT: Herb Grower Press, 1966), 14.

1 George Percy, "Observations Gathered Out of a Discourse of the Plantation of the Southern Colony in Virginia by the English, 1606," in *Jamestown Narratives: Eyewitness Accounts of the Virginia Colony; The First Decade: 1607–1617,* ed. Edward Wright Haile (Champlain, VA: RoundHouse, 1998), 90, 95.

2 Gabriel Archer, "A Relation of the Discovery of Our River from James Fort into the Main, Made by Captain Christofer Newport, and Sincerely Written and Observed by a Gentleman of the Colony," in Haile, *Jamestown Narratives,* 104, 106, 110; William Strachey, "The History of Travel into Virginia Britannia: The First Book of the First Decade," in Haile, *Jamestown Narratives,* 636; Mark Catesby, *The Natural History of Carolina, Florida, and the Bahama Islands: Containing the Figures of Birds, Beasts, Fishes, Serpents, Insects, and Plants. . . .* (London, 1771), 1:x, xix.

3 Peter Martin, *The Pleasure Gardens of Virginia: From Jamestown to Jefferson* (Princeton, NJ: Princeton University Press, 1991), xx; Archer, "Relation of the Discovery," 116; Percy, "Observations Gathered," 98; Gabriel Archer, "The Description of the Now-Discovered River and Country of Virginia, with the Likelihood of Ensuing Riches by England's Aid and Industry," in Haile, *Jamestown Narratives,* 120; William Strachey, "A True Reportory of the Wrack and Redemption of Sir Thomas Gates, Knight, upon and from the Islands of the Bermudas; His Coming to Virginia, and the Estate of That Colony Then, and After under the Government of the Lord La Warre. July 15, 1610," in Haile, *Jamestown Narratives,* 422.

4 Strachey, "History of Travel," 680; Archer, "Description of River and Country," 121; Strachey, "True Reportory," 429.

5 Robert Johnson, "The New Life of Virginea: Declaring the Former Success and Present Estate of That Plantation, Being the Second Part of [the Tract] Nova Britannia," in Haile, *Jamestown Narratives,* 561.

6 Ralphe Hamor, "A True Discourse of the Present Estate of Virginia, and the Success of the Affairs There till the 18 of June, 1614. . . . ," in Haile, *Jamestown Narratives,* 816, 819.

7 David Muraca, "Martin's Hundred: A Settlement Study" (master's thesis, College of William and Mary, Williamsburg, VA, 1993), 74; Martin, *Pleasure Gardens,* 6.

8 Stephenson B. Andrews, ed., *Bacon's Castle* (Richmond, VA: Association for the Preservation of Virginia Antiquities, 1984), 6–7; Nicholas Luccketti, "Archaeological Excavations at Bacon's Castle, Surry County, Virginia" in *Earth Patterns: Essays in Landscape Archaeology,* ed. William M. Kelso and Rachel Most (Charlottesville: University Press of Virginia, 1990), 27, 35.

9 Kathleen McCormick, "History Unearthed," *Historic Preservation* 42, no. 4 (July/August 1990): 60–61.

10 Louis R. Caywood, "Green Spring Plantation/Excavations at Green Spring Plantation" (archaeological report, Virginia 350th Anniversary Commission and Jamestown-Williamsburg-Yorktown Celebration Commission, 1955), 3; J. Paul Hudson, *This Was Green Spring: Plantation, Refuge, Prison, Statehouse* (Jamestown, VA: Jamestown Foundation, n.d.), 4; Martha W. McCartney, "The History of Green Spring Plantation, Colonial National Historical Park, James City County, Virginia" (research report, Colonial National Historical Park, National Park Service, 1998), 19.

11 M. Kent Brinkley, "The Green Spring Plantation Greenhouse/Orangery and the Probable Evolution of the Domestic Area Landscape" (research report, Colonial National Historical Park, National Park Service, 2003), 54–55.

12 William Waller Hening, ed., *The Statutes at Large; Being a Collection of All the Laws of Virginia, from the First Session of the Legislature, in the Year 1619* (Philadelphia, 1823), 3:483; H. R. McIlwaine, ed., *Legislative Journals of the Council of Colonial Virginia* (Richmond, VA, 1919), 3:1557.

13 Martin, *Pleasure Gardens,* 40.

14 Virginia's James River Plantations, Westover, http://www.jamesriverplantations.org/Westover.html; Martin, *Pleasure Gardens,* 72; Richmond Croom Beatty, *William Byrd of Westover* (Boston: Houghton Mifflin, 1932), 179.

15 McCartney, "History of Green Spring," 61; *Thomas Jefferson's Garden Book, 1766–1824, with Relevant Extracts from His Other Writings,* annotated by Edwin Morris Betts (Philadelphia: American Philosophical Society, 1944), 75–76; Hudson, "This Was Green Spring," 4.

16 Martin, *Pleasure Gardens,* 56; E. G. Swem, *Brothers of the Spade: Correspondence of Peter Collinson of London, and of John Custis, of Williamsburg, Virginia. 1734–1746* (Barre, MA: Barre Gazette, 1957).

17 *The Letterbook of John Custis IV of Williamsburg, 1717–1742,* ed. Josephine Little Zuppan (Lanham, MD: Rowman and Littlefield, 2005), 35.

18 Don McKelvey, Survey of garden tools in York County probate inventories and properties with gardens in the *Virginia Gazette* (report, Landscape and Facilities Services Department, Colonial Williamsburg Foundation, Williamsburg, VA, n.d.), 1–2.

19 McKelvey, Survey, 5, 7, 8; Rind's *Virginia Gazette* (Williamsburg), Dec. 14, 1769; Purdie and Dixon's *Virginia Gazette* (Williamsburg), August 22, 1766; ibid., July 9, 1772; Dixon and Hunter's *Virginia Gazette* (Williamsburg), August 8, 1777.

20 Bernard McMahon, "A Catalogue of Garden, Grass, Herb, Flower, Tree, & Shrub-Seeds, Flower-Roots, &c. &c." (broadside, Philadelphia, ca. 1800; repr., Ambridge, PA: Old Economy Village, 1992).

21 United States Department of Agriculture (USDA), Natural Resources Conservation Service, Plants Database, http://plants.usda.gov/. Each subsequent citation for the database provides the scientific name that can be used to search the specific plant in question; Liberty Hyde Bailey Hortorium, *Hortus Third: A Concise Dictionary of Plants Cultivated in the United States and Canada* (New York: Macmillan, 1976); Royal Horticultural Society, *Dictionary of Gardening: A Practical and Scientific Encyclopaedia of Horticulture,* ed. Fred J. Chittenden; 2nd ed. by Patrick M. Synge, 4 vols. (Oxford: Clarendon Press, 1956); *Taylor's Guide to Annuals* (Boston: Houghton Mifflin, 1986); *Taylor's Guide to Bulbs* (Boston: Houghton Mifflin, 1986); *Taylor's Guide to Perennials* (Boston: Houghton Mifflin, 1986); *Taylor's Guide to Vegetables & Herbs* (Boston: Houghton Mifflin, 1987).

A NOTE ON THE SOURCES (pages 16–21)

1 Lucia Tongiorgi Tomasi, *An Oak Spring Flora: Flower Illustration from the Fifteenth Century to the Present Time; A Selection of the Rare Books, Manuscripts and Works of Art in the Collection of Rachel Lambert Mellon* (Upperville, VA: Oak Spring Garden Library, 1997), 40.

2 Theophrastus, *Enquiry into Plants and Minor Works on Odours and Weather Signs,* trans. Sir Arthur Hort, 2 vols. (Cambridge, MA: Harvard University Press, 1961).

3 Agnes Arber, *Herbals: Their Origin and Evolution; A Chapter in the History of Botany, 1470–1670,* 3rd ed., with an introduction and annotations by William T. Stearn (Cambridge: Cambridge University Press, 1986), 2; Theophrastus, *Enquiry into Plants,* 1:xxii.

4 Dioscorides, *De materia medica: Being an Herbal with Many Other Medicinal Materials Written in Greek in the First Century of the Common Era,* trans. T. A. Osbaldeston and R. P. A. Wood

(Johannesburg: Ibidis, 2000), xiv, xv.

5   *The Great Herbal of Leonhart Fuchs: De historia stirpium commentarii insignes, 1542 (Notable Commentaries on the History of Plants)*, ed. Frederick G. Meyer, Emily Emmart Trueblood, and John L. Heller (Stanford, CA: Stanford University Press, 1999), 1:60–61.

6   Lucia Tongiorgi Tomasi and Gretchen A. Hirschauer, *The Flowering of Florence: Botanical Art for the Medici* (Washington, DC: National Gallery of Art, 2002), 30–32; Fuchs, *Great Herbal*, 1:46.

7   John Gerard, *The Herbal or General History of Plants: The Complete 1633 Edition as Revised and Enlarged by Thomas Johnson* (London, 1633; repr., New York: Dover, 1975), vi, and Arber, *Herbals*, 70; The Vienna Codex, in progress when the author died in 1566, is an unpublished work now in the Austrian National Library in Vienna. Extensive commentary about the work as well as illustrations from the work can be found in volume one of Fuchs, *Great Herbal*, ed. Meyer, Trueblood, and Heller.

8   *The Besler Florilegium: Plants of the Four Seasons*, introduction and commentary by Gérard G. Aymonin, trans. Eileen Finletter and Jean Ayer (New York: Abrams, 1989).

9   *The Florilegium of Alexander Marshal in the Collection of Her Majesty the Queen at Windsor Castle*, ed. Prudence Leith-Ross (London: Royal Collection, 2000), 8, 10.

10 Gerard, *Herbal*, vi; Anna Pavord, *The Naming of Names: The Search for Order in the World of Plants* (New York: Bloomsbury, 2005), 332.

11 Marshal, *Florilegium*, 3, 5; Prudence Leith-Ross, *The John Tradescants: Gardeners to the Rose and Lily Queen* (London: Peter Owen, 1984), 102, 108–9. Leith-Ross, *The John Tradescants*, includes the Tradescant plant catalogs, 199, 207, 252.

12 Joan Parry Dutton, *Plants of Colonial Williamsburg: How to Identify 200 of Colonial America's Flowers, Herbs, and Trees* (Williamsburg, VA: Colonial Williamsburg Foundation, 1979), 161; Joseph and Nesta Ewan, *John Banister and His Natural History of Virginia, 1678–1692* (Urbana, IL: University of Illinois Press, 1970), xviii, xx, xxii.

13 Ewan, *John Banister,* 102. Ewan includes an annotated "Catalogus Stirpium Rariorum," 167–265.

14 John Josselyn, *New-Englands Rarities Discovered* (London, 1672; repr., Boston: Massachusetts Historical Society, 1972), v.

15 John Lawson, *A New Voyage to Carolina*, ed. Hugh Talmage Lefler (Chapel Hill: University of North Carolina Press, 1967).

16 Lawson, *New Voyage to Carolina*, 80–84.

17 Swem, *Brothers* (see Introduction, n. 16).

18 [John Clayton] and Joh. Fred. Gronovio, *Flora Virginica exhibens plantas quas v.c. Johannes Clayton in Virginia observavit atque collegit*, 2 vols. (Leiden, 1739–1743). The author cites a reprint of the 1762 edition throughout this publication: [John Clayton] and Joh. Fred. Gronovio [Johannes Fredericus Gronovius], *Flora Virginica exhibens plantas, quas nobilissimus vir D. D. Johannes Claytonus, med. doct. etc. etc. in Virginia crescentes observavit, collegit & obtulit* (Leiden, 1762; repr., Cambridge, MA: Arnold Arboretum, 1946); John Clayton Herbarium database, Natural History Museum, London, http://www.nhm.ac.uk/research-curation/projects/clayton-herbarium/aboutdatabase .html. Each subsequent citation for the database provides a bar code number that can be used to search the specific plant in question. Also provided is a citation to the plant's appearance in *Flora Virginica*, a product of Clayton's collection process; Thomas Jefferson, *Notes on the State of Virginia*, ed. David Waldstreicher (Boston: Bedford/St. Martin's, 2002), 107.

19 Sue Minter, *The Apothecaries' Garden: A History of the Chelsea Physic Garden* (Stroud, UK: Sutton, 2000), 16, 27; Philip Miller, *The Gardeners Dictionary: Containing the Methods of Cultivating and Improving the Kitchen, Fruit and Flower Garden. As Also, the Physick Garden, Wilderness, Conservatory, and Vineyard, According to the Practice of the Most Experience'd Gardeners of the Present Age. . . .* (London, 1731); Philip Miller, *The Gardeners Dictionary: Containing the Methods of Cultivating and Improving All Sorts of Trees, Plants, and Flowers. For the Kitchen, Fruit, and Pleasure Gardens. . . . ,* 4th ed., 3 vols. (London, 1754); Philip Miller, *The Gardeners Dictionary: Containing the Best and Newest Methods of Cultivating and Improving the Kitchen, Fruit, Flower Garden, and Nursery. . . . ,* 8th ed., 2 vols. (London, 1768). Throughout this publication, the author cites the fourth edition of *The Gardeners Dictionary* (1754) except as indicated; Peggy Cornett, "In the Company of Gardeners: The Flower Diaries of Jefferson, Skipwith, and Faris," *Twinleaf Journal* 12 (January 2000): 9.

20 Philip Miller, *Figures of the Most Beautiful, Useful, and Uncommon Plants Described in the Gardeners Dictionary, Exhibited on Three Hundred Copper Plates. . . . ,* 2 vols. (London, 1760).

21 Carl Linnaeus, *Species Plantarum: A Facsimile of the First Edition, 1753,* with an introduction by W. T. Stearn, 2 vols. (London: Ray Society, 1957–1959); Wilfrid Blunt, *Linnaeus: The Compeat Naturalist* (London: Frances Lincoln, 2001), 222.

22 Flora Ann L. Bynum, "Old World Gardens in the New World: The Gardens of the Moravian Settlement of Bethabara in North Carolina, 1753–72," *Journal of Garden History* 16, no. 2 (1996): 77, 83.

23 Jefferson, *Garden Book* (see Introduction, n. 15).

24 Lady Jean Skipwith's List of Flowers, Skipwith Family Papers, 1760–1977, Mecklenburg County, Virginia, Manuscript and Rare Books Department, Earl Gregg Swem Library, College of William and Mary, Williamsburg, Virginia. Lady Skipwith's notes were published as "The Garden Notes of Lady Jean Skipwith" in three parts in *Garden Gossip: Recording the Activities of Gardening in the Mid-South* in the following issues: 10, no. 2 (February 1935): 9–10; 10, no. 4 (April 1935): 3–4; and 10, no. 6 (June 1935): 2–3.

25 McMahon, "Catalogue of Seeds" (see Introduction, n. 20).

26 Bernard McMahon, *The American Gardener's Calendar, 1806* (Philadelphia, 1806; repr., Charlottesville, VA: Thomas Jefferson Memorial Foundation, 1997), vii, 579ff.

27 "Southern Plant Lists" can be found on the Southern Garden History Society's Web site at http://www.southerngardenhistory.org/plantlists.html.

FLOWERS (pages 22–23)

Epigraph. John Evelyn, *Elysium Britannicum, or The Royal Gardens,* ed. John E. Ingram (Philadelphia: University of Pennsylvania Press, 2001), 401.

1   Theophrastus, *Enquiry into Plants*, 2:37, 49, 51, 53.

2   Meleager, *Garland,* in *The Greek Anthology and Other Ancient Epigrams: A Selection in Modern Verse Translations*, ed. Peter Jay (Middlesex, UK: Penguin Books, 1981), 375–76.

ADONIS (*Adonis aestivalis*) (pages 24–27)

1   McMahon, "Catalogue of Seeds," and McMahon, *American Gardener's Calendar*, third page of "Introduction to the Facsimile Edition," 607; David and James Sutherland, *Plants from the Past* (Harmondsworth, UK: Viking, 1987), 68.

2   Ippolito Pizzetti and Henry Cocker, *Flowers: A Guide for Your Garden; Being a Selective Anthology of Flowering Shrubs, Herbaceous Perennials, Bulbs, and Annuals, Familiar and Unfamiliar, Rare and Popular, with Historical, Mythological, and Cultural Particulars* (New York: Abrams, 1975), 1:27–28.

3   Royal Horticultural Society, *Dictionary of Gardening*, 1:48–49; Gerard, *Herbal*, 386; Miller, *Figures*, 1:10.

4   Pizzetti and Cocker, *Flowers*, 1:28.

BALSAM PEAR (*Momordica charantia*) and BALSAM APPLE (*Momordica balsamina*) (pages 28–31)

1   Fuchs, *Great Herbal*, 1:355; Besler, *Florilegium*, 477.

2   Deni Bown, *New Encyclopedia of Herbs and Their Uses*, rev. ed. (London: Dorling Kindersley, 2001), 279–80; Andrew Chevallier, *The*

Encyclopedia of Medicinal Plants (London: Dorling Kindersley, 1996), 234.

3 Skipwith, "Garden Notes," 10.

GLOBE CANDYTUFT (*Iberis umbellata*) (pages 32–35)

1 Royal Horticultural Society, *Dictionary of Gardening*, 2:1042; Marshal, *Florilegium*, 180; Gerard, *Herbal*, 265.

2 John Parkinson, *A Garden of Pleasant Flowers (Paradisi in Sole: Paradisus Terrestris)* (London, 1629; repr., New York: Dover, 1991), 390.

3 Rudy J. Favretti and Joy Putman Favretti, *Landscapes and Gardens for Historic Buildings: A Handbook for Reproducing and Creating Authentic Landscape Settings* (Nashville, TN: American Association for State and Local History, 1978), 125; *Boston Evening-Post*, March 31, 1760.

4 As quoted in Tomasi and Hirschauer, *Flowering of Florence*, 39; Marshal, *Florilegium*, 180.

CASTOR BEAN (*Ricinus communis*) (pages 36–39)

1 Theophrastus, *Enquiry into Plants*, 1:275.

2 Mrs. M[aud] Grieve, *A Modern Herbal: The Medicinal, Culinary, Cosmetic and Economic Properties, Cultivation and Folk-Lore of Herbs, Grasses, Fungi, Shrubs and Trees with All Their Modern Scientific Uses* (New York: Harcourt, Brace, 1931; repr., New York: Dover, 1971), 1:170; Dioscorides, *De materia medica*, 37–38.

3 Fuchs, *Great Herbal*, 1:402–3.

4 Gerard, *Herbal*, 496–97.

5 *The Diary of Colonel Landon Carter of Sabine Hall, 1752–1778*, ed. Jack P. Greene (Charlottesville: University Press of Virginia, 1965), 1:203.

6 Bown, *New Encyclopedia of Herbs*, 345.

7 Besler, *Florilegium*, 362, 363.

8 Jefferson, *Garden Book*, 447, 644.

CHINA ASTER (*Callistephus chinensis*) (pages 40–43)

1 *"Forget not Mee & My Garden . . .": Selected Letters, 1725–1768, of Peter Collinson, F.R.S.*, ed., Alan W. Armstrong (Philadelphia: American Philosophical Society, 2002), 29.

2 Alice M. Coats, *The Plant Hunters: Being a History of the Horticultural Pioneers, Their Quests and Their Discoveries; From the Renaissance to the Twentieth Century* (New York: McGraw-Hill, 1970), 90–91; Peggy Cornett Newcomb, *Popular Annuals of Eastern North America, 1865–1914* (Washington, DC: Dumbarton Oaks, 1985), 46; Horace Walpole, *The History of the Modern Taste in Gardening*, with an introduction by John Dixon Hunt (New York: Ursus, 1995), 27.

3 Swem, *Brothers of the Spade*, 36; Barbara Wells Sarudy, *Gardens and Gardening in the Chesapeake, 1700–1805* (Baltimore: The Johns Hopkins University Press, 1998), 163.

CRESTED COCKSCOMB (*Celosia argentea* var. *cristata*) (pages 44–47)

1 *Paxton's Botanical Dictionary Comprising the Names, History, and Culture of All Plants Known in Britain; With a Full Explanation of Technical Terms. New Edition Including All the New Plants Up to the Present Year*, rev. Samuel Hereman (London, 1868), 119.

2 Gerard, *Herbal*, 323.

3 Swem, *Brothers of the Spade*, 58; Favretti and Favretti, *Landscapes and Gardens*, 131; Jefferson, *Garden Book*, 4.

4 Pizzetti and Cocker, *Flowers*, 1:203.

CYPRESS VINE (*Ipomoea quamoclit*) (pages 48–51)

1 Monticello Museum Shop, the Thomas Jefferson Foundation, http://monticellostore.stores.yahoo.net/631020.html.

2 Gerard, *Herbal*, 1598.

3 Tomasi and Hirschauer, *Flowering of Florence*, 42; Miller, *Figures*, 2:143.

DEVIL'S CLAW (*Proboscidea louisianica*) (pages 52–55)

1 Richard J. Schmidt, ed., the Botanical Dermatology Database (BoDD), Cardiff University, http://bodd.cf.ac.uk/BotDermFolder/BotDermM/MART.html; L. H. Bailey Hortorium, *Hortus Third*, 912.

2 Miller, *Figures*, 2:191.

3 L. H. Bailey Hortorium, *Hortus Third*, 912.

4 McMahon, *American Gardener's Calendar*, 610.

FLAX (*Linum usitatissimum*) (pages 56–61)

1 Pizzetti and Cocker, *Flowers*, 2:776.

2 *The Greek Herbal of Dioscorides: Illustrated by a Byzantine A.D. 512; Englished by John Goodyer A.D. 1655; Edited and First Printed A.D. 1933*, ed. Robert T. Gunther (1934; repr., London: Hafner, 1968), 136. The author has chosen here to site a seventeenth-century translation of *De materia medica* rather than the modern translation by Osbaldeston and Wood for the flavor of its language.

3 Gerard, *Herbal*, 557.

4 American Heart Association, http://www.americanheart.org/presenterjhtml?identifier=4632; Chevallier, *Encyclopedia of Medicinal Plants*, 226–27.

5 Lawson, *New Voyage to Carolina*, 90, 120.

FLOSSFLOWER (*Ageratum houstonianum*) (pages 62–65)

1 Miller, *Gardeners Dictionary*, 8th ed. (1768), 1:E1v.

2 Royal Horticultural Society, *Dictionary of Gardening*, 1:66; Miller, *Gardeners Dictionary*, 8th ed. (1768), 1:E1v.

3 Denise Wiles Adams, *Restoring American Gardens: An Encyclopedia of Heirloom Ornamental Plants, 1640–1940* (Portland, OR: Timber, 2004), 212.

4 USDA Plants Database, "Ageratum houstonianum" (see Introduction, n. 21).

FOUR-O'CLOCK (*Mirabilis jalapa*) (pages 66–71)

1 Gerard, *Herbal*, 343, 344.

2 Besler, *Florilegium*, 490; Marshal, *Florilegium*, 332, 334.

3 Jefferson, *Garden Book*, 6.

4 Favretti and Favretti, *Landscapes and Gardens*, 125.

JOB'S TEARS (*Coix lacryma-jobi*) (pages 72–75)

1 James A. Duke, "*Coix lacryma-jobi* L.," Handbook of Energy Crops (Center for New Crops and Plants Products, Purdue University, 1983), http://www.hort.purdue.edu/newcrop/duke_energy/Coix_lacryma-jobi.html.

2 The Vienna Codex, in progress when the author died in 1566, is an unpublished work now in the Austrian National Library in Vienna. Extensive commentary about the work can be found in volume one of Fuchs, *Great Herbal*, ed. Meyer, Trueblood, and Heller; ibid., 172; Gerard, *Herbal*, 88.

3 Miller, *Gardeners Dictionary*, 354 (see A Note on the Sources, n. 19).

4 Clayton Herbarium database, BM000042711 (see A Note on the Sources, n. 18); Clayton and Gronovius, *Flora Virginica*, 143–44.

LARKSPUR (*Consolida orientalis*) (pages 76–81)

1 Theophrastus, *Enquiry into Plants*, 1:51.

2 L. H. Bailey Hortorium, *Hortus Third*, 308; Fuchs, *Great Herbal*, 1:304, plate 35; Besler, *Florilegium*, 272–73.

3 Gerard, *Herbal*, 1082–83.

4 Marshal, *Florilegium*, 220–23, 226–27, 236–39, 262–63; Evelyn, *Elysium Britannicum*, 277.

5 *Boston Evening-Post*, March 31, 1760; Jefferson, *Garden Book*, 6.

LOVE-IN-A-MIST (*Nigella damascena*) (pages 82–87)

1 Lys de Bray, *Manual of Old-Fashioned Flowers* (Sparkford, UK: Oxford Illustrated Press, 1984), 141; Gerard, *Herbal*, 1085; L. H. Bailey Hortorium, *Hortus Third*, 767; Miller, *Figures*, 2:125.

2 Chevallier, *Encyclopedia of Medicinal Plants*, 237; Bown, *New Encyclopedia of Herbs*, 237, 289.

3 Christopher Lloyd and Richard Bird, *The Cottage Garden* (New York: Prentice Hall, 1990), 52.

4 *Boston Evening-Post*, March 31, 1760.

LOVE-LIES-BLEEDING (*Amaranthus caudatus*) (pages 88–91)

1 Royal Horticultural Society, *Dictionary of Gardening*, 1:95; Gerard, *Herbal*, 322–23; John Rea, *Flora: Seu, de Florum Cultura. Or, a Complete Florilege, Furnished with All Requisites Belonging to a Florist* (London, 1665), 185.

2 Evelyn, *Elysium Britannicum*, 354; J[ohn]Mortimer, *The Whole Art of Husbandry: Or, the Way of Managing and Improving of Land. . . .*, 5th ed. (London, 1721), 2:208; Miller, *Figures*, 1:15.

3 Miller, *Figures*, 1:15; Daniel K. Early, "Amaranth Production in Mexico and Peru," in *Advances in New Crops: Proceedings of the First National Symposium New Crops: Research, Development, Economics, Indianapolis, Indiana, October 23–26,*

1988, ed. Jules Janick and James E. Simon (Portland, OR: Timber, 1990), 140–42; V. Apaza-Gutierrez, A. Romero-Saravia, F. R. Guillén-Portal, and D. D. Baltensperger, "Response of Grain Amaranth Production to Density and Fertilization in Tarija, Bolivia," in *Trends in New Crops and New Uses,* ed. Jules Janick and Anna Whipkey (Alexandria, VA: ASHS Press, 2002), 107–9.

4 Lawson, *New Voyage to Carolina,* 84; *Boston Evening-Post,* March 31, 1760; Jefferson, *Garden Book,* 5.

YELLOW LUPINE (*Lupinus luteus*) (pages 92–95)

1 Skipwith, "Garden Notes," 4; Receipt of Minton Collins, March 1, 1793, Skipwith Family Papers, 1760–1977, Mecklenburg County, Virginia, Manuscript and Rare Books Department, Earl Gregg Swem Library, College of William and Mary, Williamsburg, Virginia.

2 Pizzetti and Cocker, *Flowers,* 2:807.

3 Theophrastus, *Enquiry into Plants,* 1:29, 55; Publius Virgilius Maro [Virgil], *The Georgics,* trans. John Dryden (New York: Heritage, 1953), 10–11.

4 Virgil, *Georgics,* 11.

5 Dioscorides, *De materia medica,* 257; Fuchs, *Great Herbal,* 1:393.

6 Pizzetti and Cocker, *Flowers,* 2:808.

7 Gerard, *Herbal,* 1217–18; William Hanbury, *A Complete Body of Planting and Gardening. Containing the Natural History, Culture, and Management of Deciduous and Evergreen Forest-Trees. . . .* (London, 1771), 2:202.

STRIPED FRENCH MARIGOLD (*Tagetes patula* 'Striped') (pages 96–99)

1 Fuchs, *Great Herbal,* 1:167; Gerard, *Herbal,* 750.

2 The Vienna Codex, in progress when the author died in 1566, is an unpublished work now in the Austrian National Library in Vienna. Extensive commentary about the work can be found in volume one of Fuchs, *Great Herbal,* ed. Meyer, Trueblood, and Heller; ibid., 167, plates 9, 11.

3 Parkinson, *Garden of Pleasant Flowers,* 303.

4 [John Hill], *Eden: Or, A Compleat Body of Gardening. Containing Plain and Familiar Directions for Raising the Several Useful Products of a Garden, Fruits, Roots, and Herbage. . . .* (London, 1757), 160; Favretti and Favretti, *Landscapes and Gardens,* 126; Jefferson, *Garden Book,* 363; Receipt of Minton Collins, Skipwith Family Papers.

NASTURTIUM (*Tropaeolum majus*) (pages 100–103)

1 Gerard, *Herbal,* 251–52; Newcomb, *Popular Annuals,* 37.

2 Newcomb, *Popular Annuals,* 37; Gerard, *Herbal,* 251–52.

3 [Robert] Furber, *The Flower-Garden Display'd, In above Four Hundred Curious Representations of the Most Beautiful Flowers; Regularly Dispos'd in the Respective Months of Their Blossom, Curiously Engrav'd on Copper-Plates from the Designs of Mr. Furber and Others, and Coloured to the Life. . . .* (London, 1732), 58.

4 Bynum, "Old World Gardens," 77, 83; [John Randolph], *A Treatise on Gardening* (Richmond, VA, 1793; repr., Williamsburg, VA: The Printing Office, Colonial Williamsburg Foundation, 1999), 26.

5 Jefferson, *Garden Book,* 61.

SCARLET PENTAPETES (*Pentapetes phoenicia*) (pages 104–7)

1 Linnaeus, *Species Plantarum,* 2:698; Miller, *Figures,* 2:133.

2 James L. Reveal, Cornell University, Alphabetical Listing by Genera of Validly Published Supragenetic Names, Plant Biology, http://www.plantsystematics.org/reveal/pbio/fam/inspv7.html; Tropicos.org, Missouri Botanical Garden, 14 May 2008, http://www.tropicos.org/Name/30400641.

3 Jefferson, *Garden Book,* 449; McMahon, *American Gardener's Calendar,* 611.

4 Miller, *Figures,* 2:133.

CORN POPPY (*Papaver rhoeas*) (pages 108–13)

1 Gerard, *Herbal,* 370; *Proserpina,* in *The Complete Works of John Ruskin* (New York: Thomas Y. Crowell, [1905?]), 16:54.

2 Theophrastus, *Enquiry into Plants,* 1:281.

3 Fuchs, *Great Herbal,* 1:459; Gerard, *Herbal,* 372.

4 Marshal, *Florilegium,* facing 300; Thomas Fairchild, *The City Gardener. Containing the Most Experienced Method of Cultivating and Ordering Such Ever-greens, Fruit-Trees, Flowering Shrubs, Flowers, Exotick Plants, &c. As Will Be Ornamental, and Thrive Best in the London Gardens* (London, 1722), 30–31.

5 "Shirley Poppies," *The Garden: An Illustrated Weekly Journal of Horticulture in All Its Branches* 64 (Christmas 1903): 199.

6 Jefferson, *Garden Book,* 6, 24; Bynum, "Old World Gardens," 83.

MEXICAN POPPY (*Argemone mexicana*) (pages 114–17)

1 Gerard, *Herbal,* 372.

2 Royal Horticultural Society, *Dictionary of Gardening,* 1:172; Gerard, *Herbal,* 372.

3 Miller, *Figures,* 1:34.

4 Jefferson, *Garden Book,* 6.

YELLOW HORNED POPPY (*Glaucium flavum*) (pages 118–21)

1 L. H. Bailey Hortorium, *Hortus Third,* 260, 512; Theophrastus, *Enquiry into Plants,* 1:279, 281, 2:137.

2 Theophrastus, *Enquiry into Plants,* 1:281.

3 Fuchs, *Great Herbal,* 1:460; Gerard, *Herbal,* 366.

4 Clayton Herbarium database, BM000042230 (see A Note on the Sources, n. 18); Clayton and Gronovius, *Flora Virginica,* 79–80; Monticello Museum Shop, the Thomas Jefferson Foundation, http://monticellostore.stores.yahoo.net/600019.html; Royal Horticultural Society, *Dictionary of Gardening,* 2:897; Jefferson, *Garden Book,* 335.

HORMIUM SAGE (*Salvia viridis*) (pages 122–25)

1 Marshal, *Florilegium,* 330; Bynum, "Old World Gardens," 83.

2 Marshal, *Florilegium,* 330; Gerard, *Herbal,* 770–71.

3 Lloyd and Bird, *Cottage Garden,* 55–56.

SCABIOUS (*Scabiosa atropurpurea*) (pages 126–29)

1 Besler, *Florilegium,* 368; De Bray, *Manual,* 167; Marshal, *Florilegium,* 206.

2 Marshal, *Florilegium,* 84, 103, 107.

3 William Coles, *Adam in Eden: Or, Natures Paradise. The History of Plants, Fruits, Herbs and Flowers. . . .* (London, 1657), 111 (chapter 85).

4 David Stuart, *Gardening with Antique Plants* (London: Conran Octopus, 1997), 73; Lloyd and Bird, *Cottage Garden,* 148–49.

5 *Boston Evening-Post,* March 31, 1760; Skipwith "Garden Notes," 10; Receipt of Minton Collins, Skipwith Family Papers.

SUNFLOWER (*Helianthus annuus* 'Italian White') (pages 130–33)

1 Royal Horticultural Society, *Dictionary of Gardening,* 2:972; Fuchs, *Great Herbal,* 1:182; Gerard, *Herbal,* 751; Rea, *Flora,* 191; George London and Henry Wise, *The Retir'd Gardner: The Second Volume; Containing the Manner of Planting and Cultivating All Sorts of Flowers, Plants, Shrubs, and Under-Shrubs, Necessary for the Adorning of Gardens: In Which Is Explained. . . .* (London, 1706), 566.

2 Besler, *Florilegium,* 304.

3 Ibid., 304, 318.

4 Clayton Herbarium database, BM000032582, BM000038159, and Clayton number 136 (no bar code available) (see A Note on the Sources, n. 18); Clayton and Gronovius, *Flora Virginica,* 128–29; Jefferson, *Garden Book,* 24.

5 Thomas Harriot, *A Briefe and True Report of the New Found Land of Virginia,* with a new introduction by Paul Hulton (Frankfurt, 1590; repr., New York: Dover, 1972), 14.

6 John White drawings/Theodor De Bry engravings, Virtual Jamestown, Virginia Center for Digital History, University of Virginia, http://www.virtualjamestown.org/images/white_debry_html/introduction.html and Paul Hulton, *America 1585: The Complete Drawings of John White* (Chapel Hill: University of North Carolina Press, 1984), 31, 66, 126, 190; Harriot, *Briefe and True Report,* 68–69.

7 Josselyn, *New-Englands Rarities,* 56; Gerard, *Herbal,* 751.

8 Lawson, *New Voyage to Carolina,* 96.

SMALL-FLOWERED ZINNIA (*Zinnia pauciflora*) (pages 134–35)

1 Royal Horticultural Society, *Dictionary of Gardening*, 4:2311.

2 McMahon, *American Gardener's Calendar*, 609; Arthur Shurcliff, memo, May 21, 1936, Colonial Williamsburg Foundation, Williamsburg, VA.

MALVA (*Malva sylvestris* 'Brave Heart') (pages 136–41)

1 Backyardgardener, Federal Way, WA, http://www.backyardgardener.com/seeds/product/1224/1.html.

2 Gerard, *Herbal*, 930.

3 Hesiod, *Works and Days and Theogeny*, trans. Stanley Lombardo, with an introduction and notes by Robert Lamberton (Indianapolis, IN: Hackett, 1993), 24; Theophrastus, *Enquiry into Plants*, 2:103, 105; Dioscorides, *De materia medica*, 156–57; Fuchs, *Great Herbal*, 1:457.

4 Gerard, *Herbal*, 928–35.

5 Josselyn, *New-Englands Rarities*, 85, 87–88.

6 Lawson, *New Voyage to Carolina*, 83; *Sturtevant's Edible Plants of the World*, ed. U. P. Hedrick (Albany, NY: J. B. Lyon, 1919; repr., New York: Dover, 1972), 351.

VIPER'S BUGLOSS (*Echium vulgare*) (pages 142–45)

1 Theophrastus, *Enquiry into Plants*, 2:117.

2 Fuchs, *Great Herbal*, 1:425; Gerard, *Herbal*, 803.

3 Miller, *Gardeners Dictionary*, 458 (see A Note on the Sources, n. 19); De Bray, *Manual*, 77.

4 Clayton Herbarium database, BM000051775 (see A Note on the Sources, n. 18); Clayton and Gronovius, *Flora Virginica*, 26; Linnaeus, *Species Plantarum*, 1:139; Lawson, *New Voyage to Carolina*, 83.

5 Fuchs, *Great Herbal*, 1:17; Gerard, *Herbal*, 801.

6 Marshal, *Florilegium*, 304.

ALL-HEAL (*Prunella grandiflora* 'Pagoda') (pages 146–49)

1 Paxton, *Botanical Dictionary*, 464, and Royal Horticultural Society, *Dictionary of Gardening*, 3:1692; John H. Harvey, *The Availability of Hardy Plants of the Late Eighteenth Century* (n.p.: Garden History Society, 1988), 69; William Curtis, *The Botanical Magazine; or, Flower-Garden Displayed: In Which the Most Ornamental Foreign Plants, Cultivated in the Open Ground, the Green-House, and the Stove, Are Accurately Represented in Their Natural Colours. . . .* (London, 1796), 10:plate 337; William Robinson, *The English Flower Garden* (New York: Amaryllis, 1984), 591.

2 Grieve, *Modern Herbal*, 2:731; Gerard, *Herbal*, 633.

3 Fuchs, *Great Herbal*, 1:495.

4 Miller, *Figures*, 1:47; Chevallier, *Encyclopedia of Medicinal Plants*, 122.

5 USDA Plants Database, "Prunella vulgaris" (see Introduction, n. 21); Richard Mabey, *The Frampton Flora* (London: Century, 1985), 41; F. Schuyler Mathews, *Field Book of American Wild Flowers: Being a Short Description of Their Character and Habits, a Concise Definition of Their Colors, and Incidental References to the Insects Which Assist in Their Fertilization* (New York: Knickerbocker, 1902; repr., New York: Sterling, 2001), 406; Nancy Kober, *With Paintbrush & Shovel: Preserving Virginia's Wildflowers* (Charlottesville: University Press of Virginia, 2000), 7, 151.

6 Clayton Herbarium database, BM000051131 (see A Note on the Sources, n. 18); Clayton and Gronovius, *Flora Virginica*, 91.

ANISE HYSSOP (*Agastache foeniculum*) (pages 150–53)

1 L. H. Bailey Hortorium, *Hortus Third*, 35.

2 USDA Plants Database, "Agastache foeniculum" (see Introduction, n. 21).

3 Lesley Bremness, *Herbs* (New York: Dorling Kindersley, 1994), 138; Bown, *New Encyclopedia of Herbs*, 105; Royal Horticultural Society, *Dictionary of Gardening*, 1:63.

4 Clayton Herbarium database, BM000038851, BM000098022 (see A Note on the Sources, n. 18); Clayton and Gronovius, *Flora Virginica*, 88.

5 Bown, *New Encyclopedia of Herbs*, 105.

BLUE PIMPERNEL (*Anagallis monelli*) (pages 154–57)

1 L. H. Bailey Hortorium, *Hortus Third*, 72; Royal Horticultural Society, *Dictionary of Gardening*, 1:104.

2 Marshal, *Florilegium*, 194, 216, 318.

3 Theophrastus, *Enquiry into Plants*, 2:103, 105.

4 Dioscorides, *De materia medica*, 350.

5 Ibid., 350, 353.

6 Miller, *Gardeners Dictionary*, 75 (see A Note on the Sources, n. 19); Favretti and Favretti, *Landscapes and Gardens*, 137; Arthur A. Shurcliff, "Catalog of Herbs and Flowers" (report, Landscape and Facilities Services Department, Colonial Williamsburg Foundation, Williamsburg, VA, n.d.), s.v. "scarlet pimpernel."

BONESET (*Eupatorium perfoliatum*) (pages 158–61)

1 Russell Page, *The Education of a Gardener* (New York: Random House, 1983), 35.

2 Grieve, *Modern Herbal*, 2:118, 119; Charlotte Erichsen-Brown, *Medicinal and Other Uses of North American Plants: A Historical Survey with Special Reference to the Eastern Indian Tribes* (Aurora, Ontario, CAN: Breezy Creeks, 1979; repr., New York: Dover, 1989), 262, 263; Chevallier, *Encyclopedia of Medicinal Plants*, 206.

3 Linnaeus, *Species Plantarum*, 2:838–39; Erichsen-Brown, *Medicinal and Other Uses*, 262.

CARDOON (*Cynara cardunculus*) (pages 162–65)

1 For example, see L. H. Bailey Hortorium, *Hortus Third*, 355.

2 Theophrastus, *Enquiry into Plants*, 2:21, 31.

3 Dioscorides, *De materia medica*, 385.

4 Gerard, *Herbal*, 1152–53.

5 Randolph, *Treatise*, 3–4.

6 Ibid., 4–5.

7 Receipt of Minton Collins, Skipwith Family Papers.

8 Gerard, *Herbal*, 1154.

9 Robinson, *English Flower Garden*, 386.

CINNAMON VINE (*Apios americana*) (pages 166–69)

1 Ed Klekowski, Groundnut *Apios americana* Medic, the Connecticut River Web site, Department of Biology and the College of Natural Sciences and Mathematics, University of Massachusetts Amherst, 1997, http://www.bio.umass.edu/biology/conn.river/groundnt.html.

2 Lawson, *New Voyage to Carolina*, 182; Clayton and Gronovius, *Flora Virginica*, 107; Linnaeus, *Species Plantarum*, 2:753.

3 Harriot, *Briefe and True Report*, 16.

4 Josselyn, *New-Englands Rarities*, 47.

5 Sturtevant, *Edible Plants*, 54–55.

6 Furber, *The Flower-Garden Display'd*, 73.

7 Adams, *Restoring American Gardens*, 137.

8 Robinson, *English Flower Garden*, 312.

COLUMBINE (*Aquilegia canadensis*) (pages 170–75)

1 Pizzetti and Cocker, *Flowers*, 1:78; L. H. Bailey Hortorium, *Hortus Third*, 93.

2 Leith-Ross, *The John Tradescants*, 189; Marshal, *Florilegium*, 156; as cited in Coats, *Flowers and Their Histories*, 27; Besler, *Florilegium*, 235; Bynum, "Old World Gardens," 83.

3 As cited in Ewan, *John Banister*, 172; John Parkinson, *Theatrum Botanicum. The Theater of Plantes. Or, an Universall and Compleate Herball* (London, 1640), 1367; Clayton Herbarium database, BM000040271 (see A Note on the Sources, n. 18); Clayton and Gronovius, *Flora Virginica*, 82; Linnaeus, *Species Plantarum*, 1:533; Jefferson, *Garden Book*, 162.

ORANGE CONEFLOWER (*Rudbeckia fulgida* 'Goldsturm') (pages 176–79)

1 L. H. Bailey Hortorium, *Hortus Third*, 986; Royal Horticultural Society, *Dictionary of Gardening*, 4:1837; Clayton Herbarium database, BM000042612 (see A Note on the Sources, n. 18); Clayton and Gronovius, *Flora Virginica*, 131; Linnaeus, *Species Plantarum*, 2:907.

PURPLE CONEFLOWER (*Echinacea purpurea*) (pages 180–83)

1 Ewan, *John Banister*, 189; Clayton Herbarium database, BM000051216 (see A Note on the Sources, n. 18); Clayton and Gronovius, *Flora Virginica*, 130; Linnaeus, *Species Plantarum*, 2:907.

2 Chevallier, *Encyclopedia of Medicinal Plants*, 90; Bown, *New Encyclopedia of Herbs*, 199.

INDIAN-SHOT (*Canna indica*) (pages 184–87)

1 Swem, *Brothers of the Spade*, 31.

2 Thomas Walter, *Flora Caroliniana* (London, 1788), 59; L. H. Bailey Hortorium, *Hortus Third*, 217.

3 Fuchs, *Great Herbal*, 1:176; Paxton, *Botanical Dictionary*, 108; Royal Horticultural Society, *Dictionary of Gardening*, 1:384; W. P. Armstrong,

Canna indica: Indian shot, "Seeds Shot from Guns?" Wayne's Word Noteworthy Plant for June 1998, Palomar College Arboretum, http://waynesword.palomar.edu/pljune98.htm.

4 Armstrong, http://waynesword.palomar.edu/pljune98.htm.

MALTESE CROSS (*Lychnis chalcedonica*) (pages 188–91)

1 Parkinson, *Garden of Pleasant Flowers*, 253.

2 Paxton, *Botanical Dictionary*, 346; De Bray, *Manual*, 127, and L. H. Bailey Hortorium, *Hortus Third*, 688.

3 Fuchs, *Great Herbal*, 1:188; Gerard, *Herbal*, 466, 467.

4 Marshal, *Florilegium*, 238, 240; Evelyn, *Elysium Britannicum*, 338, 370.

5 Favretti and Favretti, *Landscapes and Gardens*, 125; Adams, *Restoring American Gardens*, 193; McMahon, "Catalogue of Seeds," and McMahon, *American Gardener's Calendar*, third page of "Introduction to the Facsimile Edition"; Jefferson, *Garden Book*, 334–35.

COMMON MILKWEED (*Asclepias syriaca*) (pages 192–95)

1 Lesley Adkins and Roy A. Adkins, *Dictionary of Roman Religion* (New York: Facts on File, 1996), 21.

2 David J. White, "The Milkweeds of Canada (Asclepias spp.): Status, Distribution, and Potential Impact from Noxious Weed Legislation," report prepared for the Canadian Wildlife Service, Ottawa, March 31, 1996; repr., Monarch Watch Reading Room, Kansas Biological Survey, University of Kansas, http://www.monarchwatch.org/read/articles/canweed2.htm.

3 Royal Horticultural Society, *Dictionary of Gardening*, 1:191; Clayton Herbarium database, BM000051181 (see A Note on the Sources, n. 18); Clayton and Gronovius, *Flora Virginica*, 37; Linnaeus, *Species Plantarum*, 1:214.

4 Sturtevant, *Edible Plants*, 71.

PILEWORT (*Ranunculus ficaria*) (pages 196–99)

1 Dioscorides, *De materia medica*, 227.

2 Fuchs, *Great Herbal*, 1:581; Pizzetti and Cocker, *Flowers*, 2:1085.

3 Fuchs, *Great Herbal*, 1:581; Gerard, *Herbal*, 816; Bown, *New Encyclopedia of Herbs*, 340.

4 Swem, *Brothers of the Spade*, 48.

5 Ibid.; USDA Plants Database, "Ranunculus ficaria" (see Introduction, n. 21).

RAGGED ROBIN (*Lychnis flos-cuculi*) (pages 200–203)

1 Jessica Kerr, *Shakespeare's Flowers* (New York: Thomas Y. Crowell, 1969), 13, 15, 18; *Hamlet*, with an introduction and annotations by Burton Raffel (New Haven: Yale University Press, 2003), act 4, scene 7, lines 167–68.

2 Gerard, *Herbal*, 599.

3 Pizzetti and Cocker, *Flowers*, 2:816; Gerard, *Herbal*, 600.

4 Gerard, *Herbal*, 599; Mabey, *Frampton Flora*, 123.

5 USDA Plants Database, "Lychnis flos-cuculi" (see Introduction, n. 21); Mathews, *Field Book of Wild Flowers*, 122.

RUE ANEMONE (*Thalictrum thalictroides*) (pages 204–7)

1 Clayton and Gronovius, *Flora Virginica*, 85; Linnaeus, *Species Plantarum*, 1:542; USDA Plants Database, "Thalictrum thalictroides" (see Introduction, n. 21).

2 PlantFinder, Kemper Center for Home Gardening, Missouri Botanical Garden, 2001–2008, www.mobot.org/gardeninghelp/plantfinder/Plant.asp?code=J350.

SPRING BEAUTY (*Claytonia virginica*) (pages 208–11)

1 Jefferson, *Notes on Virginia*, 107.

2 Edmund Berkeley and Dorothy Smith Berkeley, *John Clayton: Pioneer of American Botany* (Chapel Hill: University of North Carolina, 1963), 105, 179.

3 Ibid., 7–13.

4 Ibid., 16, 17, 22–23, 24; Harriet Frye, *The Great Forest: John Clayton and Flora; A Narrative Biography of America's First Botanist* (Hampton, VA: Dragon Run Books, 1990), 14.

5 Berkeley and Berkeley, *John Clayton*, 10, 14, 15.

6 Ibid., 27, 72.

7 Kober, *With Paintbrush & Shovel*, 266; Wilbur H. Duncan and Marion B. Duncan, *Wildflowers of the Eastern United States* (Athens: University of Georgia Press, 1999), 7–8.

8 Ewan, *John Banister*, 222; Clayton Herbarium database, BM000540495 (see A Note on the Sources, n. 18); Clayton and Gronovius, *Flora Virginica*, 35.

9 Sturtevant, *Edible Plants*, 177.

BLUE VERVAIN (*Verbena hastata*) (pages 212–15)

1 Mathews, *Field Book of Wild Flowers*, 386.

2 Dioscorides, *De materia medica*, 607.

3 Gerard, *Herbal*, 717; Miller, *Gardeners Dictionary*, 1439 (see A Note on the Sources, n. 19).

4 Grieve, *Modern Herbal*, 2:831–32; Bown, *New Encyclopedia of Herbs*, 401–2.

5 Vergil, *The Aeneid*, trans. Patric Dickinson (New York: New American Library, 1961), 276; Allen Mandelbaum, *The Aeneid of Virgil: A Verse Translation* (New York: Bantam, 1972), 309; Rolfe Humphries, *The Aeneid of Virgil: A Verse Translation* (New York: Charles Scribner's Sons, 1951), 340; Coles, *Adam in Eden*, 36; Gerard, *Herbal*, 718; Grieve, *Modern Herbal*, 2:831.

WALLFLOWER (*Erysimum cheiri*) (pages 216–19)

1 Theophrastus, *Enquiry into Plants*, 2:51; De Bray, *Manual*, 50.

2 Pizzetti and Cocker, *Flowers*, 1:221–22; Fuchs, *Great Herbal*, 1:440.

3 Gerard, *Herbal*, 457.

4 Robinson, *English Flower Garden*, 352.

5 Lloyd and Bird, *Cottage Garden*, 52; Pizzetti and Cocker, *Flowers*, 1:222.

6 Favretti and Favretti, *Landscapes and Gardens*, 124; Skipwith, "Garden Notes," 10; Receipt of Minton Collins, Skipwith Family Papers; McMahon, "Catalogue of Seeds."

HERBS (pages 220–21)

Epigraph. Evelyn, *Elysium Britannicum*, 403.

1 Theophrastus, *Enquiry into Plants*, 2:251.

2 Ibid., 51.

3 Coles, *Art of Simpling*, 12; as quoted in Darrett B. and Anita H. Rutman, *A Place in Time: Middlesex County, Virginia, 1650–1750* (New York: Norton, 1984), 65.

4 Coles, *Art of Simpling*, 24, 25.

5 Ibid., 25.

6 Ibid., 58–60.

7 Deborah Donovan, "Duchess Recalls Transformation of England's Alnwick Garden," *Chicago Daily Herald*, February 2, 2008.

BLESSED THISTLE (*Cnicus benedictus*) (pages 222–25)

1 Theophrastus, *Enquiry into Plants*, 2:25, 27; Dioscorides, *De materia medica*, 493.

2 Fuchs, *Great Herbal*, 1:334.

3 Gerard, *Herbal*, 1171, 1172; Grieve, *Modern Herbal*, 2:795.

4 Miller, *Figures*, 2:165–66.

5 Lawson, *New Voyage to Carolina*, 83–84; Bynum, "Old World Gardens," 83.

6 Grieve, *Modern Herbal*, 2:795, 796.

BORAGE (*Borago officinalis*) (pages 226–29)

1 Gerard, *Herbal*, 796.

2 Dioscorides, *De materia medica*, 680.

3 Gerard, *Herbal*, 797–98.

4 Bown, *New Encyclopedia of Herbs*, 145.

5 Lawson, *New Voyage to Carolina*, 83; Bynum, "Old World Gardens," 83.

CALENDULA (*Calendula officinalis*) (pages 230–33)

1 Fuchs, *Great Herbal*, 1:415, 416.

2 "Christ's Hospital Five-and-Thirty Years Ago," in *The Complete Works and Letters of Charles Lamb*, ed. Bennett A. Cerf and Donald S. Klopfer (New York: Modern Library, 1935), 13.

3 Chevallier, *Encyclopedia of Medicinal Plants*, 69; L'Occitane, http://usa.loccitane.com/FO/Catalog/Product.aspx?prod=15MA075O7&cat=Search.

4 Royal Horticultural Society, *Dictionary of Gardening*, 1:357; Gerard, *Herbal*, 738; Marshal, *Florilegium*, facing 146, facing 134.

5 Besler, *Florilegium*, 304.

6 Jefferson, *Garden Book*, 4.

7 Lloyd and Bird, *Cottage Garden*, 23.

DARK-LEAVED ORACH (*Atriplex hortensis* 'Cupreata') (pages 234–37)

1 Elizabeth Waggener to Lawrence Griffith, May 21, 1992, in the author's possession.

2 Theophrastus, *Enquiry into Plants*, 2:61; Dioscorides, *De materia medica*, 269–70;

Gerard, *Herbal*, 327.

3 Gerard, *Herbal*, 326, 327.

4 Miller, *Gardeners Dictionary*, 156, 157 (see A Note on the Sources, n. 19).

5 Harriot, *Briefe and True Report*, 14; Josselyn, *New-Englands Rarities*, 85; Lawson, *New Voyage to Carolina*, 83.

ST. MARY'S THISTLE (*Silybum marianum*) (pages 238–41)

1 Gerard, *Herbal*, 1149–50.

2 Bown, *New Encyclopedia of Herbs*, 368.

3 Chevallier, *Encyclopedia of Medicinal Plants*, 71; Bown, *New Encyclopedia of Herbs*, 368.

4 Dioscorides, *De materia medica*, 719; Grieve, *Modern Herbal*, 2:797; Chevallier, *Encyclopedia of Medicinal Plants*, 71; Gerard, *Herbal*, 1150.

5 Bynum, "Old World Gardens," 83.

STRAWBERRY BLITE (*Chenopodium foliosum* 'Strawberry Sticks') (pages 242–45)

1 Gerard, *Herbal*, 325, 326.

2 Marshal, *Florilegium*, 232; Robinson, *English Flower Garden*, 353.

3 Gerard, *Herbal*, 329.

4 Ewan, *John Banister*, 176; Lawson, *New Voyage to Carolina*, 84; Bown, *New Encyclopedia of Herbs*, 166.

MOTH MULLEIN (*Verbascum blattaria*) (pages 246–49)

1 Miller, *Figures*, 1:45.

2 Ibid.

3 Ibid.

4 Fuchs, *Great Herbal*, 1:353; Gerard, *Herbal*, 778; Charles S. Raddin, "The Mullen," *Birds and Nature* 10, no. 1 (June 1901), http://www.birdnature.com/jun1901/mullen.html.

5 Robinson, *English Flower Garden*, 689; Pizzetti and Cocker, *Flowers*, 2:1340.

6 USDA Plants Database, "Verbascum blattaria" (see Introduction, n. 21); Clayton and Gronovius, *Flora Virginica*, 31; Lawson, *New Voyage to Carolina*, 83–84; Gerard, *Herbal*, 774; Bown, *New Encyclopedia of Herbs*, 401.

ELECAMPANE (*Inula helenium*) (pages 250–53)

1 Theophrastus, *Enquiry into Plants*, 2:269; Dioscorides, *De materia medica*, 30, 33.

2 Arthur O. Tucker and Thomas DeBaggio, *The Big Book of Herbs: A Comprehensive Illustrated Reference to Herbs of Flavor and Fragrance* (Loveland, CO: Interweave, 2000), 302.

3 Fuchs, *Great Herbal*, 1:373.

4 Josselyn, *New-Englands Rarities*, 90; Lawson, *New Voyage to Carolina*, 83–84.

MOTHERWORT (*Leonurus cardiaca*) (pages 254–57)

1 Bown, *New Encyclopedia of Herbs*, 258; Chevallier, *Encyclopedia of Medicinal Plants*, 225.

2 Fuchs, *Great Herbal*, 1:420; Grieve, *Modern Herbal*, 2:555; [Floridus Macer], *Macers Herbal Practysyd by Doctor Lynacro, Translated Out of Laten, into Englysshe. . . .* ([London, ca. 1552]), "Motherworte"; Nicholas Culpeper, *Culpeper's Complete Herbal and English Physician, Enlarged* (London, 1814; Glenwood, IL: Meyerbooks, 1990), 121; Gerard, *Herbal*, 705.

3 Hugh T. Lefler, "Promotional Literature of the Southern Colonies," *Journal of Southern History* 33, no. 1 (February 1967): 19–20; *Neu-gefundenes Eden* (Bern, Switzerland, 1737) was translated back into English and published, in 1940, as *William Byrd's Natural History of Virginia, or The Newly Discovered Eden* by Richmond Croom Beatty and William J. Mulloy (Richmond, VA: Dietz). Byrd, however, never wrote a line of it; Miller, *Figures*, 1:54.

4 USDA Plants Database, "Leonurus cardiaca" (see Introduction, n. 21); Michael Pollan, *The Botany of Desire: A Plant's-Eye View of the World* (New York: Random House, 2001), 32.

5 Miller, *Figures*, 1:54.

PASSIONFLOWER (*Passiflora incarnata*) (pages 258–61)

1 Strachey, "History of Travel," 678 (see Introduction, n. 2).

2 Ewan, *John Banister*, 183; Lawson, *New Voyage to Carolina*, 102; Clayton Herbarium database, BM000038183 (see A Note on the Sources, n. 18); Clayton and Gronovius, *Flora Virginica*, 140.

3 Pizzetti and Cocker, *Flowers*, 2:953.

4 Ibid.

5 Parkinson, *Garden of Pleasant Flowers*, 394; Marshal, *Florilegium*, 234.

6 Chevallier, *Encyclopedia of Medicinal Plants*, 117; William H. Banks Jr., *Plants of the Cherokee: Medicinal, Edible, and Useful Plants of the Eastern Cherokee Indians* (Gatlinburg, TN: Great Smoky Mountains Association, 2004), 79; J. T. Garrett, *The Cherokee Herbal: Native Plant Medicine from the Four Directions* (Rochester, VT: Bear, 2003), 233.

7 USDA Plants Database, "Passiflora incarnata" (see Introduction, n. 21).

PENNYROYAL (*Mentha pulegium*) (pages 262–63)

1 Dioscorides, *De materia medica*, 406; Bown, *New Encyclopedia of Herbs*, 277; Chevallier, *Encyclopedia of Medicinal Plants*, 233.

2 Theophrastus, *Enquiry into Plants*, 2:295, 297; Chevallier, *Encyclopedia of Medicinal Plants*, 233; Gerard, *Herbal*, 672.

3 Josselyn, *New-Englands Rarities*, 41, 44, 87, 89; Grieve, *Modern Herbal*, 2:625; *Every Man His Own Doctor: or, The Poor Planter's Physician. Prescribing Plain and Easy Means for Persons to Cure Themselves. . . .*, 3rd ed. (Williamsburg, VA, and Annapolis, MD, 1736), 11, 12, 14.

GENERAL PLANTING INFORMATION (pages 267–73)

Epigraph. Thomas Hill, *The Gardener's Labyrinth*, ed. Richard Mabey (London, 1577; Oxford: Oxford University Press, 1987), 53.

Image Credits

Courtesy of the Colonial Williamsburg Foundation, Williamsburg, Virginia. Page 3: "Wolverton, the House of William Acton," 1753, oil on canvas, artist unknown (1976-84); page 5: Detail from the Bodleian Plate (G1938-196/R1974-34); and page 16: Philip Miller's *Figures of the Most Beautiful, Useful, and Uncommon Plants Described in the Gardeners Dictionary, Exhibited on Three Hundred Copper Plates, Accurately Engraven after Drawings Taken from Nature. . . .*, 2 vols. London, 1771.

From Libri Picturati by permission from the Jagiellonian Library (Biblioteka Jagiellonska), Kraków, Poland. Page 24: Pheasant's Eye (*Adonis annua*) (vol. A19, plate 14) and page 88: Love-Lies-Bleeding (*Amaranthus paniculatus*) (vol. A28, plate 18), sixteenth-century watercolors by unknown artist(s) in the Netherlands.

From *The New Herbal of 1543 (Kräuterbuch)* by Leonhart Fuchs by permission courtesy of the City Library of Ulm (Stadtbibliothek Ulm), Germany. Page 28: Balsam Apple (*Momordica balsamina*) (plate 105); page 118: Yellow Horned Poppy (*Glaucium flavum*) (plate 294); page 142: Viper's Bugloss (*Echium vulgare*) (plate 229); page 196: Pilewort (*Ranunculus ficaria*) (plate 497); page 234: Orach (*Atriplex hortensis*) (plate 64); page 250: Elecampane (*Inula helenium*) (plate 134); and page 262: Pennyroyal (*Mentha pulegium*) (plate 110), colored woodcuts.

By permission from the Uffizi Gallery (Gabinetto Disegni e Stampe degli Uffizi), Florence, Italy. Page 32: Globe Candytuft (*Iberis umbellata*) with a Hazel Hen (*Tetrastes bonasia*) and page 48: Cypress Vine Morning Glory (*Ipomoea quamoclit*), gouaches on paper by Jacopo Ligozzi, ca. 1576.

From the Codex Liechtenstein by permission from the Collections of the Prince of Liechtenstein, Vaduz and Vienna (Sammlungen des Fürsten von und zu Liechtenstein, Vaduz Wien). Page 40: *Callistephus chinensis* (vol. 8, plate 124) and page 238: *Carduus marianus [Silybum marianum]* (vol. 3, plate 67), watercolors by Franz and Ferdinand Bauer, before 1788 and ca. 1777.

From the Vienna Codex by Leonhart Fuchs (1566) by permission from the Austrian National Library, Vienna (ÖNB/Wien). Page 72: Job's Tears (*Coix Lacryma-jobi*) (vol. 2, plate 363) and page 130: Sunflower (*Helianthus annuus*) (vol. 2, plate 391), colored woodcuts, ca. 1560 or earlier.

By permission from Rollo Clifford, Frampton Court Estate, Gloucester, England. Page 200: Ragged Robin (*Lychnis flos-cuculi*), watercolor by the Clifford family, 1849.

By permission courtesy of the Petersburg Garden Club, Petersburg, Virginia. Page 204: Rue-Anemone (*Thalictrum thalictroides*), watercolor by Bessie Niemeyer Marshall, ca. 1937.

By permission courtesy of the National Arbor Day Foundation, Nebraska City, Nebraska. Page 273: ArborDay.org 2006 Hardiness Zone Map.

Courtesy of the Colonial Williamsburg Foundation. All of the following images were originally produced as copperplates for eighteenth- and nineteenth-century publications.

From Philip Miller, *Figures of the Most Beautiful, Useful, and Uncommon Plants Described in the Gardeners Dictionary, Exhibited on Three Hundred Copper Plates, Accurately Engraven after Drawings Taken from Nature. . . .*, 2 vols. London, 1771. Page 36: *Ricinus foliis peltatis inequaliter serratis . . .* (vol. 2, plate 219); page 52: *Martynia caule ramoso, foliis cordato-ovatis pilosis* (vol. 2, plate 286); page 56: *Linum calycibus . . .* (vol. 2, plate 166); page 82: *Nigella petalis subtricuspidatis . . .* (vol. 2, plate 187); page 104: *Pentapetes foliis hastato-lanceolatis serratis* (vol. 2, plate 200); page 114: *Argemone Mexicana* (vol. 1, plate 50); page 222: *Cnicus foliis Cordatis . . .* (vol. 2, plate 248); page 246: *Blattaria alba* (vol. 1, plate 67); and page 254: *Cardiaca foliis tenuis* (vol. 1, plate 80).

From John Edwards, *The British Herbal, Containing One Hundred Plates of the Most Beautiful and Scarce Flowers and Useful Medicinal Plants Which Blow in the Open Air of Great Britain, Accurately Coloured from Nature, with Their Botanical Characters, and a Short Account of Their Cultivation, &c. &c.* London, 1770. Page 44: *Amaranthus cristatus.* Crested Amaranth (plate 75); page 76: *Delphinum hortense.* Garden Larkspur (plate 60); page 100: *Cardamindum ampliore folio & majore flore. . . .* Indian Nasturtium with a larger Leaf & Flower (plate 32); page 108: *Papaver erraticum, rubrum, campestre.* Common, red field Poppy (plate 7); page 136: *Malva sylvestris.* Wild Mallow (plate 31); page 188: *Lychnis hirsuta flore coccineo major.* Greater hairy Campion with a Scarlet Flower (plate 58); and page 226: *Borrago floribus caeruleis.* Borage with blue Flowers (plate 21).

From B[enjamin] Maund, *The Botanic Garden; Consisting of Highly Finished Representations of Hardy Ornamental Flowering Plants, Cultivated in Great Britain; with Their Names, Classes, Orders, History, Qualities, Culture, and Physiological Observations.* Vol. 13. London, [1851?]. Page 62: *Ageratum Mexicanum [syn. A. houstoniaum].* Mexican ageratum (plate 1083).

From William Curtis, *The Botanical Magazine; or, Flower-Garden Displayed: In Which the Most Ornamental Foreign Plants, Cultivated in the Open Ground, the Green-House, and the Stove, Will Be Accurately Represented in Their Natural Colours. . . .* London, 1787–1833. Page 66: *Mirabilis Jalapa.* Common Marvel of Peru (vol. 11, plate 371); page 92: *Lupinus Luteus.* Yellow Lupine (vol. 4, plate 140); page 96: *Tagetes Patula.* Spreading Tagates, or French Marigold (vol. 5, plate 150); page 126: *Scabiosa Atropurpurea.* Sweet Scabious (vol. 7, plate 247); page 134: *Zinnia Tenuiflora.* Slender-Flowered Zinnia (vol. 16, plate 555); page 146: *Prunella Grandiflora.* Great-Flowered Self-Heal (vol. 10, plate 337); page 154: *Anagallis Monelli.* Italian Pimpernel (vol. 9, plate 319); page 158: *Eupatorium salviaefolium.* Sage-leaved Eupatorium (vol. 45, vol. 3 of the new series, plate 2010); page 162: *Cynara cardunculus*, var. Common Cardoon (vol. 60, vol. 7 of the new series, plate 3241); page 166: *Glycine Apios.* Tuberous-Rooted Glycine (vol. 30, plate 1198); page 170: *Aquilegia Canadensis.* Canadian Columbine (vol. 7, plate 246); page 176: *Rudbeckia fulgida.* Small Hairy Rudbeckia (vol. 45, vol. 3 of the new series, plate 1996); page 180: *Rudbeckia purpurea.* Purple Rudbeckia (vol. 1, plate 2); page 184: *Canna Indica.* Common Indian Reed or Shot (vol. 13, plate 454); page 208: *Claytonia Virginica.* Virginian Claytonia (vol. 24, plate 941); page 216: *Cheiranthus Armeniacus.* Armenian Wall-Flower (vol. 22, plate 835); page 230: *Calendula officinalis.* Common Marigold (vol. 59, vol. 6 of the new series, plate 3204); page 242: *Blitum Virgatum.* Strawberry Blite (vol. 8, plate 276); and page 258: *Passiflora coerulea.* Common Passion-Flower (vol. 1, plate 28).

Plant Index

Bold numbers indicate the pages on which the plant is featured.

columbine (*Aquilegia canadensis*), **170–75**, 206
columbine (*Aquilegia chrysantha*), 170
columbine, garden (*Aquilegia vulgaris*), 174
Consolida ambigua (larkspur), 76
Consolida orientalis (larkspur), 11, 18, 27, 41, **76–81**, 87, 91, 194, 233, 269
Consolida regalis (larkspur), 76
Convallaria majalis (lily of the valley), 204
cool-tankard, 229. See also *Borago officinalis*
corn cockle (*Agrostemma githago*), 270
costmary (*Chrysanthemum balsamita*), 9
cotton (*Gossypium* sp.), 107, 136
cress (*Barbarea* spp.), 27, 32, 242
Crinum spp. (crinum lily), 20
crowflower, 200, 203. See also *Lychnis flos-cuculi*
cuckoo flower, 203. See also *Lychnis flos-cuculi*
Cynara cardunculus (cardoon), **162–65**, 229
Cynara scolymus (artichoke), 162, 165, 238
Cynoglossum officinale (hound's-tongue), 1, 9
cypress vine (*Ipomoea quamoclit*), **48–51**, 74, 168, 268

dandelion (*Taraxacum officinale*), 154
Daucus carota (Queen Anne's lace), 176
delphinium, annual, 81. See also *Consolida orientalis*
devil's claw (*Proboscidea louisianica*), **52–55**
Dianthus barbatus (sweet William), 48, 51, 200, 233
Digitalis purpurea (foxglove), 18, 27
dittany (*Origanum dictamnus*), 262
Dracocephalum moldavica (dragonwort), 125, 270

Echinacea purpurea (purple coneflower), 161, **180–83**, 221
Echinops sp. (globe thistle), 222
Echium vulgare (viper's bugloss), 20, 56, 122, 126, **142–45**
Echium vulgare 'Blue Bedder' (viper's bugloss), 145
elecampane (*Inula helenium*), 19, 183, 224, **250–53**
Endymion non-scriptus (bluebell), 206
Erysimum cheiri (wallflower), 27, 32, **216–19**, 233, 267
Erysimum hieraciifolium (wallflower), 218
Eupatorium perfoliatum (boneset), 9, 47, **158–61**, 221, 257
Eupatorium purpureum (joe-pye weed), 9, 180
Euphorbia pulcherrima (poinsettia), 23

false saffron (*Carthamus tinctorius*), 270
fennel flower, 87. See also *Nigella damascena*
fenugreek (*Trigonella foenum-graecum*), 56
figgewoort, 198. See also *Ranunculus ficaria*
flax (*Linum usitatissimum*), **56–61**
flax, common, 61. See also *Linum usitatissimum*
flax, golden, 61. See also *Linum usitatissimum*
flos Adonis, 27. See also *Adonis aestivalis*
floscampi, 203. See also *Lychnis flos-cuculi*

flossflower (*Ageratum houstonianum*), **62–65**. See also ageratum
foamflower (*Tiarella cordifolia*), 204
four-o'clock (*Mirabilis jalapa*), 64, **66–71**, 134
foxglove (*Digitalis purpurea*), 18, 27
French spinach, 237. See also *Atriplex hortensis* 'Cupreata'
fringe tree (*Chionanthus virginicus*), 174

garden aster, 42. See also *Callistephus chinensis*
garden impatiens (*Impatiens balsamina*), 28, 270
garden orach, 237, 242. See also *Atriplex hortensis* 'Cupreata'
Gelsemium sempervirens (yellow jessamine), 261
Gibraltar mint, 263. See also *Mentha pulegium*
ginger, wild (*Asarum canadense*), 204
Glaucium corniculatum (scarlet horned poppy), 118
Glaucium flavum (yellow horned poppy), 87, **118–21**
globe amaranth (*Gomphrena globosa*), 270
Gomphrena globosa (globe amaranth), 270
Good-King-Henry (*Chenopodium bonus-henricus*), 242
Gossypium sp. (cotton), 107, 136
groundnut, American, 2, 9, 166, 168. See also *Apios americana*

Hedera helix (ivy), 263
Helianthus annuus 'Italian White' (sunflower), 39, 122, **130–33**
Heliotropium arborescens (heliotrope), 71, 270
Hibiscus sp. (hibiscus), 107, 136
high mallow, 141. See also *Malva sylvestris* 'Brave Heart'
Hippeastrum spp. (amaryllis), 20
hollyhock (*Alcea rosea*), 136, 141
honeywort (*Cerinthe major*), 270
hormium, 122, 125. See also *Salvia viridis*
horseheal, 253. See also *Inula helenium*
horsemint (*Monarda punctata*), 9, 176, 270
hound's-tongue (*Cynoglossum officinale*), 1, 9
Hypochoeris sp. (cat's ear), 154
hyssop, anise (*Agastache foeniculum*), 9, **150–53**, 257
hyssop, blue giant, 150, 153. See also *Agastache foeniculum*
hyssop, lavender, 153. See also *Agastache foeniculum*
hyssop, purple giant (*Agastache scrophulariifolia*), 153
hyssop, wrinkled giant (*Agastache rugosa*), 150
hyssop, yellow giant (*Agastache nepetoides*), 153, 270
Hyssopus officinalis (hyssop), 19

Iberis amara 'Coronaria' (rocket candytuft), 32, 270
Iberis umbellata (globe candytuft), **32–35**, 122, 125, 219

Iberis umbellata 'Appleblossom' (globe candytuft), 35
Impatiens balsamina (garden impatiens), 28, 270
Indian cress, 100, 103. See also *Tropaeolum majus*
Indian frill, 187. See also *Canna indica*
Indian sage, 161. See also *Eupatorium perfoliatum*
Indian-shot (*Canna indica*), 9, 20, 74–75, **184–87**, 269
Inula helenium (elecampane), 19, 183, 224, **250–53**
Ipomoea quamoclit (cypress vine), **48–51**, 74, 168, 268
Isatis tinctoria (woad), 270
ivy (*Hedera helix*), 263

jack-in-prison, 82, 87. See also *Nigella damascena*
jack-in-the-pulpit (*Arisaema triphyllum*), 204
Jerusalem-cross, 191. See also *Lychnis chalcedonica*
Job's tears (*Coix lacryma-jobi*), **72–75**, 221
joe-pye weed (*Eupatorium purpureum*), 9, 180
Joseph's-coat (*Amaranthus tricolor*), 133, 270

knapweed (*Centaurea* sp.), 126
knight's-spur, 81. See also *Consolida orientalis*

lamb's-quarters (*Chenopodium album*), 90, 234, 237, 242, 245
larkes-heal, 81. See also *Consolida orientalis*
larkspur (*Consolida ambigua*), 76
larkspur (*Consolida orientalis*), 11, 18, 27, 41, **76–81**, 87, 91, 194, 233, 269
larkspur (*Consolida regalis*), 76
Lavandula spp. (lavender), 19
Leonurus cardiaca (motherwort), 9, **254–57**
Levisticum officinale (lovage), 270
licorice mint, 153. See also *Agastache foeniculum*
lily, crinum (*Crinum* spp.), 20
lily of the valley (*Convallaria majalis*), 204
Linaria vulgaris (toadflax), 56, 126
Linum usitatissimum (flax), **56–61**
Lobelia siphilitica (blue lobelia), 180
London-pride, 191. See also *Lychnis chalcedonica*
Lonicera sempervirens (woodbine), 261
lovage (*Levisticum officinale*), 270
love-entangle, 82, 87. See also *Nigella damascena*
love-in-a-mist (*Nigella damascena*), **82–87**, 276
love-in-a-puzzle, 82, 87. See also *Nigella damascena*
love-lies-bleeding (*Amaranthus caudatus*), 44, **88–91**, 98, 122
Lupinus albus (white lupine), 92, 95
Lupinus luteus (yellow lupine), **92–95**
Lychnis chalcedonica (Maltese cross), **188–91**
Lychnis coronaria (rose campion), 200
Lychnis flos-cuculi (ragged robin), 9, **200–203**

Magnolia spp. (magnolia), 174
Maltese cross (*Lychnis chalcedonica*), **188–91**
Malva sylvestris 'Brave Heart' (malva), 91, **136–41**

sweet-evening-stock (*Matthiola incana*), 270
sweet flag (*Acorus calamus*), 269, 270
sweet scabious, 125, 126, 128. See also *Scabiosa atropurpurea*
sweet-sultan (*Centaurea moschata*), 270
sweet William, 51. See also *Ipomoea quamoclit*
sweet William (*Dianthus barbatus*), 48, 51, 200, 233

Tagetes erecta (African marigold), 96, 267, 268, 269
Tagetes patula 'Striped' (striped French marigold), 64, 91, **96–99**, 128, 134, 267, 268, 269
talewort, 229. See also *Borago officinalis*
Taraxacum officinale (dandelion), 154
tassel flower, 91. See also *Amaranthus caudatus*
Thalictrum thalictroides (rue anemone), **204–7**, 211
thistle, distaff (*Carthamus lanatus*), 222
thistle, globe (*Echinops* sp.), 222
thistle, golden (*Scolymus hispanicus*), 222
thistle, holy, 225. See also *Cnicus benedictus*
thistle, holy, 240. See also *Silybum marianum*
thistle, milk. 222, 240. See also *Silybum marianum*
thistle, star- (*Centaurea solstitialis*), 222
thoroughwort, common, 161. See also *Eupatorium perfoliatum*
Thymus spp. (thyme), 19
Tiarella cordifolia (foamflower), 204
toadflax (*Linaria vulgaris*), 56, 126
Tropaeolum majus (nasturtium), **100–103**, 221
Tropaeolum minus (small nasturtium), 100
tree-of-heaven (*Ailanthus altissima*), 28
Trigonella foenum-graecum (fenugreek), 56
Trollius europaeus (trollius), 27
trumpet creeper (*Campsis radicans*), 261

unicorn plant, 55. See also *Proboscidea louisianica*

Verbascum blattaria (moth mullein), 56, **246–49**
Verbascum thapsus (common mullein), 118, 224, 249
Verbena hastata (blue vervain), 158, 161, **212–15**
Verbena officinalis (vervain), 19, 212, 215, 224
Veronica officinalis (speedwell), 188, 270
Veronica spicata (speedwell), 47
vervain (*Verbena officinalis*), 19, 212, 215, 224
vervain, blue (*Verbena hastata*), 158, 161, **212–15**
viper's bugloss (*Echium vulgare*), 20, 56, 122, 126, **142–45**
Virginia creeper (*Parthenocissus quinquefolia*), 261
Vitex agnus-castus (vitex), 149, 263

wallflower (*Erysimum cheiri*), 27, 32, **216–19**, 233, 267
wallflower (*Erysimum hieraciifolium*), 218
wild cotton, 195. See also *Asclepias syriaca*
wild quinine (*Parthenium integrifolium*), 158
winter greens (*Barbarea* spp.), 27, 242
winter greens (*Brassica* spp.), 27, 242
woodbine (*Lonicera sempervirens*), 261
wormseed (*Chenopodium ambrosioides*), 245

yarrow (*Achillea millefolium* 'Roseum'), 47
yellow jessamine (*Gelsemium sempervirens*), 261
yellow starwort, 253. See also *Inula helenium*

Zinnia pauciflora (small-flowered zinnia), 64, 91, 98, 128, **134–35**, 191, 268
Zinnia peruviana (zinnia), 134

General Index

Adam in Eden (Coles), 126, 215
Adonis (god), 24, 27
advertisements: for property with gardens in
    Virginia Gazette, 6; for seeds in Boston Evening-
    Post, 32, 78, 82, 90, 128; for seeds in McMahon
    broadside, 7, 21, 24, 191, 218
Aeneid (Virgil), 215
Age of Exploration, 21
alkamides, 183
Allen, Arthur, 4
American Gardener's Calendar, The (McMahon), 21;
    on Adonis, 24; on devil's claw, 55; on Maltese
    cross, 191; on scarlet pentapetes, 104; on
    small-flowered zinnia, 134; on wallflower, 218
American Heart Association, 60
Amerindians. See indigenous peoples
Aphrodite, 24, 27
Apollo, 192
Appleseed, Johnny, 257
Archer, Gabriel, 2
Aristotle, 17, 36
Art of Simpling (Coles), 221
asclepions, 192
Asclepius, 192
aster yellows, 41, 42
Austrian National Library (Vienna), 278n7, 279n2
    (Job's Tears), 280n2 (Striped French Marigold)

back breeding, 145, 269–70
Bacon's Castle, 4
Banister, John, 19, 174, 180, 211, 245, 258
barley, 2, 19, 108, 138
Bartram, John, 40, 270
Beauclerk, Henry, 210
bees, 150, 203, 270
Berkeley, William, 4
Besler, Basilius, 18. See also Hortus Eystettensis
Besler Florilegium, The (Besler), 18. See also Hortus
    Eystettensis
Bethabara, 21; and blessed thistle, 224; and borage,
    226; and columbine, 174; and corn poppy,
    112; and hormium sage, 122; and nasturtium,
    100, 103; and St. Mary's thistle, 238
Big Book of Herbs, The (Tucker and DeBaggio), 250
binomial nomenclature, 20, 104, 138, 211. See also
    taxonomy
Bodleian Plate, 5
borage seed oil, 226, 229
Boston Evening-Post, 32, 78, 82, 90, 128
botanical gardens, 1, 7, 17, 20, 104
Botanical Magazine, The (Curtis), 146
Botany of Desire, The (Pollan), 257
Bray, Lys de, 142
Briefe and True Report of the New Found Land of
    Virginia, A (Harriot), 132
Brinkley, Kent, 4
Brothers of the Spade (Swem), 6, 19

Bry, Theodor de, 132
bulbs, 198, 267
Burgesses, House of, 5
butterflies, 192, 195, 203, 249
Byrd, William, I, 6
Byrd, William, II, 5, 6, 208, 220, 283n3
    (Motherwort)

caffeoyl derivatives, 183
calendula oil, 230
Carter, Judy, 36, 39
Carter, Landon, 36, 39
castor bean oil, 36, 39
"Catalogus Stirpium Rariorum" (Banister), 19,
    278n13
Catesby, Mark, 208
Charles I, 32, 188, 242, 258
Charles II, 208, 210
Charles V (Holy Roman Emperor), 96
Chelsea Physic Garden (botanical garden), 7, 20,
    52, 215
Clayton, Sir Jasper (great-grandfather of JC), 208
Clayton, Gen. Jasper (uncle of JC), 210
Clayton, John (father of JC), 208
Clayton, Sir John (grandfather of JC), 208
Clayton, John (JC), 20, 208, 210, 278n18; and
    all-heal, 148; and boneset, 158; and cinnamon
    vine, 166; and columbine, 174; and hyssop,
    153, 270; and Job's tears, 74; and milkweed,
    192; and mullein, 249; and orange coneflower,
    176; and passionflower, 258; and purple
    coneflower, 180; and rue anemone, 204; and
    spring beauty, 208, 210–11; and sunflower,
    130; and viper's bugloss, 142; and yellow
    horned poppy, 118, 121
Clayton, Thomas (brother of JC), 210
Clifford, George, 211
Clifford family, 148, 203
climate, 2, 7, 11, 273
Cocker, Henry. See Flowers
Coles, William, 1, 126, 215, 221
College of William and Mary, 5
Collins, Minton, 92, 96, 128, 165, 218
Collinson, Peter, 6, 19; on bulbs, 198; on China
    aster, 40; and cockscomb, 44; and Indian-shot,
    184, 187; and pilewort, 198
colonial American herbal, 10, 21
Colonial Williamsburg: and anise hyssop, 150,
    153; and calendula, 233; and cinnamon vine,
    168; Colonial Nursery of, 196, 269; and
    cypress vine, 48; and flossflower, 64; and globe
    candytuft, 32; historical window of, 7; and
    hormium sage, 122; landscape nursery of, 9,
    203; and Maltese cross, 191; and pilewort,
    196; and plants, 166; and ragged robin, 203;
    research by, 6; and scarlet pentapetes, 104; and
    scarlet pimpernel, 157; and small-flowered

zinnia, 134; and "Southern Plant Lists," 21;
    St. George Tucker House of, 48. See also
    Williamsburg
Compton, Henry, 19, 174, 180, 211, 261
cottage garden, 2, 7, 11, 23, 103, 122, 126, 175,
    218
Cottage Garden, The (Lloyd and Bird), 122
Coys, William, 126
cucumber beetle, 91
Curtis, William, 146
Custis, John, IV, 5, 6, 19, 210; and China aster 40;
    and cockscomb, 44; and Indian-shot, 184, 187;
    and pilewort, 198

deadheading, 269
DeBaggio, Thomas, 250
De materia medica (Dioscorides), 17, 133, 279n2
    (Flax); on artichoke and cardoon, 162; on
    blessed thistle, 222; on blue pimpernel, 157;
    on borage, 226; on castor bean, 36; on corn
    poppy, 108; on elecampane, 250; on flax, 56;
    on love-in-a-mist, 82; on malva, 136; on moth
    mullein, 249; on orach, 234; on pilewort, 196;
    on scabious, 126; on St. Mary's thistle, 238; on
    vervain, 212; on yellow lupine, 95
De simplicium medicamentorum temperamentis ac
    facultatibus (Galen), 220–21
Dictionary of Gardening (Royal Horticultural
    Society), 13, 62, 104, 121, 154, 176
Dioscorides, 17, 133, 220. See also De materia
    medica
doctrine of signatures, 1, 17

Edinburgh (botanical garden), 7
Eichstätt, 18
elecampane oil, 250
Elysium Britannicum, or The Royal Gardens (Evelyn),
    190
English Flower Garden, The (Robinson), 146, 242,
    249
Enlightenment, 5
Enquiry into Plants (Theophrastus), 17; on blessed
    thistle, 222; on blue pimpernel, 154; on
    calendula, 230; on cardoon and artichoke, 162;
    on castor bean, 36; on corn poppy, 108; on
    elecampane, 250; on flowers, 22–23; on herbs,
    220; on larkspur, 76; on malva, 136; on orach,
    234; on pennyroyal, 262; on viper's bugloss,
    142; on wallflower, 216; on white lupine, 92;
    on yellow horned poppy, 118
Evelyn, John, 22, 76, 88, 190–91, 220
evening primrose oil, 226
Every Man His Own Doctor: or, The Poor Planter's
    Physician, 262

Fairchild, Thomas, 111
Faris, William, 40